jMonkeyEngine 3.0
Game Development:
A Practical Guide

Richard Reese & Justin Johnson

P 8
t e c h

Published in 2015 by P8tech, an imprint of Play Technologies (England) Limited

Copyright © Play Technologies (England) Limited

ISBN: 978-0-9929105-8-7

P8Tech
6 Woodside
Churnet View Road
Oakamoor
ST10 3AE

www.P8Tech.com

About the Authors

Richard Reese has written several Java and C books and brings a concise and easy-to-follow approach to topics at hand. He currently teaches at Tarleton State University where he is able to apply years of industry experience to enhance his classes. Richard is the author of P8's book: *Java 8 New Features: A Practical Heads-Up Guide.*

Justin Johnson enjoys playing and developing computer games. He finds writing about JME3 to be a very rewarding experience. He has developed across different game engines, and feels that JME3 is the most versatile and customizable open source game engine about.

Code

Download this book's code package from *www.P8tech.com/JME.zip*

Errata

Despite best efforts, mistakes can sometimes creep into books. If you spot a mistake, please feel free to email us at errata@p8tech.com (with the book title in the subject line). The errata page for the book is hosted at *www.P8tech.com/JME*

Table of Contents

1

Introduction to JME3

Introduction

jMonkeyEngine3 (JME3) is a 3D game development environment for Java programmers. It is based on the Lightweight Java Game Library (LWJGL) and supports a number of target platforms. JME3 has been used for a number of games including Boardtastic, Ships with Cannons, and Mythruna. A more complete list can be found at http://jmonkeyengine.org/showcase/.

In this book we will cover all of the significant aspects of game development using JME3 and will develop a game as we go along. When you are done you will have a good understanding of how a game can be developed using JME3 and you will have a working game that you can play and build upon. While JME3 has some excellent documentation, a book such as this is able to pull it together into a more structured package, organized around a specific game. In addition, the numerous code examples go a long way towards improving the reader's understanding of game development and JME3.

The game we will be developing is a space-based game called *Shades of Infinity*. It will incorporate a first person shooter view, and features such as support for multiple players and special effects. The game is based on the premise that - in the future - a rogue AI entity escapes from Earth after nearly being destroyed and inhabits space, periodically attacking Earth's ships. The goal of the game is to destroy the entity.

Let's examine JME3 in more depth starting with why JME3 is a good choice for game development.

Why JME3?

There are many Java-based game engines available. JME3 will often be the best choice because it is actively being developed and has a large development and user community. It is designed for use with high end computers and supports a wide range of features. These include support for 3D graphics, networking, terrain development, physics, multiple players, and many other aspects of a game that you would expect. Being based on LWJGL, it leverages the work done there and adds more support.

As a Java programmer you can leverage your expertise without having to learn a new language. JME3 uses OpenGL libraries which makes it fast and takes advantage of the underlying graphics hardware. It supports the import of graphic models from many sources including Blender. In addition, JME3 is open source and free. JME3 currently supports Java 7.

Installing JME3

JME3 runs on a number of operating systems. The examples used in this book were developed on a Windows 7 platform. It is recommended that a graphics card supporting OpenGL 2.0, or better, be used. The Java JDK is included in the download so it is not necessary to download it separately.

The download site is at http://hub.jmonkeyengine.org/downloads/. The installation process is simple; the specifics depend on the operating system you are using.

The JME3 Development Environment

The JME3 development environment is based on NetBeans. If you are familiar with this environment, then JME3 will be easy to pickup. If not, then you should not have much difficulty using JME3 as it is well organized. We will point out those features that you are most likely to encounter when developing your game.

Figure 1 - JME3 SDK shows the initial JME3 window. In this section we will cover the basic components of the system and how to use them. As you progress through the book we will introduce other useful features including screen snapshots of important menu and dialog selections.

Many features of the SDK are accessed using the file menu or access keys. The Project Window will display the relevant parts of a project such as its assets and files. We will learn more about this structure in this chapter. The Info Screen found in the middle of the SDK is replaced by your game's file contents when developing the application. While console tab Output - Application is not used directly in a game, it is can be useful for debugging purposes.

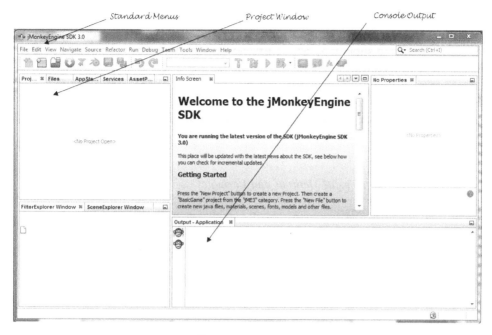

Figure 1 - JME3 SDK

Once you have set up JME3 and understand its basics, you are ready to start the game development process. Important JME3 links to assist you in your development effort are listed in *Table 1 - JME3 Useful Links*.

Table 1 - JME3 Useful Links

Topic	URL
Main JME3 Site	http://hub.jmonkeyengine.org/tag/jme3/
Downloads	http://hub.jmonkeyengine.org/downloads/
Current status	http://hub.jmonkeyengine.org/
General Documentation	http://hub.jmonkeyengine.org/wiki/doku.php
API Documentation	http://hub.jmonkeyengine.org/javadoc/
Forums	http://hub.jmonkeyengine.org/forum/
JME3 Troubleshooting	http://hub.jmonkeyengine.org/forum/board/troubleshooting/
Blogs	http://hub.jmonkeyengine.org/blog/
Twitter	https://twitter.com/jmonkeyengine

Structure of a JME3 Application

A JME3 application is derived from the class `SimpleApplication`. This class provides the standard methods to support a game's lifecycle plus a number of variables to provide access to important features of a game. These methods and variables are detailed in *Table 2 - SimpleApplication Useful Methods and Variables*. In the next section we will explain the essential methods and variables used in a basic game. In later chapters we will expand upon the remaining methods and variables and introduce other methods and variables as they become useful.

Table 2 - SimpleApplication Useful Methods and Variables

Methods	Purpose
main	The starting point for Java applications and JME3 games
simpleInitApp	Used to initialize the game
simpleUpdate	Used to update the state of the game
simpleRender	Used to render unique GUI elements of a game
destroy	Supports game termination tasks
Variables	**Purpose**
assetManager	Used to manage the game's assets such as its objects and their appearance
rootNode	The root of the game's elements
guiNode	Used to support the Heads Up Display (HUD)

The BasicGame Project

JME3 provides a simple game project called `BasicGame`. This game can be created using the File - New Project menu selection. Go ahead and start up JME3. Use this menu selection to create a game. The New Dialog box should appear as illustrated in *Figure 2 - New Project Dialog Box*. Select BasicGame and then the Next button.

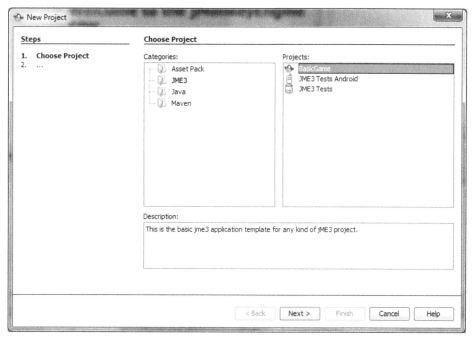

Figure 2 - New Project Dialog Box

The next dialog box will appear as shown in *Figure 3 - Name and Location Dialog Box*. Leave the name as it is and select Finish.

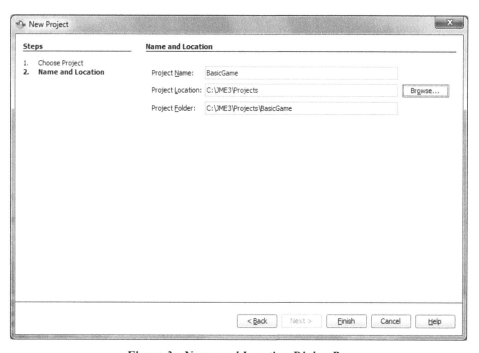

Figure 3 - Name and Location Dialog Box

Expand the `BasicGame` project by clicking on the + in the Project window. Expand the Source Packages and mygame folders also. Double click on Main.java and this will display the source code for the game. Alternately, you can right click on the file and select Open. When you have done this, your project should appear as shown in *Figure 4 - BasicGame Project*.

Figure 4 - BasicGame Project

Execute the game by either pressing the F6 key, the Run Project button (the green arrow) or select the menu combination Run – Run Project. The game will appear with a blue cube located at its origin as shown in *Figure 5 - BasicGame Executing*. To terminate the game, use the escape key.

The text on the bottom left-hand side of the game is the default **Heads Up Display** (HUD). A HUD is a convenient technique to display information about the state of a game. In the default game it displays basic information about the GUI. The HUD will be discussed in more detail in Using the HUD.

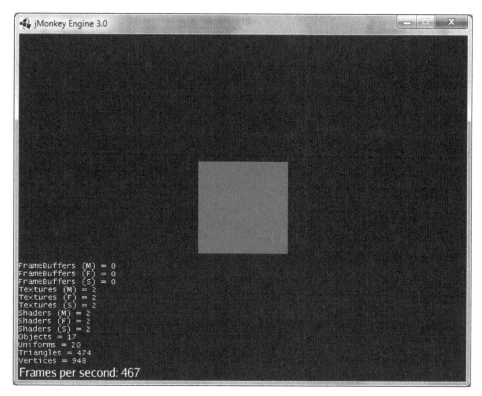

FrameBuffers (M) = 0
FrameBuffers (F) = 0
FrameBuffers (S) = 0
Textures (M) = 2
Textures (F) = 2
Textures (S) = 2
Shaders (M) = 2
Shaders (F) = 2
Shaders (S) = 2
Objects = 17
Uniforms = 20
Triangles = 474
Vertices = 948
Frames per second: 467

Figure 5 - BasicGame Executing

For the user to interact with the game, some sort of input device is needed. Often this is a combination of the keyboard and mouse. The keys are referred to as **Navigation keys**. When the game is started, the default navigation is in effect as described in *Table 3 - Navigation Keys*. Assuming the player is at the same position as the camera, the effect of the navigation keys can be interpreted as the camera and the player moving. That is, the view is from the perspective of the player. As the player moves, the camera moves. This is reflected in the last two columns of the table.

Table 3 - Navigation Keys

Input	Camera	Player
W and S keys	Moves forward and backward	Walks back and forth
A and D keys	Moves left and right	Walks left and right
Q and Y keys	Moves up and down	Flies up and down
Mouse left and right	Rotates left and right	Looks left and right
Mouse forward and backward	Rotates up and down	Looks up and down

Application Lifecycle

Every game is started by invoking the `SimpleApplication` class' `start` method which will eventually invoke the `simpleInitApp` method. The `simpleInitApp` method is used to initialize the game's objects, e.g. geometries and nodes, before the game starts. The `simpleInitApp` is only run once, at the start of the game.

The `simpleUpdate` method keeps the game data, e.g. the player's score or location, up to date. The `simpleUpdate` method is called repeatedly throughout the game and does not normally need to be invoked explicitly. After every update, JME3 automatically redraws the screen and calls the `simpleRender` method. The game will continue running until the user escapes the current application, or the `stop` method is called.

In *Figure 6 - JME3 Simple Lifecycle Model*, a simple version of a JME3 life cycle is shown. The `start` method will start the game. Once the `simpleInitApp` method has completed, the `simpleUpdate` and `simpleRender` methods are called repeatedly. When the `stop` method is called, the `destroy` method is executed so that termination tasks can be performed.

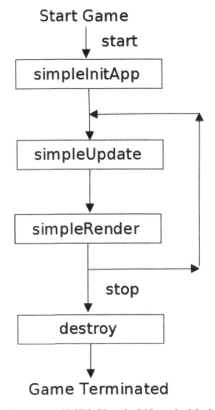

Figure 6 - JME3 Simple Lifecycle Model

In Chapter 3 we will introduce the `AppState` class. This class provides a convenient way to maintain the game state from a global perspective. In Chapter 3 we will also introduce the `Controls` class which implements the behavior of a game's entities.

Understanding the Scene Graph

The **Scene Graph** data structure is the virtual representation of the 3D world in JME3. This is the primary component of the world you see on the screen in front of you. All of the visual and non-visual elements of a game are attached to the scene graph. The top of the scene graph is denoted by the `rootNode` variable declared in the `SimpleApplication` class. The scene graph is built by adding elements to the `rootNode`.

The scene graph is a tree structure consisting of **Spatials** which are abstract data types that are able to store information about elements of the scene graph. They are represented by the `Spatial` class located in `com.jme.scene.Spatial`.

Every `Spatial` that is going to be part of the scene graph must be attached to the `rootNode`. Likewise, detaching an object from the `rootNode` removes the object from the scene. The scene graph is normally composed of numerous sub-nodes which represent elements of the game. When a node is moved, rotated, or scaled (referred to as **transforming** in JME3) the objects attached to it are similarly affected.

There are two types of spatials: **Nodes** and **Geometries**. A node is a spatial that can have other spatials as children. Nodes are invisible to the actual game play. There are several predefined nodes provided by JME3. The most important one is the `rootNode`.

A **geometry** represents a visible element of the game. It consists of a **Mesh** which gives it a shape and a **Material** which describes the 'covering' of a mesh. This can be as simple as a solid color or a sophisticated fabric whose appearance varies depending on the lighting situation.

A node is represented by an instance of the `Node` class while a geometry is represented by the `Geometry` class. JME3 provides several predefined meshes including a box, sphere, and cylinder. Geometries and materials will be covered in more detail in Chapter 2.

Figure 7 - Scene Graph illustrates a scene graph consisting of nodes and geometries. The spatial types are summarized in *Table 4 - Nodes versus Geometries* and *Table 5 - Geometry Supporting Classes*. All of these classes are found in the `com.jme3.scene` package. Nodes and geometries can hold user data if necessary. Geometries are always attached to nodes.

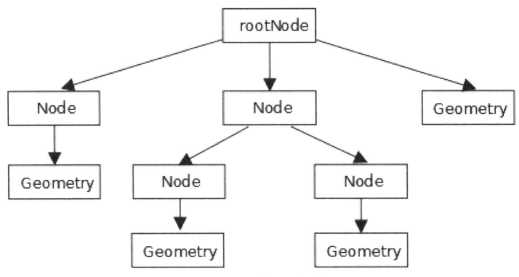

Figure 7 - Scene Graph

Table 4 - Nodes versus Geometries

Element	Class	Visible	Can be Transformed	Description
Node	`Node`	No	Yes	Invisible element of the game used to group other elements together
Geometry	`Geometry`	Yes	Yes	A visible element of a game

Table 5 - Geometry Supporting Classes

Element	Class	Visible	Can be Transformed	Description
Mesh	`Mesh`	Yes	No	Provides the framework for the element
Material	`Material`	Yes	No	Covers the mesh

The Coordinate System

The scene graph uses a right-handed coordinate system, similar to OpenGL. The origin is a single point in space located at (0, 0, 0) which is initially at the center of most games. The coordinate system consists of an x, y, and z axis.

From the center point, the X-Axis runs positive to the right and negative to the left. The Y-Axis runs positive in the upward direction and negative in the downward direction, relative to the starting position. The Z-Axis runs positive toward the player and negative away from the player in the starting position. Every point in space is located at an X,Y,Z coordinate where the interception of the three axes has the coordinate of (0,0,0).

Figure 8 - XYZ Axes illustrates these axes.

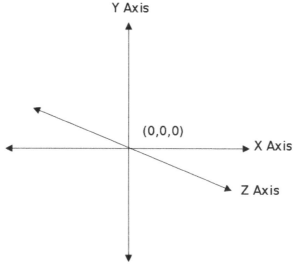

Figure 8 - XYZ Axes

The unit of measurement used in JME3 with an axis is called the **World Unit**, or WU. The WU will vary depending on the nature of a particular game. For example, a jet piloting game could have a WU of feet or miles. A game where the user controls a marble, or small object, might have a WU of inches. World Units could be thought of as the size perspective of the game. Objects will be placed throughout the game in relation to the origin and measured in WUs. For example, the location (0, 0, 20) is 20 WUs from the Z axis origin toward the viewer. These WUs could represent 20 feet or 20 inches, depending on the nature of the game.

Understanding the BasicGame's Code

The default source code for the BasicGame, as shown in the next code sequence, consists of two methods:

- main – Creates an instance of SimpleApplication and starts the game

- simpleInitApp – Creates the GUI interface for the application

The BasicGame is derived from the SimpleApplication class which is found in the com.jme3.app package. Every JME3 game is an instance of this class. The class controls the behavior of the machine. The SimpleApplication class extends the Application, class also found in the com.jme3.app package. However, the Application class should not be extended for game development. We will start with the main method then we will move on to the simpleInitApp method.

11

```
public class Main extends SimpleApplication {

    public static void main(String[] args) {
        Main app = new Main();
        app.start();
    }

    @Override
    public void simpleInitApp() {
        Box b = new Box(1, 1, 1);
        Geometry geom = new Geometry("Box", b);

        Material mat = new Material(assetManager,
                "Common/MatDefs/Misc/Unshaded.j3md");
        mat.setColor("Color", ColorRGBA.Blue);
        geom.setMaterial(mat);

        rootNode.attachChild(geom);
    }
}
```

Understanding the `main` Method

The BasicGame was created with a `Main` class. We can change the project name and class name to any valid name. There are two actions performed in the `main` method:

1. A new instance of the `Main` class is instantiated and assigned to the `app` variable

2. The `start` method is then executed which opens up the application window and initializes the scene.

When the `start` method executes, it will call the `simpleInitApp` method.

Understanding the `simpleInitApp` Method

In the `simpleInitApp` method, a geometry is created and attached to the `rootNode`. The object being created in BasicGame is a blue cube. First, a box shape is created that is 1x1x1 WUs in size, using the `Box` class. This is the mesh for the scene's only visible object.

Next, a `Geometry` object is created using the box mesh. The constructor's first argument assigns a name to the element and the mesh is supplied as the second argument. The name can be used later to work with the element if necessary.

A material is then loaded using the `Unshaded.j3md` material and the `assetManager`. This is a simple material. The `assetManager` object controls the application's assets such as materials.

The `setColor` method sets the color of a material. The `ColorRGBA` class (`com.jme3.math` package) possesses a number of constants representing commonly used colors as listed in *Table 6 - Static ColorRGBA Colors*. RGB stands for the Red, Green, and Blue components of a color. The A represents the Alpha value which is the transparency of the element.

Table 6 - Static ColorRGBA Colors

ColorRGBA.Black	ColorRGBA.Gray	ColorRGBA.Pink
ColorRGBA.Blue	ColorRGBA.Green	ColorRGBA.Red
ColorRGBA.Brown	ColorRGBA.LightGray	ColorRGBA.White
ColorRGBA.Cyan	ColorRGBA.Magenta	ColorRGBA.Yellow
ColorRGBA.DarkGray	ColorRGBA.Orange	

The material is attached to the geometry using the `setMaterial` method. In the last statement, the geometry is attached to the `rootNode` adding it to the scene graph.

In *Figure 9 - BasicGame with Axes*, the axes have been explicitly drawn to show the position of the box in the game. The additional code for displaying these axes can be found at `www.p8tech.com`. Using these explicit axes will help visualize the placement of objects in a game. We will use these axes periodically in our examples to better convey the placements of objects.

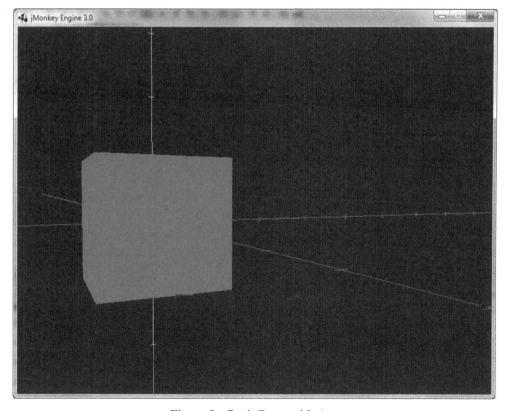

Figure 9 - BasicGame with Axes

In every game there are two `SimpleApplication` class methods that are usually overridden in a JME3 application: `simpleUpdate` and `simpleRender`. These methods will be covered in more depth in a later chapter.

Adding a Library

Several examples in this chapter will use assets found in the test-data library. This library is provided by JME3, but is not included by default. Adding additional libraries to your project is a simple task. First, right click on Libraries in the Project Window and select Add Library, as seen in *Figure 10 - Add Library Part 1*.

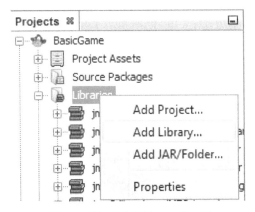

Figure 10 - Add Library Part 1

This will open a new window where you can choose the library you want to add. Scroll to the bottom of the list and find jme3.est-data. Click on jme3.est-data, highlighting this option. Finally, click on the Add Library button at the bottom of the window, as seen in *Figure 11 - Add Library Part 2*. This will incorporate the jme3.est-data library into your project. This library provides several textures, materials, sounds, models, and pictures.

We will use the assets found in this library for many of our examples. However, we may not always explicitly mention the library. It is a good idea to also add this library to any of the projects you create for the examples in this book.

Figure 11 - Add Library Part 2

Using the HUD

The **HUD**, or Head-Up-Display, is part of the visual user interface of a game. The HUD basically sits on top of the game's scene graph and displays additional state information. Some typical examples of HUD elements include health bars, ammunition, current score, or mini-maps. Any information you want the player to have access to throughout the game can be added to the HUD.

Although very useful, a HUD can clutter the game screen so it is good practice to only display essential information. If a game does not have anything important to display, it may be best to avoid using a HUD altogether.

The default JME3 HUD shows only a few basic game details, called **Display Settings**. This is shown in *Figure 5 - BasicGame Executing*. The number at the bottom of the screen displays the current **Frames Per Second**, or fps. A frame is essentially the application's display. The frame rate is the rate at which the frame is updated (i.e. redrawn or rendered). When this happens, the frame is said to be refreshed. Most common games have an fps of 60. This means that the frame is redrawn around 60 times every second. A higher fps means more fluid gameplay.

The first part of the HUD is called the **StatsView** and it displays information about **Textures, FrameBuffers**, and **Shaders**. The values with an (M) indicate how many of these elements are in memory. The values with an (F) indicate how many were used in the previous frame. The values with an (S) indicate how many were switched during the previous frame. These various statistics are used to pinpoint performance issues.

Textures: Textures are a type of material that is not a solid color.

Frame Buffers: These are rendering surfaces allowing off-screen rendering and render-to-texture functionality. Instead of the scene rendering to the screen, it is rendered into the Frame Buffer; the result can be either a texture or a buffer.

Shaders: A shader is an instruction sequence that executes on a GPU and is used to enhance the display. There are several types of shaders which are used for effects (shading, blur, lighting, glow, etc) and for accelerating the rendering of an object.

Performance and fps

In order to maintain optimal game play performance it is best to keep the fps close to 60 or above. An fps below 30 is an indicator of poor performance. Another indication of poor performance is an (M) value that is higher than an (F) value. A higher (M) value shows that there are more objects in memory than need be. These problems can be solved by de-allocating unnecessary objects and reducing high polygon counts for objects.

The **Polygon count** refers to the number of vertices and triangles that make up an object. This basically means that the higher level of detail, the higher the polygon count. A lower level of detail is easier to load because it has fewer vertices and lines to draw to the screen. Sometimes we need to replace high polygon objects with lower polygon objects for our game to run more smoothly.

Controlling the Default Display Settings

When the game appears to be working at an acceptable level, or if they are getting annoying, the display settings can be disabled. To disable the settings two methods can be called with `false` as the parameter:

```
setDisplayFps(false);      // Disables the fps display
setDisplayStatView(false);// Disables the StatsView display
```

With the default display settings disabled, the HUD is now clear and ready to be utilized for game customization. As mentioned, the HUD can be used to display text, pictures, and other elements. The primary way to access the HUD is through the `guiNode` which is declared in the `SimpleApplication` class. The `guiNode` is the 2-dimensional equivalent of the 3-dimensional `rootNode`.

Adding Text to the HUD

To add text to the HUD we need to:

1. Create a `BitmapText` object

2. Set the text to display

3. Set the size, color, and location

4. Attach it to the `guiNode`

To demonstrate this technique we will create a simple HUD with the string "Infinite Recursion" displayed in the lower left hand portion of the display. This will be the name of our ship. Add this code to the `simpleInitApp` method.

In order to add text to the HUD, a `BitmapText` object is used. The `BitmapText` constructor takes a `BitmapFont` as an argument as shown in the next code sequence. The `SimpleApplication` class provides a default `BitmapFont` object called `guiFont` that can be used as the parameter. In addition, a boolean `rightToLeft` parameter can be added. We used `false` which indicates the text will be drawn from left to right. This option can be useful when using languages other than English. For example, if we wanted to use Chinese characters we would probably want to set the boolean value to `true`.

```
BitmapText text = new BitmapText(guiFont, false);
```

`BitmapText` objects have several useful methods including `setSize`, `setColor`, `setText`, and `setLocalTranslation`. The `setLocalTranslation` method is the primary method for positioning a `BitmapText` object. The size of the font was specified by using the default rendered size of the `guiFont` character set. We do this by running the `getCharSet` and `getRenderedSize` methods against `guiFont` as shown next. However, the `setSize` method will accept any float value as a parameter.

```
text.setSize(guiFont.getCharSet().getRenderedSize());
```

Set the color was set to red with the text set to "Infinite Recursion" as shown in the code that follows:

```
text.setColor(ColorRGBA.Red);
text.setText("Infinite Recursion");
```

The three parameters of the `setLocalTranslation` method correspond to the x, y, and z coordinates of the text. The lower left point of the screen coordinate is (0, 0). To access the top right point of the screen we can use the `settings.getWidth` and `settings.getHeight` values as the x and y parameters. These are used in the next statement to position the text:

```
text.setLocalTranslation(100, 50, 0);
```

Each visible element in a scene graph has an origin point. The origin point for text is its lower left corner. For this example, let's set the x value to 100, the y value to 50, and leave the z value at 0. The left hand side of the text string is 100 pixels from the left side of the screen. The bottom of the text screen is 50 pixels from the bottom of the text screen. These values will give us an idea of the scale of the HUD. This is illustrated in *Figure 12 - HUD Text Example*.

The third argument, which usually represents a point on the z axis, is useful when HUD elements overlap. In most cases this value, the depth order z, will be 0. A relative negative value will move the text behind other objects, and a relative positive value will move text to the front. For example, `text.move(100, 100, 1)` would move the text object 100 units to the right, 100 units up, and bring the object to the foreground (in front of any other objects with a lesser z value).

Finally, in order for the object to appear in the HUD it must be attached to the `guiNode` using the familiar `attachChild` method:

```
guiNode.attachChild(text);
```

When the application executes the resulting HUD will appear as shown in *Figure 12 - HUD Text Example*.

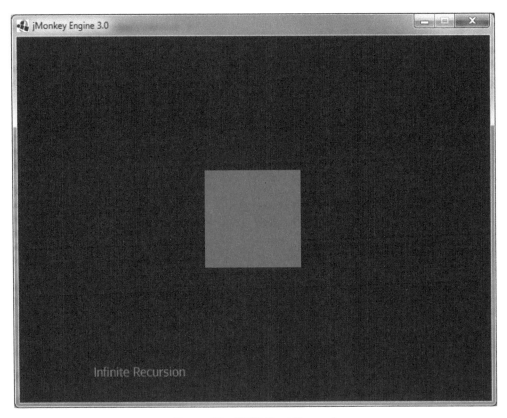

Figure 12 - HUD Text Example

When using the HUD to keep track of score or health points, it will be necessary to update the text or image periodically. This is done using the simpleUpdate method which will be covered in a later chapter.

Adding a Picture to the HUD

To add a picture to the HUD:

1. Create a Picture object

2. Assign an image to it

3. Set its size and location

4. Attach it to the guiNode

In this example we will add a monkey image to the center of the screen. This is a similar process to adding text. We will add this code to the simpleInitApp method.

Add a picture to the HUD using a Picture object with the picture name as the parameter as shown in the next code sequence. To set an image to the Picture object, the setImage method is used. This method has three parameters: the assetManager, the location of the image, and a boolean argument indicating whether or not the image will be transparent. The assetManager is inherited from the SimpleApplication class. The image we chose to use for this example, Monkey.png, can be found in the jme3-test-data library's Texture folder.

```
Picture picture = new Picture("Monkey Image");
picture.setImage(assetManager,
    "Textures/ColoredTex/Monkey.png", true);
```

The Picture object also has setWidth, setHeight, and setPosition methods. Use these as shown next to position the picture. The setPosition method takes an X and Y pixel value as the parameter. The origin of a Picture object is at its center.

```
picture.setWidth(settings.getWidth()/2);
picture.setHeight(settings.getHeight()/2);
picture.setPosition(settings.getWidth()/4,
    settings.getHeight()/4);
```

The Picture object must be attached to the guiNode in the same way that any object is attached to the rootNode, using the attachChild method:

```
guiNode.attachChild(picture);
```

When the application executes the resulting HUD will appear as shown in *Figure 13 - HUD Picture Example*.

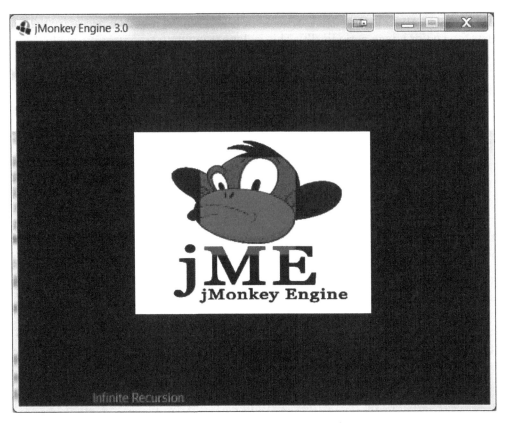

Figure 13 - HUD Picture Example

When working with HUD elements, specifying the scope of HUD variables is an important consideration. We frequently want to be able to access the variable from multiple locations in the project. It is recommended that you:

- When possible, declare HUD elements, such as font, as private instance variables. If they don't change then make them final.

- Initialize HUD values in `simpleInitApp`.

- Update HUD values in `simpleUpdate`.

Part of this process will be illustrated in the next section where we develop an initial HUD for our game. Support is provided for more sophisticated HUDs using the Nifty GUI library which we do not cover.

Shades of Infinity Initial HUD

For our game, Shades of Infinity, we will be using a custom class called `SpaceShip` to manage some HUD components. The `SpaceShip` class holds various data about the player's current space ship and location. Part of this class is found listed in the next code sequence. The complete listing for this version is found on the publisher's website.

The `SpaceShip` class stores the ship's name, location, shield level, power level, and torpedo count in private variables. The class has a 5 argument constructor to initialize these variables. The rest of the class consists of getters and setters for the 5 variables.

```java
public class SpaceShip {
    private Vector3f locationVector;
    private String name;
    private int shieldLevel;
    private int powerLevel;
    private int numberOfTorpedoes;

    public SpaceShip(String name, Vector3f locationVector,
            int shieldLevel, int powerLevel,
            int numberOfTorpedoes) {
        this.locationVector = locationVector;
        this.name = name;
        this.shieldLevel = shieldLevel;
        this.powerLevel = powerLevel;
        this.numberOfTorpedoes = numberOfTorpedoes;
    }
    ...
}
```

In the `Main` class we can call a method, `initializeHUD`, to initialize these variables. We use the `line` variable to keep track of the placement of the elements on the HUD so they don't overlap. Since all the current elements we are adding to the HUD are text-based, we can follow the process of adding text to the HUD as discussed in Adding Text to the HUD. The helper method, `getBitmapText`, that follows is used to simplify the code.

```java
    // HUD Fields
    BitmapText hudShipName;
    BitmapText hudShipPosition;
    BitmapText hudShipShieldLevel;
    BitmapText hudShipPowerLevel;
    BitmapText hudShipNumberOfTorpedoes;

    private BitmapText getBitmapText(String text, int line) {
        BitmapText bmt = new BitmapText(guiFont, false);
        bmt.setSize(guiFont.getCharSet().getRenderedSize());
        bmt.setColor(ColorRGBA.Blue);
        bmt.setLocalTranslation(0,
            bmt.getLineHeight() * line, 0);
        bmt.setText(text);
        return bmt;
    }

    private void initializeHUD() {
        int line = 5;
        // Initialize Ship's name
        hudShipName = getBitmapText(
            spaceShip.getName(), line--);
```

```
                guiNode.attachChild(hudShipName);

                // Initialize Ship's position
                hudShipPosition = getBitmapText(
                    "Position: " +
                    spaceShip.getLocationVector(), line--);
                guiNode.attachChild(hudShipPosition);

                // Initialize Ship's shield level
                hudShipShieldLevel = getBitmapText(
                    "Shields: " + spaceShip.getShieldLevel(), line--);
                guiNode.attachChild(hudShipShieldLevel);

                // Initialize Ship's power level
                hudShipPowerLevel = getBitmapText(
                    "Power: " + spaceShip.getPowerLevel(), line--);
                guiNode.attachChild(hudShipPowerLevel);

                // Initialize Ship's number of torpedoes
                hudShipNumberOfTorpedoes = getBitmapText(
                    "Torpedoes: " +
                    spaceShip.getNumberOfTorpedoes(), line--);
                guiNode.attachChild(hudShipNumberOfTorpedoes);
        }
```

Add the following code sequence to the `simpleInitApp` method:

```
        spaceShip = new SpaceShip("Infinite Recursion",
                new Vector3f(cam.getLocation()),
                100, 100, 50);
        initializeHUD();
```

When executed, the game will appear as shown in *Figure 14 - Shades of Infinity HUD*.

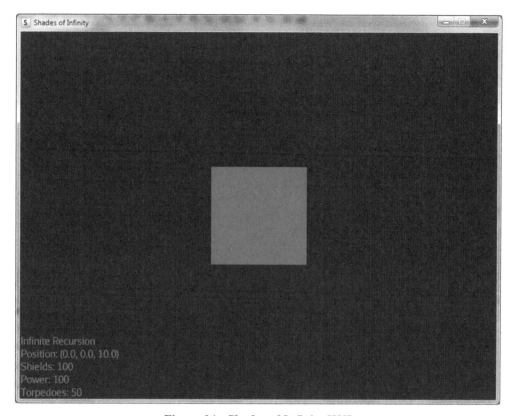

Figure 14 - Shades of Infinity HUD

When using the HUD to keep track of score, health points, or anything that changes over time, it will be necessary to update the text or image periodically. This is done using the `simpleUpdate` method. We will discuss the `simpleUpdate` method, and update our current HUD elements in a later chapter.

Creating a Simple Background Sound

Sounds are a crucial component of any good game. Sounds can be used to set the mood or provide excitement to a situation. Sounds also give the user instant feedback such as a weapon firing, or situational cues like an alarm going off.

There are 3 primary types of sound in JME3, **Situational**, **Positional**, and **Ambient.** Ambient sounds are typically played continuously at lower volume. Background music is usually referred to as ambient. Ambient sounds in games are not usually tied to a specific position in the game, but are heard equally well regardless of position. Situational sounds are tied to some event, like a gunshot. Situational sounds are not ambient, because they do not play continuously. Positional sounds emanate from a specific point in the game space such as a waterfall or the creaking of a door. Positional sounds can be either situational or ambient.

JME3 provides support for two primary sound file formats: Ogg Vorbis and Waveform. Waveform, or .wav, files tend to have a bigger file size and better quality. Ogg Vorbis, or .ogg, files are compressed with a smaller file size and some loss of quality.

JME3 uses a special node for sound called the `AudioNode`. This node is found in the `com.jme3.audio` package. An `AudioNode` object is created using the `assetManager` and the location of the audio file as constructor parameters. There is also an optional third boolean argument to the `AudioNode` constructor. When set to `true` the sound will be streamed. When set to `false` the sound will be pre-buffered. Streamed files will start playing before they are completely loaded. Pre-buffered sounds will be fully loaded before the sound is played.

Use the pre-buffered approach with short sounds like a gunshot. Remember, pre-buffered sounds use the `false` parameter. Optionally, you can leave this parameter out since pre-buffered is the default.

Use the streamed approach for long sound files like music or dialogue. Remember, for streamed sounds use the `true` parameter.

The `AudioNode` class possesses a `setVolume` method that takes a float as an argument. The default volume is 1.0. The `setLooping` method determines whether or not the sound will be repeating. This will be set to `true` for background music and ambient sounds. It is important to note that `setLooping` cannot be set to `true` if the sound is streamed. Because ambient music cannot be streamed, we will use the default pre-buffered approach.

Like all nodes, the `AudioNode` object must be attached to either the `rootNode` or a child of the `rootNode`. The `play` method will start the sound and it will play continuously until the `stop` method is called. We will illustrate how an `AudioNode` can be used to play some background music. We will use one of the default sound files. The code in this example should be placed in the `simpleUpdate` method.

Declare an `AudioNode` using the `assetManager` and the location of the sound as parameters as shown in the next statements. We want ambient music so we can either leave out the optional third parameter or use `false`. We set the volume to 0.3f, which is a fairly quiet level of volume.

```
AudioNode background = new AudioNode(assetManager,
    "Sound/Environment/Ocean Waves.ogg");
background.setVolume(0.3f);
```

With background music you want to avoid overpowering the rest of the game. When an `AudioNode` is created, its volume is to set to 1. Using the `setVolume` method with a value of 0 will make it silent. A value of 2 doubles the volume.

For continuous background music we want to set the looping to `true`, causing the sound file to repeat indefinitely as shown here:

```
background.setLooping(true);
```

As usual we must attach our new audio node to the `rootNode`. Then, we need to call the `play` method to get our background music started.

```
rootNode.attachChild(background);
background.play();
```

In Java, if we use a float value that is a decimal, we must include an `f` after the number! For example, 0.3 will not work in the `setVolume` method. We must use `0.3f` because the `setVolume` method expects a float rather than a double. This is true of many common methods in JME3.

Try running the code a few times with different volume values to get a feel for effect of different sound levels in JME3. We will examine positional and situational sounds in Chapter 5.

Using the Camera

The camera typically shows the game from the user's perspective, or first person perspective. However, it is possible to use multiple cameras in a game. This can be useful for using a third person perspective or from behind the player character. JME3 provides a default camera with the standard game.

The position of a camera, and other elements, is specified by a **Vector**. Vectors are used extensively in JME3. They can be thought of as a point in space. Vectors are used to place objects, nodes, and even sounds at particular points in the game space. All vectors are relative to the coordinate system. The data type used for vectors in JME3 is the `Vector3f` found in the `com.jme3.math` package. In JME3, a vector located at the origin of the game space, or (0, 0, 0), can be defined as follows:

```
Vector3f vector = new Vector3f(0, 0, 0);
```

The default camera position is defined as `Vector3f(0, 0, 10)`. From the starting position the camera is on the positive Z-Axis, looking toward the origin.

JME3 uses the `Camera` class to represent a camera. The `Camera` class is found in the `com.jme3.renderer` package. A default `Camera` object is provided and is represented by the variable `cam`. The `cam` object starts off with several default properties. The width and height of `cam` are set to the current game's `settings.getWidth` and `settings.getHeight` values, respectively. This means that cameras view is in the same scale as the game. There are also several useful methods associated with the `cam` object laid out in *Table 7 – Default Camera Methods*.

Table 7 – Default Camera Methods

Methods	Use
`getLocation` and `setLocation`	Gets and sets the camera's position
`getRotation` and `setRotation`	Gets and sets the camera's rotation
`getLeft` and `setLeft`	Gets and sets the camera's left axis
`getUp` and `setUp`	Gets and sets the camera's up axis
`setAxes`	Sets the camera's left, up, and direction properties
`resize`	Adjusts the camera object's width and height and optionally the aspect ratio
`lookAt()`	Faces the camera toward a set of coordinates
`getDirection`	Returns the vector that the camera is facing

The **frustum** is basically the viewing box of the camera. This is the 3-dimensional region that is visible on the screen. The frustum is defined by a six-sided box with a near, far, left, right, top, and bottom plane relative to eye point. The default frustum consists of:

- A frame of view angle of 45 ° along the Y axis

- An aspect ratio of width divided by height

- The near plane of 1 World Unit distant

- The far plane of 1000 World Units distant

A graphical depiction of a frustum is shown in *Figure 15 - Frustum*.

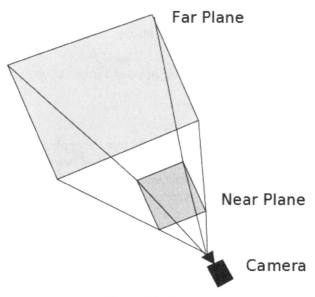

Figure 15 - Frustum

JME3 also supports a fly camera and a chase camera. They are used to support movement of a player and a third person perspective. They are discussed in Chapter 6.

Application and Display Settings

The application and display settings are related to each other. Application settings refer to the characteristics of a game such as the state of the game. Displays settings are concerned with visual elements such as its height or title. In general, we will refer to these collectively as application settings.

Controlling the Application Settings

The `AppSettings` class stores the configuration of the application. It contains a number of methods to get and save the characteristics of an application. The class is final and is found in the `com.jme3.system package`. It also extends `HashMap` which gives it methods to easily access application settings.

The `AppSettings` class possesses a single constructor that uses a boolean argument. If this argument is set to `true` then the default settings are used. If `false` is used, then the application will load the settings from a previous launch of the application.

To specify an application's settings:

1. Create an instance of the `AppSettings` class
2. Customize the application's settings
3. Using the `SimpleApplication` class' `setSettings` to assign the settings to the application

This is illustrated in the following sequence. The statement, `settings.set…`, refers to a number of methods that are used to configure an application. Some of these are discussed in Controlling the Display Settings.

```
AppSettings settings = new AppSettings(true);
settings.set…
app.setSettings(settings);
```

The configuration of an application must be set before the application starts. It is best to set the configuration of the application in the `main` method before the `start` method is called. If the configuration needs to be changed when the application is running, then the `restart` method must be called for the changes to take effect.

```
settings.set…
app.setSettings(settings);
app.restart();
```

Always configure and set your settings before calling the `start` method. Otherwise, they will not take effect.

The `SimpleApplication` class' `restart` method will restart a game. It does not reinitialize the entire game but will apply any update settings.

Controlling the Display Settings

The display settings control the size and general appearance of the application. This includes:

- The title of the application

- Its width and height

- Whether it is full screen

- Details of the resolution

Controlling an Application's Title

The title is controlled using the `setTitle` method. It is illustrated in the following code where we set the title of the application to "Shades of Infinity":

```
settings.setTitle("Shades of Infinity");
```

The `getTitle` method will return the current title if needed.

Controlling an Application's Resolution

The height and width of the application is set using the setHeight, setWidth, and/or setResolution methods. The **resolution** of a screen is the number of pixels used by each dimension of the screen. This is normally expressed as width by height.

The setResolution method uses two integer parameters: width and height. The default resolution is 640 pixels width by 480 pixels high. The resolution specified must be one supported by the system. If an invalid resolution is specified, then the default resolution for the system is used.

In the following example, the initial size is then set to 1024 pixels wide and 768 pixels high:

```
settings.setResolution(1024, 768);
```

We can achieve the same effect using the setWidth and setHeight methods as shown:

```
settings.setWidth(1024);
settings.setHeight(768);
```

We can also set the minimum width and height of an application using the setMinWidth and setMinHeight methods.

Controlling Full Screen

To render the application in full screen we use the setFullScreen method. In this code sequence the application will appear using the full screen:

```
settings.setFullscreen(true);
```

The isFullScreen method will return true if the screen is currently set to full screen.

Controlling Icons

The icons used by an application's window are controlled by the AppSettings class' setIcons method. An array of Objects representing icons is passed to the method. This is normally an array of BufferedImages.

The icons are used for the Display Settings dialog box and the main window. At minimum, a 16x16 and a 32x32 pixel icons should be supplied. The 16x16 is used for the title bar icon and the 32x32 is used the alt-tab icon. Linux uses a 32x32 and Mac OS X uses a 128x128 pixel icon. A variety of sizes should be used to support multiple platforms.

In the following code sequence an array is created and passed to the setIcons method. We used a single 16x16 pixel icon representing a simple S for the Windows game. This icon can be found at www.p8tech.com.

```
try {
    settings.setIcons(new BufferedImage[]{
        ImageIO.read(new FileImageInputStream(
        new File("assets/Images/Sicon16x16.png")))
    });
} catch (IOException e) {
    //
}
app.setSettings(settings);
```

The resulting window is shown in *Figure 16 - Icon Example*.

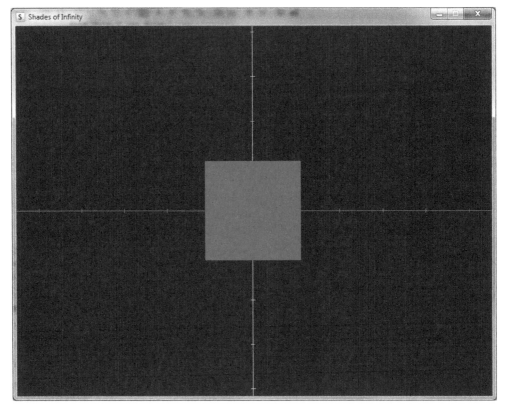

Figure 16 - Icon Example

Input Devices Settings

There are several input device-related settings available. Most of these are of an advanced nature and will be discussed later. For applications that do not use a keyboard or mouse, the setUseInput and useInput methods can disable their use. These types of applications are called headless applications and are discussed in Chapter 10.

Joysticks are another possible input device. The setUseJoysticks and useJoysticks methods control whether they are used or not.

On touch screen devices equivalent mouse actions are facilitated using the setEmulateMouse method. Screen taps or finger movements are translated to mouse movements. There are also methods to flip the X and Y axis if necessary.

Audio Settings

The renderer used for sound is specified by the setAudioRenderer method. Currently only one renderer is supported: OpenAL which is set by default. The following code sets it explicitly:

```
settings.setAudioRenderer(AppSettings.LWJGL_OPENAL);
```

To disable sound we can use null as an argument:

```
settings.setAudioRenderer(null);
```

3D stereo is enabled using the setStereo3D method. Its boolean argument is set to true to enable 3D audio. However, this support requires help from the GPU and most GPUs do not support it. The useStereo3D method returns true if 3D stereo is being used.

Saving and Loading an Application's Settings

It can be desirable to save, and subsequently load, the settings for an application. The AppSettings class' save and load methods are used for this purpose. There is also a copyFrom and mergeFrom method that copies settings from one AppSettings object to another.

The save method is overloaded and supports two versions. The first one uses a string that corresponds to the name of a setting. This name is used to uniquely identify a set of settings. In the following example we use the string, "Shades of Infinity", for the name of the setting. All of the settings for a game will be saved under this name. Since the save method throws a BackingStoreException exception we need to handle it.

```
try {
    settings.save("Shades of Infinity");
} catch (BackingStoreException ex) {
    //
}
```

The location of these settings depends on the operating system. On Windows 7 you will find these settings saved in the registry under HKEY_CURRENT_USER\Software\JavaSoft\Prefs\/Shades of/Infinity as shown in *Figure 17- Registry Settings for Shades of Infinity.*

.../B_/Use/Input	REG_SZ	true
/B_/V/Sync	REG_SZ	false
/L_/Bits/Per/Pixel	REG_SZ	24
/L_/Depth/Bits	REG_SZ	24
/L_/Frame/Rate	REG_SZ	-1
/L_/Frequency	REG_SZ	-1
/L_/Height	REG_SZ	600
/L_/Min/Height	REG_SZ	0
/L_/Min/Width	REG_SZ	0

Figure 17- Registry Settings for Shades of Infinity

To access the regedit application, type regedit from the Window's 'command' line as demonstrated in *Figure 18 - Starting the regedit Tool.*

Figure 18 - Starting the regedit Tool

JME3 will save the setting in an operating system specific location as listed in *Table 8 - Default System Settings Location*. On windows it is stored in the registry. On Linux and Mac it is stored in an XML file.

Table 8 - Default System Settings Location

Operating System	Location
Windows	HKEY_CURRENT_USER\Software\JavaSoft\Prefs\KeyName
Linux	$HOME/.java/.userPrefs/KeyName
Mac	$HOME/Library/Preferences/KeyName.plist

To load a setting use the overloaded load method. Using a string as an argument to the method will load the settings using that name as shown next. The BackingStoreException exception needs to be dealt with.

```
try {
    settings.load("Shades of Infinity");
} catch (BackingStoreException ex) {
    //
}
```

Using a File to Save/Load Settings

If you need to save the settings to a specific file then using IO streams will work. The `save` method takes an `OutputStream` representing the destination of the settings. In the following example, we use the file `Shades of Infinity.dat`:

```
try {
    FileOutputStream fos =
        new FileOutputStream("Shades of Infinity.dat");
    settings.save(fos);
} catch (BackingStoreException | IOException ex) {
    //
}
```

In this example, the file will be located at the root of the JME3 project directory.

To load the settings we use the `load` method with the `FileInputStream` object referencing the file as shown here:

```
try {
    FileInputStream fos =
        new FileInputStream("Shades of Infinity.dat");
    settings.load(fos);
} catch (BackingStoreException | IOException ex) {
    //
}
```

Conclusion

In this chapter we introduced the basics of a JME3 game and provided a number of details regarding its settings and configuration. Several basic terms were introduced including the concepts of geometry, node, and material. These are used to create the scene graph for an application.

We learned that all JME3 applications are derived from the `SimpleApplication` class which provides the basic methods and variables used in a game. The `simpleInitApp` method is where the initialization of the game occurs including the initialization of the scene graph.

The 3D coordinate system was detailed along with how the camera and other elements of a game can be positioned. The internals of the `BasicGame` were explained and augmented to support the space-based game we will be developing.

We also covered the HUD and how text and images can be added to it. A game's settings are an important part of a game: we investigated how these are set and saved.

In the next chapter we will look more closely at the use of materials and textures!

2

Objects in Space

When we create a game, we are interested in creating a scene graph populated with the elements of the game. These elements are represented in JME3 by Spatial objects, some of which may represent the players of the game.

Spatials may be either nodes or geometries. A geometry is normally assigned a mesh that defines its shape. A material is then applied to the mesh to give a "skin". Working with nodes and geometries are an essential part of game development. In this chapter we will focus on the basics of how this is done. Some aspects, such as lighting, will be postponed until a later chapter.

In this chapter, we will address several techniques including:

- Managing a scene graph

- The use of spatials including nodes, geometries, and meshes

- Transformations of objects

- Working with predefined shapes

Transformations include moving an object to a different location, making it bigger or smaller (by scaling it), and changing its orientation by rotating it.

In the *Working with Meshes* section, we will look at how to display the wireframe view of an object and how several JME3 provided shapes can be used. We will also illustrate how a custom mesh can be created.

To help you better understand this chapter's topics, we have developed a simple scene graph consisting of several elements. Two of these are spheres, one which represents a planet and the second a moon. There is a group of AI ships found between the planet and the moon. AI ships will be the ships controlled by the game's Artificial Intelligence nemesis. This is shown in *Figure 1 - Planetary System with AI Ships*.

The two spheres have been given different rotations. The two AI ships have been given different colors. As with previous applications, the player is able to move around the scene entering the various spheres and shapes freely. In Chapter 3 we will demonstrate how to handle collisions.

The objects in the scene are displayed using their wireframes. This highlights their shapes and simplifies our discussions. We will learn how to add materials to a geometry, alongside a detailed discussion of materials and how they are affected by lighting, in Chapter 5.

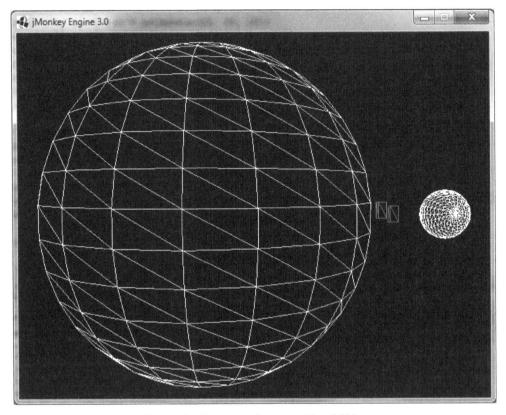

Figure 1 - Planetary System with AI Ships

This program is detailed and explained as we move through the chapter. The complete program can be downloaded from www.p8tech.com. It is recommended that you download and execute the program to see how it behaves.

Creating and Managing a Scene Graph

As seen in Chapter 1, a scene graph represents the visual world the user sees and manipulates. The head of this tree structure is **rootNode**. In this section we will focus on the creation and manipulation of the scene graph.

Spatials make up the scene graph. They can be loaded from a file, transformed, and saved. They possess many attributes including:

- Their positions on the screen

- How large they are (their scale)

- How they are oriented/rotated on the screen

Spatials, Nodes, and Geometries

There are two kinds of spatial: nodes and geometries. **Nodes** can be very useful when objects need to be grouped together. For example, a model solar system could have a parent node in the center with all the planets having their own node attached to the parent. If the entire solar system needed to be moved or resized, changes need only be applied to the parent node and the rest would follow.

A **geometry** is a visible element of a scene such as a character or building. It has a shape, appearance, and is normally visible. The `rootNode` is a node that contains all of the elements of the scene graph in a tree structure.

Understanding Nodes

The `Node` class is an invisible handle for a group of objects in JME3, located in the `com.jme3.scene` package. Like the `rootNode`, all nodes can have geometries and other nodes attached to them.

Nodes can be very helpful when you need to create a complex object. In this chapter we will provide several examples of creating a complex object. The first example is a planetary system and the second is a space station. Both of these examples have two or more nodes and geometries attached to a parent node.

Changes and transformations applied to a parent node are applied to all child spatials, geometries, and nodes. As we will see in the Using Transformations section, nodes are used extensively to effect transformations of objects.

Our planetary system example will make use of a node that we will call the `baseNode`. This node will be the base for the geometries we will create. All nodes need to be attached to the `rootNode` before they appear in the scene as illustrated using a method like the following `attachChild` method:

```
Node baseNode = new Node("Base node");
rootNode.attachChild(baseNode);
```

Understanding Geometries

The `Geometry` class represents a visible 3D object and is found in the `com.jme3.scene` package. Geometries support an object's appearance in a game. They are the main building block for visible parts of the game space and are made up of shapes, colors, materials, and textures. Some common examples of geometries include walls, players, spheres, buildings, vehicles, terrains, and pretty much any visible object in the game space!

To create a `Geometry`, the steps are:

1. Create a mesh object

2. Instantiate a `Geometry` object with the mesh object

3. Create a material

4. Attach the material to the geometry

The mesh provides the shape. The material covers it and they are tied together using a `Geometry` object.

The mesh created for the geometry can either be a custom mesh or a pre-defined mesh like the `Box` object, or the `Sphere` object. Creating custom meshes is discussed in the *Creating a Custom Mesh* section.

To illustrate the process of creating and using a geometry, we will use a sphere mesh to represent a planet in our planetary system. If you plan to create many geometries of the same shape, it is a good idea to create a helper method to make this process easier. We will be using the `getSphere` method for this purpose (as shown next). This method takes arguments for a sphere and returns a geometry. This will save us the trouble of creating a new mesh for every sphere-shaped geometry we create.

```
public Geometry getSphere(int y, int z, float radius) {
    Sphere sphere1 = new Sphere(y, z, radius);
    Geometry sphere = new Geometry("Sphere", sphere1);
    return sphere;
}
```

The parameters of the `Sphere` constructor can be a bit confusing at first. For this example we will focus on the `radius` argument, which will determine the size of the object. The other arguments will be covered in more depth in *Using the Sphere Shape* section.

Now that we have the `getSphere` method, let's create a model planet as illustrated in the code sequence that follows. First, we get a sphere geometry using the `getSphere` method and assign it to the `planet` variable. For a material we will use the basic unshaded material provided by JME3. Once our material is created, we can attach it to the geometry with the `setMaterial` method. We then set our material to display as a wireframe. The details of this will be discussed in the *Displaying a Wireframe* section of this chapter. Then we will attach the geometry to our `baseNode` rather than directly to the `rootNode`. This gives us the first planet of our planetary system as seen in *Figure 2 - First Planet*.

```
Geometry planet = getSphere(20, 20, 2f);
Material sphereMaterial = new Material(assetManager,
    "Common/MatDefs/Misc/Unshaded.j3md");
planet.setMaterial(sphereMaterial);
sphereMaterial.getAdditionalRenderState().
    setWireframe(true);
baseNode.attachChild(planet);
```

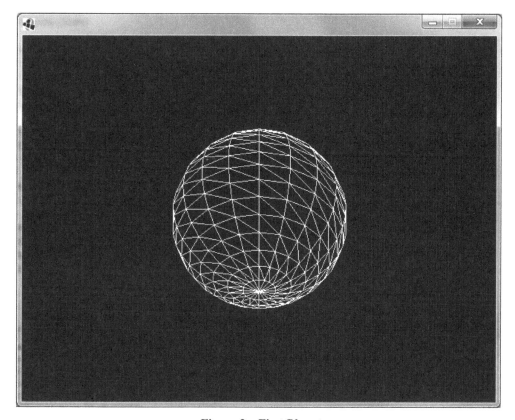

Figure 2 - First Planet

Let's add another object to our planetary system. This time we will add a sphere to represent a moon for our planet. This process will be almost identical to the creation of the planet. The main difference will be in the size of the sphere. This code segment will be shorter because we can reuse the material that we created for the planet.

```
Geometry moon = getSphere(20, 20, 0.3f);
moon.setMaterial(sphereMaterial);
baseNode.attachChild(moon);
```

Now our planetary system has a planet and a moon. As you can see in *Figure 3 - Geometry Example*, we have a wireframe planet with a wireframe moon in the very center. Of course, we do not want our planet's moon to be inside of it. We will solve this problem in *Changing the Position of an Object* section.

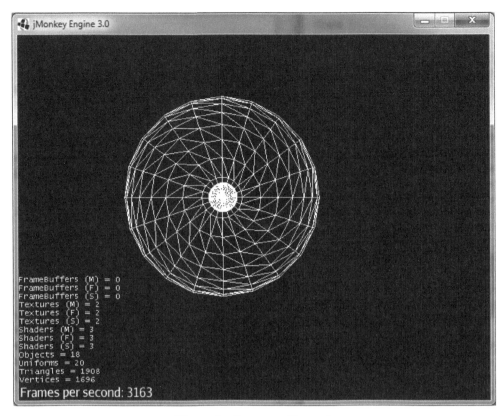

Figure 3 - Geometry Example

Using Materials

Materials give an object its external appearance. It can be as simple as a solid color or can involve many different textures and lighting conditions. In JME3, a material is basically anything that affects the surface appearance of a spatial. In this chapter, we will provide a basic introduction to the use of materials. The interaction between materials and lighting is covered in more depth in Chapter 5.

All geometries must have a material applied to them. It is a good idea to reuse materials that are the same for multiple objects. You can create one material and apply it to as many geometries as you like. This technique comes in handy when you need to create a lot of similar objects like walls or multiple background objects.

JME3 has several materials that are available to us by default. It is also possible to create your own materials and import materials from external sources. We will discuss creating materials in Chapter 5. Materials can add shininess, bumpiness, and glow to an object. They are also necessary to if we want to add a texture to an object. There are many options when it comes to materials, for now let's just take a quick look at two.

The materials that are used most often are the Unshaded and Lighting materials. The Unshaded material ignores the effects of lighting and shading. As you may have noticed running the basic game, an unshaded material, the blue cube, is visible even though there is no light source. This is typically the type of material you would use for testing out objects in your scene.

When working with materials, the methods you will commonly use are the `setTexture` method (for applying a texture) and the `setColor` method (for applying color and glow). We will look into these methods in more depth in Chapter 5.

As we have seen in previous examples, the `Unshaded` material is found in the project manager under assets, specifically: `Common/MatDefs/Misc/Unshaded.j3md`. We create materials using the `assetManager` and the material location as illustrated next.

```
Material sphereMaterial = new Material(assetManager,
    "Common/MatDefs/Misc/Unshaded.j3md");
```

The second most frequently used material is the `Lighting` material. These materials require a light source to be seen. These materials will make an object appear darker on sides that are further away from the light source. This type of material uses the same `setTexture` and `setColor` methods as the unshaded material.

However, there are more complexities due to the effects of lighting. For example, the unshaded material typically uses a `ColorMap`, where lighting materials can use other maps such as `DiffuseMap`, `NormalMap`, `SpecularMap`, `ParallaxMap`, or `AlphaMap`. These various maps and the lighting material will be examined more closely in Chapter 5. The `Lighting` material is located in: `Common/MatDefs/Light/Lighting.j3md`. This type of material is created in the same way as the unshaded material.

Maintaining a Scene Graph

The process of managing a scene graph consists of:

- Creating spatials
- Adding spatials to the scene graph
- Manipulating the spatials

In this section we will cover the basics of how these tasks are performed along with useful variations to these techniques.

Adding Objects

There are several methods we can use to add an element to the scene graph. However, the `Node` class' `attachChild` method is the most commonly used method. It is simple to use and works well for most additions. We can add a single node, a group of nodes, or a model to a scene graph.

In previous examples, we saw how we can add a single geometry to the `rootNode`. To illustrate how to add a group of objects we will create 2 AI ships and group them together as a unit. We will then add the group to the scene graph. These ships will be represented by simple cubes. In later versions of the game we will create more sophisticated ships.

In the `createAIShip` helper method shown next, a box shape is used to represent the ship. Most of these techniques have been covered earlier so we will not go into details here.

```
    private Geometry createAIShip(String name,
            float x, float y, float z, ColorRGBA color) {
        Box box = new Box(1, 2, 1);
        Geometry geom = new Geometry(name, box);

        geom.setLocalTranslation(x, y, z);
        Material mat = new Material(assetManager,
            "Common/MatDefs/Misc/Unshaded.j3md");
        mat.setColor("Color", color);
        geom.setMaterial(mat);
        mat.getAdditionalRenderState().setWireframe(true);
        return geom;
    }
```

The code sequence that follows next, illustrates how to create the group of ships. First, 2 AI ships are created, followed by 3 nodes. One is a base node and the other two nodes will be attached to the base node as sub-nodes. The `attachChild` method is used to attach the AI Ship geometries to the sub-nodes and then attach the sub-nodes to the base node. The `attachChild` method is used one more time to attach the group, represented by `baseNode`, to the scene graph.

```
    Geometry geom1 =
        createAIShip("AI Ship 1", 1, 0, 0, ColorRGBA.Blue);
    Geometry geom2 =
        createAIShip("AI Ship 2", -2, 1, 0, ColorRGBA.Red);

    Node baseNode = new Node("AI Base Node");
    Node node1 = new Node("node 1");
    Node node2 = new Node("node 2");

    node1.attachChild(geom1);
    node2.attachChild(geom2);
    baseNode.attachChild(node1);
    baseNode.attachChild(node2);

    rootNode.attachChild(baseNode);
```

This grouping is illustrated in *Figure 4 - Group Diagram* and the user interface is shown in *Figure 5 - Adding Multiple Objects*. There is also the `attachChildAt` method that adds a node at the index specified in the second parameter. Using indexes is covered in the *Locating Objects in a Scene Graph* section. In *Adding a .blend Model to Your Project*, we will see how a 3D model can be added to a graph.

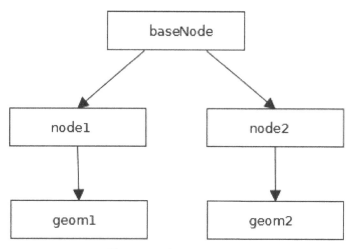

Figure 4 - Group Diagram

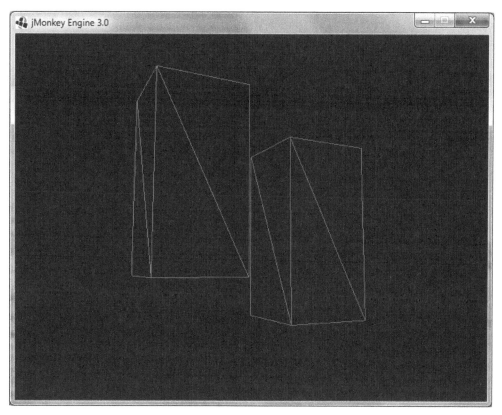

Figure 5 - Adding Multiple Objects

Removing Objects

If we want to make an object disappear from a scene, we can remove it from the scene graph using one of several methods. The most common one is the `detachChild` method, which removes the node specified by its argument. In the following statement, we remove `node2` from the graph referenced by the `baseNode`:

```
baseNode.detachChild(node2);
```

We can also use the `detachChildNamed` method to specify the method by name, as shown here:

```
baseNode.detachChildNamed("node 2");
```

The `detachChildAt` method will remove the child at the index specified by the method's parameter. Graph indexes are discussed in the *Locating Objects in a Scene Graph* section. If we want to remove all of the node's elements, we use the `detachAllChildren` method.

Swapping Objects

Sometimes it is desirable to swap two nodes in a graph to provide a more logical ordering of the nodes. We can do this using a combination of the `detachChild` and `attachChild` methods but this can be tedious, inefficient, and error prone. A simpler technique is to use the `swapChildren` method to interchange the position of two children in a graph. This method is illustrated in the next statement where `node1` and `node2` are swapped. The arguments to the method are the indexes of the nodes.

```
baseNode.swapChildren(0, 1);
```

When executed, you will not see any difference in the scene graph. The red ship will be on the left and the blue ship will be on the right. This is because the locations of the ships have not changed, only their positions in the graph. Displaying the indexes of these nodes will reveal their new order as discussed in the next section.

Locating Objects in a Scene Graph

There are times when it is useful to be able to locate an object either by its index in the graph, or by its name. When a node is created it is assigned a name. When a node is added to a graph it is assigned an index within that graph.

The overloaded `getChild` method will return a reference to a node using either its name or its index. The `getChildIndex` method will return the index of a node. Using the example shown in Adding Objects, the following code sequence illustrates how this method is used:

```
System.out.println(baseNode.getChild(0));
System.out.println(baseNode.getChild("node 1"));
System.out.println(baseNode.getChildIndex(node1));
```

The output follows:

node 1 (Node)

node 1 (Node)

0

If we are interested in accessing all of the nodes in a graph we can use the `getChldren` method to return a list. In the following example, this method is used to iterate through the list displaying the name and index of each node:

```
List<Spatial> list = baseNode.getChildren();
for(Spatial spatial :  list) {
System.out.println("Index: " +
    baseNode.getChildIndex(spatial) +
    " - " + spatial.getName());
}
```

The output of this sequence follows:

Index: 0 - node 1

Index: 1 - node 2

If we use the `rootNode` instead of the `baseNode` we get the output that follows.

Index: 0 - AI Base Node

The indexes are relative to the node we are looking at. Since the `rootNode` has only one child, that is the only one listed. `baseNode` had two children so both of its children were listed.

The `getParent` method returns the parent node of the node it is executing against. In the following example, we determine the parent of `baseNode`:

```
System.out.println(baseNode.getParent());
```

The output returns `rootNode` as we would expect:

Root Node (Node)

Scene Graph Traversal

Traversing a scene graph is the process of visiting one or more elements of a scene graph and potentially performing some operation on the element. This can be useful when:

- You need to find specific elements to modify their state
- You want to understand the scene graph

We saw how the individual elements of a scene graph can be enumerated in the *Locating Objects in a Scene Graph* section. However, this is not as convenient as traversing it as a tree. Traversing a graph can also give us a better idea of how the nodes and geometries are organized.

The `Spatial` class possesses methods that permit us to perform either a depth first traversal, or a breadth first traversal, of the scene graph's tree allowing two ways of processing scene objects. To visit all of the children of a node, use either the `Spatial` class' `depthFirstTraversal` or `breadthFirstTraversal` methods. The order of the traversal is implied by their names.

These methods are executed against a graph where its single parameter is an instance of the `SceneGraphVisitor` interface. This interface has a single method, `visit`, which is called each time an element of the graph is encountered.

To traverse a graph:

1.   Create an object that implements the `SceneGraphVisitor` interface

2.   Add functionality to its `visitor` method

3.   Execute either of the traversal methods against a graph with the `SceneGraphVisitor` object as its argument

To illustrate this process, we will first create a private class called `TraverseGraph` as shown in the code that follows. The `visit` method is passed a reference to the current spatial being processed. Within this method we call a helper method to display information about the node. The triangle and vertex information is discussed in the *Displaying a Wireframe* section. However, they simply return the number of triangles and vertexes used for a given spatial.

```
private class TraverseGraph implements SceneGraphVisitor {

    public void visit(Spatial spatial) {
        displaySpatialInformation(spatial);
    }
}

private void displaySpatialInformation(Spatial spatial) {
    System.out.println("\nSpatial Name: " +
        spatial.getName());
    if (spatial.getParent() != null) {
        System.out.println("Parent's Node: " +
            spatial.getParent().getName());
    }
    System.out.println("Triangle count: " +
        spatial.getTriangleCount());
    System.out.println("Vertex count: " +
        spatial.getVertexCount());
}
```

To perform a depth first traversal of the graph, add the following code to the `simpleInitApp` method:

```
    rootNode.breadthFirstTraversal(new TraverseGraph());
```

If we use the code found in *Adding Objects* to create a scene graph, the output of this execution follows:

Spatial Name: Root Node

Triangle count: 24

Vertex count: 48

Spatial Name: AI Base Node

Parent's Node: Root Node

Triangle count: 24

Vertex count: 48

Spatial Name: node 1

Parent's Node: AI Base Node

Triangle count: 12

Vertex count: 24

Spatial Name: node 2

Parent's Node: AI Base Node

Triangle count: 12

Vertex count: 24

Spatial Name: AI Ship 1

Parent's Node: node 1

Triangle count: 12

Vertex count: 24

Spatial Name: AI Ship 2

Parent's Node: node 2

Triangle count: 12

Vertex count: 24

JME3 has provided the `SceneGraphVisitorAdapter` class to assist in traversing nodes and geometries separately. This class uses an overloaded `visit` method, one for nodes and one for geometries. In the following sequence we extend this class and provide a simple implementation for the methods:

```
private class TraverseGraphAdapter
        extends SceneGraphVisitorAdapter {
    @Override
    public void visit(Geometry geom) {
        System.out.println("Geometry Visited: " + geom);
    }

    @Override
    public void visit(Node node) {
        System.out.println("Node Visited: " + node);
    }
}
```

To demonstrate this approach, we perform the previous traversal but use our new class instead:

```
rootNode.breadthFirstTraversal(
    new TraverseGraphAdapter ());
```

The output follows:

Node Visited: Root Node (Node)

Node Visited: AI Base Node (Node)

Node Visited: node 1 (Node)

Node Visited: node 2 (Node)

Geometry Visited: AI Ship 1 (Geometry)

Geometry Visited: AI Ship 2 (Geometry)

The adapter class list the nodes first and then the geometries

The depth-first traversal may be faster if you are looking for a specific leaf element since it will reach leaf nodes quicker. The breadth-first technique is faster if you are looking for parent nodes. The actual performance depends on the graph's construction.

Using Transformations

Transformations are used to rotate, scale, and translate spatials. These transformations can be applied to a specific geometry, or to a node. When transformations are applied directly to a geometry, only that geometry is affected. When a transformation is applied to a node, all objects attached to the node are affected. In this section, we will examine the methods provided by JME3 to effect these transformations.

Changing the Position of an Object

Translation is a type of transformation used to move or relocate a spatial. There are two primary methods used for this type of transformation: `setLocalTranslation` and `move`. They can both be used to effect the same translation operation. The method to use depends on the situation and the developer's preference.

The `setLocalTranslation` method is used to relocate a spatial to specific or absolute coordinates. We will use this method to place objects in our game. In the following example we translate the moon in our planetary system to a new location. The new location is 3 WU in the positive x direction along the x axis from the origin.

```
moon.setLocalTranslation(3f, 0, 0);
```

The `move` method, rather than specifying an absolute location, uses a relative location. In the following statement, we assume the moon is located at (3, 0, 0). When the `move` method is called, the x, y, and z arguments are added to the current location. Since we will use 0 for the x and z values, the geometry will remain at its former x and z location. This will simply move the moon in the positive y direction without affecting its other coordinates.

```
moon.move(0, 3, 0);
```

Now the moon is located at (3, 3, 0), as shown in *Figure 6 - Translation Example*.

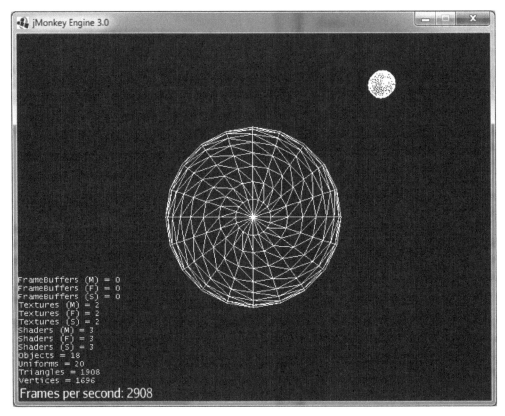

Figure 6 - Translation Example

Changing the Size of an Object

Scaling is the type of transformation used for resizing an object. The two methods used for scaling are `scale` and `setLocalScale`. Much like the methods used for translation, the `scale` method resizes the object relative to its current size and the `setLocalScale` method resizes the object relative to its initial size.

The arguments to these methods are the scaling factors in each dimension. The x, y, and z arguments correspond to a width, height, and depth. A value of 1.0f keeps the scale the same. Values between 0.0f and less than 1.0f will make the spatial smaller. Values that are greater than 1.0f will make the spatial bigger. If you use the same value for each argument, then the spatial will scale the object equally in all 3 directions.

These overloaded methods also work with a single argument. If you want to keep the size proportional, you can use 0.5f to cut the size in half or 2.0f to double the size. Using different values will stretch out the object.

In the statement that follows, we will scale our planetary system model using the `setLocalScale` method. Let's apply this to the node that holds our geometries. This will scale both our planet and moon equally. We will use 2 for all three arguments, causing our entire planetary system to double in size. Run this code and notice the resulting size of the objects.

```
baseNode.setLocalScale(2, 2, 2);
```

In the next statement, we will scale just the moon using the `scale` method. Let's make the moon a little bit bigger. We will call the `scale` method against our moon with a parameter of 1.5f. This will make our moon 50% bigger than it was previously. The `scale` method adds the scaling factor to the existing size of an object.

```
moon.scale(1.5f);
```

Take a look at *Figure 7 - Scale Example* to see how the planetary system has been affected.

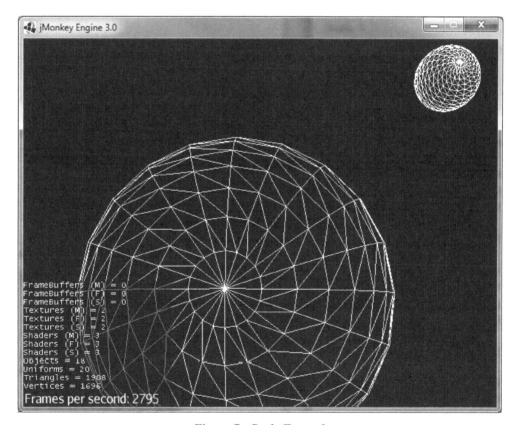

Figure 7 - Scale Example

Changing an Object's Orientation

Rotation is the type of transformation used for rotating, spinning, and tilting a spatial. Rotation can be applied to the three axes. These rotations are typically referred to as pitch, yaw, and roll.

- **Pitch** is rotation around the x axis. You can picture this as nodding your head.

- **Yaw** is rotation around the y axis. You can picture this as shaking your head.

- **Roll** is rotation around the z axis. You can picture this as cocking your head.

Nodes are very useful for rotation. If a geometry needs to rotate about a specific point in space, a node can be placed at that point and a geometry can rotate about the node. JME3 has a specific type of node used for rotation called a **Pivot Node**. Pivot nodes are used as a specific point, or pivot, to rotate one or more spatials, geometries, or nodes. A rotation can then be applied to the pivot node, instantly rotating all attached children in a single step.

The pivot point is not to be confused with an object's origin. The origin of a geometry is used to specify the geometry's location. Often, the origin and pivot point are the same but they don't have to be. In this section, we will use the `baseNode` that we created earlier as a pivot node for our planetary system.

There are two primary methods to use with rotation: `rotate` and `setLocalRotation`. The `rotate` method rotates from the current position. The `setLocalRotation` method disregards any previous rotation and replaces it. For example, if we called the `setLocalRotation` method to affect a pitch, and then called the method again with a roll, only the roll would be applied to the spatial. However, if we called the `rotate` method in the same way, both the pitch and roll would be applied to the spatial.

These methods use radians to specify the angle of rotation. If we prefer to work in degrees, then we need to convert from degrees to radians. The easiest way to accomplish to do this is with the `com.jme3.math.FastMath` class' `DEG_TO_RAD` static variable as we will demonstrate shortly. The class has several methods for using `PI` and converting between radians and degrees.

In the following statement, we will rotate our `baseNode` around the z axis to affect a roll. The `rotate` method has an x, y, and z argument. Since we are only rotating around the z axis, we will use a 0 for the x and y axes' arguments. Let's apply a 45 degree roll to the node. We need to use radians as the argument so we convert degrees to radians by multiplying our degrees, 45, by `FastMath.DEG_TO_RAD`. Use this statement in the `simpleInitApp` method and observe the pitch of the planetary system.

```
baseNode.rotate(0, 0, 45*FastMath.DEG_TO_RAD);
```

The `setLocalRotation` method works in a similar way to the previous method, except that it replaces any pre-existing rotation. The `setLocalRotation` method is more challenging to use than most of the other transformations. The reason for this is that this method uses matrix calculus in order to perform rotation. The best way to use this method is with **Quaternions**. A quaternion is a complex mathematical concept that is used in three-dimensional space.

The reason we use quaternions is to maintain our degrees of freedom in three-dimensional space. The way we implemented the rotate method is easier to do, but does not necessarily maintain the degrees of freedom. While this does not cause a problem, per se, the setLocalRotation method requires us to use more accurate techniques. Fully understanding quaternions can be quite difficult due to the advanced mathematical concepts behind them. However, there are a few simple ways to make them work for you.

In the following example, we will create a quaternion used to apply a 45 degree pitch to our planetary system. First, we will create a quaternion called pitch45, this is simply a variable name that can be anything you like. Then we will run the fromAngleAxis method against it. This method takes two arguments, the first is a predefined JME3 value called FastMath.PI, and the second is a vector defining which axes we will rotate around.

```
Quaternion pitch45 = new Quaternion();
pitch45.fromAngleAxis(FastMath.PI/4,
    new Vector3f(1, 0, 0));
baseNode.setLocalRotation(pitch45);
```

This may sound more complicated than it is. FastMath.PI is equal to 180 degrees. We want 45 degrees, so we will use FastMath.PI/4. Because we want to provide a pitch, our new vector will have the coordinates (1, 0, 0). This simply means we will rotate around the x axis. The quaternion is then applied to our planetary system using the setLocalRotation method. Conversion expressions for common angles and radians is found in *Table 1 - Degrees to Radians*.

The effect of this rotation is shown in *Figure 8 - Rotation Example*. Notice that if you run the setLocalRotation method after the rotate method, only the 45 degree pitch is applied to the node. However, if you switch the order of the methods both of the rotations will be applied. Remember that the rotate method adds on to existing orientation, while the setLocalRotation method overwrites existing orientation.

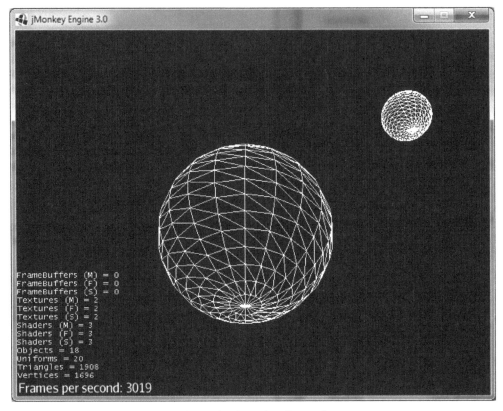

Figure 8 - Rotation Example

Table 1 - Degrees to Radians

Degrees	Radians
45 Degrees	`FastMath.PI / 4`
90 Degrees	`FastMath.PI / 2`
180 Degrees	`FastMath.PI`
270 Degrees	`FastMath.PI * 3 / 2`
360 Degrees	`FastMath.PI * 2`
X Degrees	`FastMath.PI * X / 180`

Culling

JME3 provides a useful way for a program to run more smoothly when there are many models and geometries in the scene. It does this by using a technique called **culling**. Culling is the process of rendering only the graphics currently in view of the camera. There are two types of culling in JME3.

The first type of culling is **Face Culling**. This means that certain polygons of a mesh are not drawn. There are four different face culling modes, all of which run against a `Material` as listed in *Table 2 – Face Culling Modes*.

Table 2 – Face Culling Modes

Mode	Meaning
`FaceCullMode.Back`	Only the front-sides of a mesh are drawn.
`FaceCullMode.Front`	Only the back-sides of a mesh are drawn. A mesh with front-face culling will most likely appear to be invisible.
`FaceCullMode.FrontAndBack`	Makes a mesh completely invisible.
`FaceCullMode.Off`	Everything is drawn, slows down large scenes.

In the following statement, we use the `setFaceCull` method to make a material invisible using the front and back culling option. This is how you would use any of the other face culling modes.

```
mat.getAdditionalRenderState().
    setFaceCullMode(FaceCullMode.FrontAndBack);
```

The second type of culling is called **Frustum Culling** and is used for only drawing the part of the scene that is in view of the camera. Most of the scene is out of sight of the player anyway, so it makes sense to save some computing power and leave it un-rendered. This type of culling is performed automatically in JME3, but can also be manually set to one of four modes as detailed in *Table 3 - Frustum Culling Modes*.

Table 3 - Frustum Culling Modes

Mode	Meaning
`CullHint.Dynamic`	Default, faster because it doesn't worry about objects that are out of view
`CullHint.Never`	Calculate and draw everything always, slows down the scene
`CullHint.Always`	The entire spatial is invisible
`CullHint.Inherit`	Inherit culling behavior from parent node

In the next statement, we use the `setCullHint` method using the `CullHint.Never` parameter. This option will cause the spatial it runs against to always be fully rendered. You can use the other culling options in the same way.

```
Node1.setCullHint(CullHint.Never);
```

Working with Meshes

The elements of the game that are visible consist of meshes. These meshes are made up of points, lines, or triangles. You can obtain meshes by either:

- Using JME3-provided shapes such as the `Box` class
- Creating custom meshes programmatically
- Loading 3D models

Most games are created using a combination of meshes.

Meshes can be transformed and have a **Bounding Volume**. The bounding volume is the space enclosed by a mesh and is useful when collisions between meshes need to be detected. Collisions are discussed in Chapter 3.

Meshes can be either static or dynamic. Static meshes cannot be modified while dynamic meshes can. This means that static meshes can be optimized and are rendered faster. Unless a mesh really needs to be modified on-the-fly, it should be set as static. The `setStatic` and `setDynamic` methods are used for this purpose.

Meshes are based on the `Mesh` class found in the `com.jme3.scene.mesh` package. A `Geometry` is built using a mesh. JME3 has several pre-defined meshes such as `Box`, `Sphere`, `Dome`, and `Cylinder` as will be discussed in the *Using Shapes* section. JME3 also supports custom meshes if there is no suitable pre-defined mesh for the situation.

Polygon meshes are made up of triangles. The corners of the triangles are referred to as vertices. Any shape can be broken down into triangles. For example, a simple cube can be broken down into six rectangles. The six rectangles can then be broken down into 12 triangles as we will see in the *Displaying a Wireframe* section. Mesh objects have several useful methods as detailed in *Table 4 - Useful Mesh Methods*.

Table 4 - Useful Mesh Methods

Method	Description
getId	Returns the ID of the mesh
clone	Creates a clone of the mesh
setLineWidth	Sets the line thickness of the mesh. The default is 1.
getTriangleCount	Returns how many triangles are in the current mesh
getVertexCount	Returns number of vertices in the current mesh
setBuffer	Sets the `VertexBuffer` on the current mesh
updateBound	Updates the bounding volume of the current mesh
setStatic	Specifies that the mesh cannot be modified
setDynamic	Specifies that the mesh can be modified

Displaying a Wireframe

To better understand meshes, let's examine the simple `Box` shape used in the standard game. In *Figure 9 - Box Wireframe*, the box is displayed as a wire mesh such that we can clearly see six vertices of the 3D box. The other two vertices are hidden.

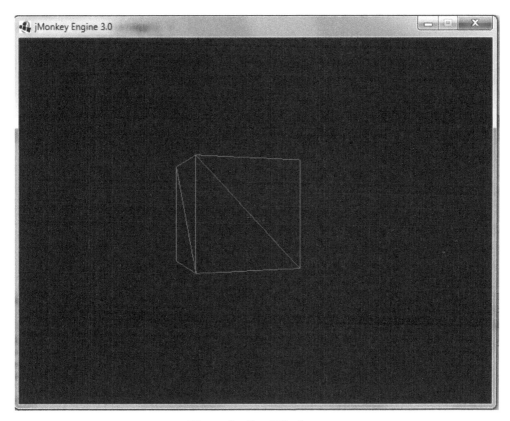

Figure 9 - Box Wireframe

Each side of the box is made of two triangles and four vertices. For the box there are a total of 12 triangles and 24 vertices. It is easy to see that there are 12 triangles since there are six sides to the box with two triangles per side. Each side of the box is drawn separately. Since each side uses four vertices and there are six sides, the box consists of a total of 24 vertices where each of the eight corners of the box has three vertices from the three adjacent sides.

To confirm these numbers we will use the following code sequence. We used the standard code for creation of the box and used the `setWireframe` method to force the display of only the box's outline. The `getTriangleCount` and `getVertexCount` methods return the number of triangles and vertices used by the box respectively.

```
Box box = new Box(1, 1, 1);
Geometry geom = new Geometry("Box", box);
```

```
Material mat = new Material(assetManager,
    "Common/MatDefs/Misc/Unshaded.j3md");
mat.setColor("Color", ColorRGBA.Blue);
geom.setMaterial(mat);

mat.getAdditionalRenderState().setWireframe(true);
rootNode.attachChild(geom);

System.out.println("Triangle count: " +
    b.getTriangleCount());
System.out.println("Vertex count: " + b.getVertexCount());
```

The output of this sequence follows:

Triangle count: 12

Vertex count: 24

Using Shapes

The `com.jme3.scene.shape` package consists of a number of predefined meshes as described in *Table 5 - Shape Classes*. The constructors for these classes differ in the number and types of parameters. They are often overloaded. For example, the `Cylinder` class has five constructors using up to seven parameters. In this section, we will introduce a few of the more commonly used shapes.

Table 5 - Shape Classes

Class	Purpose
AbstractBox	This is the base class for `Box` and `StripBox`
Box	A 3D box
Curve	Used to represent a spline
Cylinder	A cylinder
Dome	A hemisphere, that is, half of a sphere
Line	A line
PQTorus	A parameterized torus
Quad	A rectangular plane
Sphere	A full sphere
StripBox	A box with solid faces
Surface	A surface which currently only supports a Non-uniform rational basis spline (NURBS). This is a model for representing surfaces that may be irregular.
Torus	A doughnut-shaped object

Using the Box Shape

The `Box` class possesses two useful constructors as detailed in *Table 6 - Box Constructors*. Its default constructor is used only for serialization purposes and should not be used. There is also a deprecated four-argument constructor that we will not cover.

The first constructor takes the dimension of the box as its parameters and centers the box at (0,0,0). The dimensions provided are measured in each direction starting at the center, For example, an x axis size of 2 means the box is 4 WU along that axis. The `Box` class represents a cube.

Table 6 - Box Constructors

Constructor	Parameters
Box(float x, float y, float z)	The x, y, and z sizes
Box(Vector3f min, Vector3f max)	Two vectors representing two points that define the size and shape of the box

In the following example, a box with an X size of 1, a Y size of 2, and a Z size of 3 is drawn where its origin is at (1,0,0). This is illustrated in *Figure 10 - Box Example*.

```
Box b = new Box(1, 2, 3);
Geometry geom = new Geometry("Box", b);
Material mat = new Material(assetManager,
    "Common/MatDefs/Misc/Unshaded.j3md");
mat.setColor("Color", ColorRGBA.Blue);
geom.setMaterial(mat);
geom.setLocalTranslation(1, 0, 0);
rootNode.attachChild(geom);
    drawAxes();
```

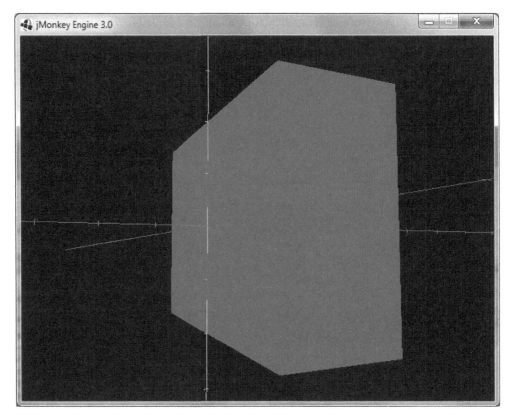

Figure 10 - Box Example

Using the Cylinder Shape

A cylinder can be useful at times. We think of a cylinder as having a radius and a height. JME3 supports the cylinder using the `Cylinder` class. Several constructors are supported using a combination of parameters as detailed in *Table 7 - Cylinder Parameters*. The axis of a cylinder can be envisioned as an imaginary line down its center. The radial of a cylinder is a cross section of the cylinder. The center of a cylinder is its origin.

Table 7 - Cylinder Parameters

Parameter	Meaning
axis samples	The number of triangle samples taken along its axis
radial samples	The number of triangle samples taken along the radial
radius one	The first radius
radius two	A second radius for the second end of the cylinder

Parameter	Meaning
height	The height of the cylinder
closed	When true, the cylinder is closed at the top and bottom
inverted	When true, the cylinder is displayed as if viewed from its center

Figure 11 - Cylinder Example shows a cylinder as a wireframe. This cylinder is rendered by the Cylinder Controller project as explained in Chapter 3. You can execute the program now to play with the parameters of a cylinder and to get a better feel for what they mean.

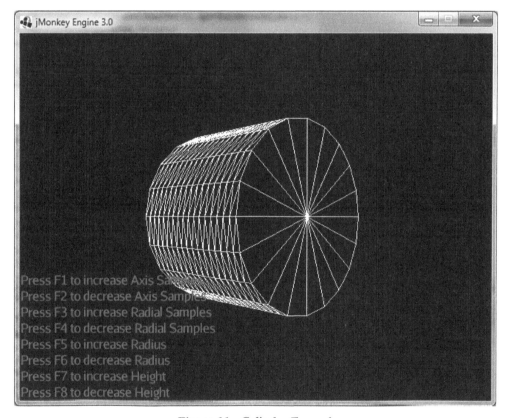

Figure 11 - Cylinder Example

Using the Sphere Shape

The sphere can be used to represent a number of objects. For our game, we will use it to represent a planet. Two constructors are supported using the parameters detailed in *Table 8 - Sphere Parameters*. The origin of a sphere is its center. The z axis refers to the axis running through the top and bottom of the sphere. The radial refers to the number of lines drawn from pole to pole corresponding to longitudinal lines. The more samples there are, the smoother the sphere will appear.

Table 8 - Sphere Parameters

Parameter	Meaning
zSamples	The number of samples along the z axis
radial Samples	The number of samples along the radial
radius	The radius of the sphere
use Even Slices	Determines if an even number of slices are used along the z axis
interior	Not documented

Figure 12 - Sphere Example illustrates a sphere. This sphere is rendered by the Sphere Controller project developed in Chapter 3. You can execute the program to play with the parameters of a sphere and to get a better feel for what they mean.

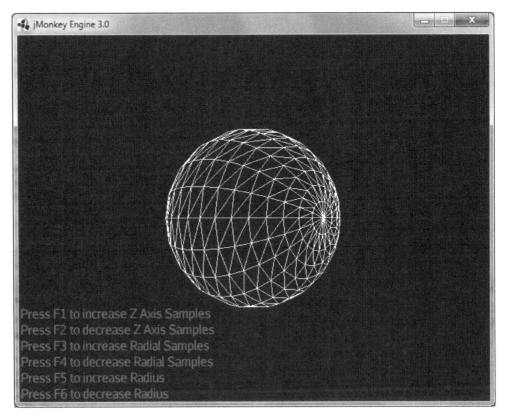

Figure 12 - Sphere Example

Using Non-3D Shapes

JME3 supports several shapes that are not 3D. They are all found in the `com.jme3.scene.shape` package. These are useful in some situations and include:

- `Quad` – A 2D rectangle with no depth

- `Line` – A line with a start and end point

- `Curve` – A curved spline

In this section we will examine the `Quad` and `Line` classes.

Rendering a Quad

The `Quad` class represents a two dimensional plane. It possesses two constructors both taking a width and a height as their first two parameters. The second constructor has a third parameter that allows the texture coordinates to be flipped along the y axis. Textures are discussed in more depth in Chapter 5.

The following example draws a simple plane at the origin. The width along the x axis is 2 and its height along the y axis is 3.

```
Quad quad = new Quad(2,3);
Geometry geom = new Geometry("Quad", quad);
Material mat = new Material(assetManager,
    "Common/MatDefs/Misc/Unshaded.j3md");
mat.setColor("Color", ColorRGBA.Red);
geom.setMaterial(mat);
geom.setLocalTranslation(0, 0, 0);
rootNode.attachChild(geom);
drawAxes();
```

The result is shown in *Figure 13 - Quad Example*.

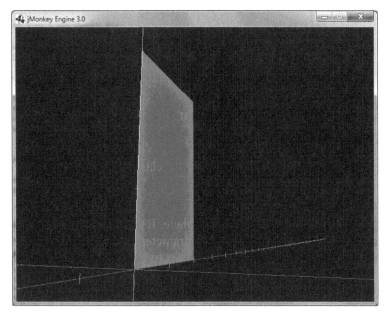

Figure 13 - Quad Example

Rendering a Line

The `Line` class will display a line giving a starting and ending point. A two argument constructor allows them to be specified as `Vector3f` objects. In the following example, We will draw a line from the origin to (1,2,3) in white:

```
Line line = new Line(new Vector3f(0,0,0),
    new Vector3f(1,2,3));
Geometry lineGeom = new Geometry("Line", line);
Material mat = new Material(assetManager,
    "Common/MatDefs/Misc/Unshaded.j3md");
mat.setColor("Color", ColorRGBA.White);
lineGeom.setMaterial(mat);
lineGeom.setLocalTranslation(0, 0, 0);
rootNode.attachChild(lineGeom);
drawAxes();
```

The result is shown in *Figure 14 - Line Example*.

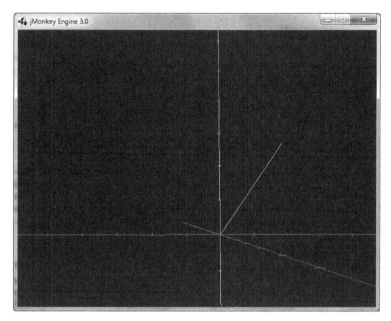

Figure 14 - Line Example

Do not confuse these `Line` and `Curve` classes with the `com.jme3.math` classes `Line` and `Curve`. The math classes represent invisible objects that are useful for collision detection. Be careful when using an IDE's completion suggestions.

Creating a Custom Mesh

Meshes can be created programmatically. These types of meshes are called custom meshes. To create a custom `Mesh`, the vertices of the triangles that make up the shape must be defined. In addition, the vertices of each triangle must be specified individually in a counter-clockwise direction. The class used for creating `Mesh` objects is found in the `com.jme3.scene` package. To demonstrate how to create a custom mesh, we will develop a mesh for a pyramid.

To create a mesh:

1. Create a new `Mesh` object
2. Create a vertices array using `Vector3fs`
3. Create a texture array of `Vector2fs` to hold a texture
4. Define the triangles of the mesh using an array of `int`
5. Store the data from steps 2, 3, and 4 into buffers

Creating a new Mesh object

We start by creating a basic `Mesh` object:

```
Mesh myMesh = new Mesh();
```

The pyramid mesh can be visualized in *Figure 15 - Custom Mesh* as if we are looking down on the x plane. The x axis is drawn horizontally and the z axis is drawn vertically. The four outer points are all at the same y level. The center point is raised above the plane. Our pyramid will be made up of four triangles. The orange vertices in the figure are represented by indexes 0 through 4 of the `vertices` array defined in the next section.

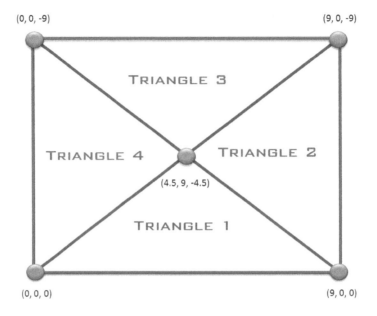

Figure 15 - Custom Mesh

Creating a Vertices Array

Our pyramid mesh will have 5 vertices at (0,0,0), (9,0,0), (4.5f,9,-4.5f), (0, 0, -9) and (9, 0, -9). These vertices will need to be stored in an array of vectors. The base of each triangle is 9 WU long, so the center is 4.5 WU in the x direction, and 4.5 WU in the negative z direction. The face of the pyramid consists of the first three coordinates listed. The remaining three triangles will only need two new vertices, or corner points. The following sequence will create the array of vertices:

```
Vector3f [ ] vertices = new Vector3f[5];
vertices[0] = new Vector3f(0,0,0);
vertices[1] = new Vector3f(9,0,0);
vertices[2] = new Vector3f(4.5f,9,-4.5f);
vertices[3] = new Vector3f(0,0,-9);
vertices[4] = new Vector3f(9,0,-9);
```

Creating the Texture Array

A texture will eventually be added to a mesh. Given the vertices of the mesh, the texture coordinates must be defined so the system will be able to determine how to attach the texture.

The vertices for the texture must be stored in an array of `Vector2fs`, in the same order as the mesh vertices as shown in the next code sequence. Using a 1 in these vertices means that the texture will fill the mesh at 100% size. Using smaller or larger values will shrink or stretch the texture respectively. Textures are covered in more detail in Chapter 5.

```
Vector2f[ ] texVertices = new Vector2f[4];
texVertices [0] = new Vector2f(0,0);
texVertices [1] = new Vector2f(1,0);
texVertices [2] = new Vector2f(0,1);
texVertices [3] = new Vector2f(1,1);
```

Defining the Triangle Array

The next step in the process is defining the four triangles for the pyramid. Each triangle will have three indexes. Remember, the triangles must be defined in counter-clockwise order. The triangles and their vertices are listed in *Table 9 - Triangle Array and Vertices*.

Table 9 - Triangle Array and Vertices

Triangle	Vertices
1	(4.5,9,-4.5) (0,0,0) (9,0,0)
2	(4.5, 9, -4.5) (9, 0, 0) (9, 0, -9)
3	(4.5,9,-4.5) (9, 0, -9) (0,0, -9)
4	(4.5, 9, -4.5) (0, 0, -9) (0, 0, 0)

The indexes that represent these vertices will be stored in an array of `int`. For example, the index that represents (4.5f,9,-4.5f) in the `vertices` array is 2. So, the indexes for the first triangle in counter-clockwise order are 2, 0, and 1. The indexes for the second triangle are 2, 1, and 4. The array is defined as:

```
int [] indexes = { 2,0,1, 2,1,4, 2,4,3, 2,3,0};
```

Storing the Mesh Data

The last step in the process is to store the data about the mesh into a buffer. There are three different buffer types for the three different types of information about the mesh: `Position`, `TextCoord`, and `Index` found in the `com.jme3.scene.VertexBuffer.Type` class. We are setting up the vertex buffers for the mesh. Vertex buffers are discussed in the *Understanding Vertex Buffers* section.

The `setBuffer()` method must be called against the `Mesh` object to assign this data. The integer parameter describes the number of components of the values. For example, each of the vertices are made up of three floats, each of the texture coordinates are made up of two floats, and each of the indices are made up of three `int` values. The `updateBound()` method must be called against the `Mesh` object to render the mesh in the scene.

```
myMesh.setBuffer(Type.Position, 3,
    BufferUtils.createFloatBuffer(vertices));

myMesh.setBuffer(Type.TexCoord, 2,
    BufferUtils.createFloatBuffer(texVertices));

myMesh.setBuffer(Type.Index, 3,
    BufferUtils.createIntBuffer(indexes));

myMesh.updateBound();
```

Our custom mesh can now be used as shown here:

```
Material mat = new Material(assetManager,
    "Common/MatDefs/Misc/Unshaded.j3md");

Geometry myGeo = new Geometry("My Mesh", myMesh);
myGeo.setCullHint(Spatial.CullHint.Never);
mat.getAdditionalRenderState().setWireframe(true);
myGeo.setMaterial(mat);
rootNode.attachChild(myGeo);
```

The geometry using the custom pyramid mesh should appear as shown in *Figure 16 - Pyramid Geometry*.

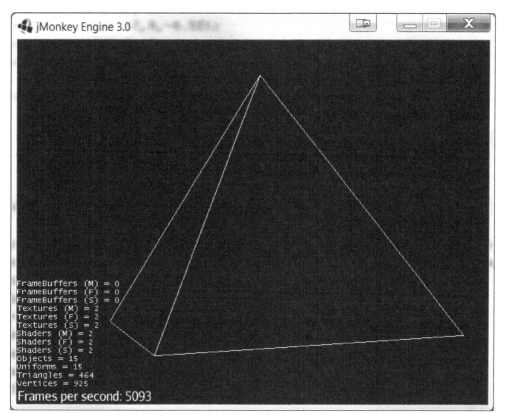

FrameBuffers (M) = 0
FrameBuffers (F) = 0
FrameBuffers (S) = 0
Textures (M) = 2
Textures (F) = 2
Textures (S) = 2
Shaders (M) = 2
Shaders (F) = 2
Shaders (S) = 2
Objects = 15
Uniforms = 15
Triangles = 464
Vertices = 925
Frames per second: 5093

Figure 16 - Pyramid Geometry

Creating Complex Shapes

Most games are designed using complex shapes. Sometimes these are created using a 3D modeler application such as Blender and at other times they are created programmatically. In this section, we will explore the issues in creating complex shapes programmatically.

To create a complex shape, we have to:

1. Create a base node and use it as the pivot point

2. Attach each shape to a geometry

3. Position the geometries around the base node or child nodes

4. Attach the base node to the scene

Transformations should be applied to the base node. Of course, complex shapes can be created by combining other complex shapes. For example, a house is a complex shape that may have other complex shapes such as windows, doors, and furniture as its elements.

In Adding Objects, we discussed how to group AI ships together. This is an example of creating a complex object from simpler objects. Another example follows where we create our planetary system. This is the body of the `getPlanets` method found in Building a Space Station.

A base node is created followed by the creation of a planet. The planet is located at (0,0,0) and then rotated. The moon is created next and placed at (3,0,0). The planet and the moon are then attached to the base node.

```
// Creating Complex Shapes
Node baseNode = new Node("Base node");
//Create Planet
Geometry centerSphere = getSphere(20, 20, 2f);
centerSphere.setLocalTranslation(0, 0, 0);
centerSphere.rotate(-1.5f, 0, 0);
Material sphereMaterial = new Material(assetManager,
    "Common/MatDefs/Misc/Unshaded.j3md");
centerSphere.setMaterial(sphereMaterial);
sphereMaterial.getAdditionalRenderState().
    setWireframe(true);
baseNode.attachChild(centerSphere);

//Create Moon
Geometry moon = getSphere(20, 20, 0.3f);
moon.setLocalTranslation(3f, 0, 0);
moon.setMaterial(sphereMaterial);    // Reuse material
baseNode.attachChild(moon);
```

> You can always create one static shape as a mesh and use it in several places making the rendering process more efficient

Using 3D Models

3D models created using other applications such as Blender are collections of meshes and can be loaded and used in a game. It is not uncommon to create a model or scene using an external editor. They are then exported and imported into JM3 using the `AssetManager` class.

Adding a .blend Model to Your Project

Blend models are produced by Blender. This application makes it easier to create 3D models. The models are saved as `.blend` files, which can then be used by JME3. The basic steps to add a `.blend` model to your project include:

1. Create a model folder

2. Move the `.blend` file to the folder

3. Convert to a `.j3o` object

It is a good idea to organize your assets such as models under the Project Assets folder. Models are best placed under the Models sub-folder. Add a new folder under your project's Asset/Model folder by right clicking on the Model's folder and selecting New – Others ... Select a folder from the Other category as shown in *Figure 17 – Creating a Folder*.

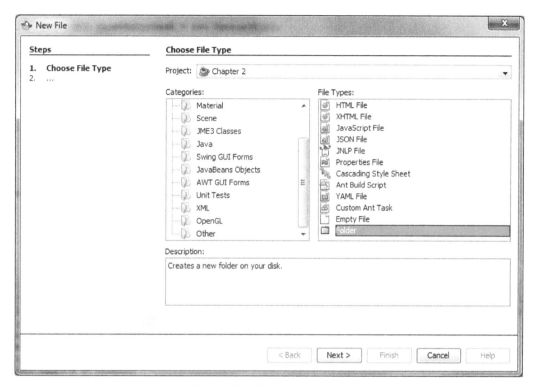

Figure 17 – Creating a Folder

Give it a name such as SpaceShips in the next dialog box as shown in *Figure 18 - Naming the Folder*.

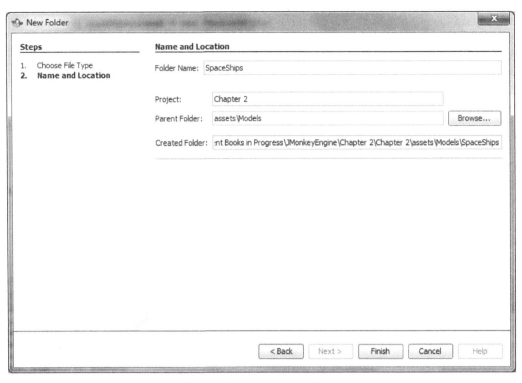

Figure 18 - Naming the Folder

Drag and drop the .blend file to the folder. Right click on the model and select Convert to j3o Binary. The new j3o file should appear shortly.

Using Different Levels of Detail

When an object is rendered, its appearance will change depending on how far the object is away from a camera. Ideally, when the object is close, a lot of detail will be shown. When it is far away, less detail will be displayed. This is referred to as the **Level of Detail**.

To achieve this effect in JME3, a different set of vertex buffers is assigned to an object for each level of detail desired. The `setLodLevels` method is passed an array of `VertexBuffer`s corresponding to the LOD desired.

Understanding Vertex Buffers

A **Vertex Buffer** is an OpenGL object that provides an efficient technique for uploading information about a vertex, such as its position and color, to a graphics device. The information will reside in the graphics card as opposed to main memory. This makes the rendering of the vertex much faster.

JME3 supports a vertex buffer using its `VertexBuffer` class. This class supports a large number of vertex attributes including position, size, color, and texture coordinates. A mesh is composed of `VertexBuffer` objects, which can be obtained using the `getBufferList` method if needed.

Building a Space Station

We now have enough information to start building objects for our game. The code that follows is used to create a basic space station. The first step in this process is creating a method called `buildSpaceStation` to build the station, so we can avoid cluttering the `simpleInitApp` method.

In the `buildSpaceStation` method, we will start with a basic unshaded material and configure it so the wireframe will be displayed. Next, we create a central node that we can use to build our station upon. This way we can scale, move, or rotate all parts of the station at once. The first part of our station is a ring-shaped model that can be found in the download from the publisher's website. We will simply load this model using the `assetManager`, apply our material, and attach it to the node.

Next let's add some geometries to the space station. The first geometry we will create using the `getSphere` method. This sphere will be the central hub of the space station. We will apply the same material as before and attach it to the `rootNode`. Then we will add two cylinders using the `getCylinder` method. The first cylinder is orientated properly to connect the sphere to the ring. The second cylinder, `cyGeo2`, needs to be rotated to provide symmetry. Let's rotate it 90 degrees using the `rotate` method we learned about in *Changing an Object's Orientation*. Next, we attach both cylinders to the `rootNode`.

Run the code and take a look at the space station. It's a little on the small side. We can scale all the parts by calling the `scale` method on the `station1Node`. Try it with a few different values and see the difference in size. If the code runs correctly you should see a space station as shown in *Figure 19 - Space Station*.

```java
public void buildSpaceStation(){
    Material mat = new Material(assetManager,
        "Common/MatDefs/Misc/Unshaded.j3md");
    mat.getAdditionalRenderState().setWireframe(true);

    Node station1Node = new Node();
    rootNode.attachChild(station1Node);

    Spatial ring = assetManager.loadModel(
        "Models/ SpaceShips/ring.obj");
    ring.setMaterial(mat);
    station1Node.attachChild(ring);

    Geometry sphereGeo = getSphere(32,32,2);
    sphereGeo.setMaterial(mat);
    station1Node.attachChild(sphereGeo);

    Geometry cyGeo = getCylinder(10,10,0.5f,12);
    cyGeo.setMaterial(mat);
    station1Node.attachChild(cyGeo);
```

```
        Geometry cyGeo2 = getCylinder(10,10,0.5f,12);
        cyGeo2.setMaterial(mat);
        cyGeo2.rotate(0,90*FastMath.DEG_TO_RAD,0);
        station1Node.attachChild(cyGeo2);

        station1Node.scale(3);
    }

    public Geometry getSphere(int y, int z, float radius) {
        Sphere sphere1 = new Sphere(y, z, radius);
        Geometry sphere = new Geometry("Sphere", sphere1);
        return sphere;
    }

    public Geometry getCylinder(int y, int z,
            float radius, float length) {
        Cylinder cyMesh = new Cylinder(y, z, radius, length);
        Geometry cylinder = new Geometry("Cylinder", cyMesh);
        return cylinder;
    }
```

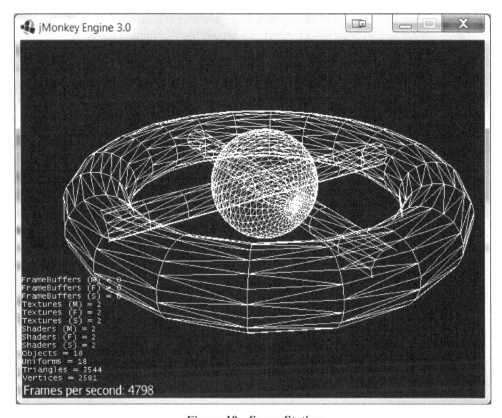

Figure 19 - Space Station

The code to develop the planetary system is shown in the following code sequence. This code brings together many of the examples used in this chapter. Adding the space station to the scene is left as an exercise for the reader.

```java
@Override
public void simpleInitApp() {
    buildPlanetarySystem();
}

private void buildPlanetarySystem() {
    Node planets = getPlanets();
    Node borgs = getAIShips();
    borgs.setLocalTranslation(2.3f, 0, 0);
    borgs.scale(0.05f);
    rootNode.attachChild(borgs);
    rootNode.attachChild(planets);
}

public Node getPlanets() {
    Node baseNode = new Node("Base node");
    //Create Planet
    Geometry centerSphere = getSphere(20, 20, 2f);
    centerSphere.setLocalTranslation(0, 0, 0);
    centerSphere.rotate(-1.5f, 0, 0);
    Material sphereMaterial = new Material(assetManager,
        "Common/MatDefs/Misc/Unshaded.j3md");
    centerSphere.setMaterial(sphereMaterial);
    sphereMaterial.getAdditionalRenderState().
        setWireframe(true);
    baseNode.attachChild(centerSphere);

    //Create Moon
    Geometry moon = getSphere(20, 20, 0.3f);
    moon.setLocalTranslation(3f, 0, 0);
    moon.setMaterial(sphereMaterial);    // Reuse material
    baseNode.attachChild(moon);

    return baseNode;
}

public Geometry getSphere(int y, int z, float radius) {
    Sphere sphere1 = new Sphere(y, z, radius);
    Geometry sphere = new Geometry("Sphere", sphere1);
    return sphere;
}

private Node getAIShips() {
    Geometry geom = createAIShip(
        "Alien Ship 1", 1, 0, 0, ColorRGBA.Blue);
    Geometry geom2 = createAIShip(
```

```
            "Alien Ship 2", -2, 1, 0, ColorRGBA.Red);

        Node baseNode = new Node("base node");
        Node node1 = new Node("node 1");
        Node node2 = new Node("node 2");

        baseNode.attachChild(node1);
        node1.attachChild(geom);
        node1.attachChild(geom2);
        baseNode.attachChild(node2);

        return baseNode;
    }

    private Geometry createAIShip(String name,
            float x, float y, float z, ColorRGBA color) {
        Box box = new Box(1, 2, 1);
        Geometry geom = new Geometry(name, box);

        geom.setLocalTranslation(x, y, z);
        Material mat = new Material(assetManager,
            "Common/MatDefs/Misc/Unshaded.j3md");
        mat.setColor("Color", color);
        geom.setMaterial(mat);
        mat.getAdditionalRenderState().setWireframe(true);
        return geom;
    }
```

Conclusion

In this chapter we introduced the fundamental concepts of JME3 objects in the scene graph and covered the basic techniques for manipulating these objects. We covered some key concepts including proper object placement, rotation, translation, scaling, and culling to fill our scene graph with various objects.

We learned how to use a single node to group multiple geometries. We used this technique to build a space station for our game, create a small planetary system, and to rotate multiple geometries around a single point in space. We also discovered that we can use a node to build complex shapes out of other nodes and geometries.

This chapter also covered the use of meshes, and to a limited extent, materials. We discovered that meshes and models are built out of vertices and triangles. We created a custom pyramid mesh. The use of the wireframe applied to materials allows us to see the vertices and triangles that make up objects easily.

In the next chapter we will examine how the user can interact with the game.

3

User Interaction

Introduction

The game loop, or update loop, is a crucial component to the application lifecycle. Recall, from Chapter 1, the sequence that every JME3 game follows. First the `start` method is called, then the `simpleInitApp` method, and then followed by the update loop. The `simpleInitApp` method only executes once, but the update loop, which includes the `simpleUpdate` method, will repeat until the game is stopped.

The update loop consists primarily of three phases:

1. Handling user input
2. Updating the game state
3. Rendering The GUI

In this chapter we will focus on handling user input. Player input can come in several forms including keyboard, mouse, and/or joystick/controller. In this chapter we will explore how JME3 supports these types of devices and how input is translated into action.

Updating the game state can be quite involved. In Chapter 4 we will examine the features of JME3 that support this need. In this chapter we will continue using the `SimpleApplication` class' `simpleUpdate` method. Rendering a GUI is largely performed automatically by JME3. However, the `simpleRender` method is used for custom processing.

We will start this chapter with coverage of how keystrokes, buttons, and mouse events arc mapped to JME3 actions. These events are mapped to a string, describing their intent and then associated with listeners which are codes sequence used to affect the intended action.

This is followed by a discussion of **Picking** which is where a user selects or targets an object in a game. Picking involves actions such as clicking on a door to open it, or firing at a target caught in a game's crosshairs.

When an event such as shooting an object occurs, there are usually visual and audible effects. In this chapter we will introduce a few simple visual effects while audible effects are handled using situational sounds.

In the last section of this chapter we will demonstrate many of this chapter's techniques as applied to the Shades of Infinity game.

Handling Player Input

Triggers are actions that originate from the player. There are specific JME3 classes that support different types of triggers for keyboard, mouse, and joystick inputs. This action eventually modifies the state of the game. JME3 uses a flexible approach to capture and process user inputs. An input such as a mouse button click event is associated with a name, called a **Mapping Name**, which represents the intended action. A mapping name is then associated with a listener.

Listeners are code sequences that respond to user actions. If the user presses the up arrow key, the game should respond to the action. The listener's code performs these actions.

When the button is pressed, the name is passed to listener code that handles the action. A keyboard input, such as pressing the A key, may be intended to have the same effect as pressing the mouse button. By tying both low level user inputs to the same mapping name, it simplifies the process and makes it more maintainable.

The generic approach to add interaction to your game includes:

1. Define one or more triggers for a user action

2. Map these triggers to a mapping name

3. Create listener(s) to handle the events

4. Register the mappings to a listener

5. Implement the actions in a listener

Figure 1 - Input Mapping Process illustrates how this process occurs. One or more event triggers are mapped to a mapping name. When one of the corresponding input events occurs, the mapping name is sent to a listener, along with other information, which then processes the input event.

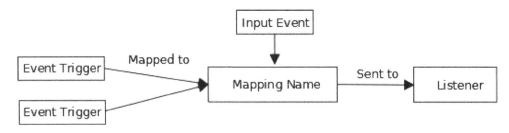

Figure 1 - Input Mapping Process

Action Versus Analog Listeners

JME3 differentiates between digital and analog action types. Digital actions are discrete events and are mapped to an `ActionListener`. These events are typified by a button click event.

Analog events are more continuous in nature. Examples include joystick movement or a mouse wheel scroll. Analog events are mapped to an instance of an `AnalogListener`.

These two types of listener interfaces are summarized in *Table 1 - Listener Interfaces Summary*.

> Listeners do not know which low level event occurred. They are only concerned with the mapping name. However, depending on the type of listener, relevant contextual information is available (such as if a key was pressed or not).

Table 1 - Listener Interfaces Summary

Listener Type	Parameters	Meaning
`ActionListener`	`name`	Name of the action
	`keyPressed`	True if the key is pressed
	`tpf`	Time Per Frame
`AnalogListener`	`name`	Name of the action
	`value`	A float value presenting the strength of the input
	`tpf`	Time Per Frame

> The **Time Per Frame** parameter is a floating point value set to the number of seconds since the last frame was rendered. It is often used to control the speed of animations. This value will vary depending on the current frames per second of the game.

Typically, an action or analog event is mapped to either an action or an analog listener. The main difference is the type of information that is available. We will map a mouse button event to both types of listeners to see how this mapping differs in Using Mouse Buttons.

Understanding the Sphere Application

The Sphere application is used in several sections of this chapter to illustrate various user input techniques. The application is straight forward enough, but it is long. The Cylinder application is similar to the Sphere application is not explained here. The source code for both of these applications can be found on the publisher's website. You may want to download and play with both of these applications to get a better feel for how they work.

The application uses numerous instance and static variables to control the appearance of the sphere as listed in *Table 2 - Sphere Application Variables*. These variables, amongst others, will be used in several examples that follow.

Table 2 - Sphere Application Variables

Variable Declaration	Purpose
`private Sphere sphere;`	The reference variable for the sphere
`private int zSamples = 20;`	Controls the number of samples along the sphere's Z axis
`private int radialSamples = 20;`	Controls the number of samples along the radial
`private float radius = 2.0f;`	Controls the sphere's radius
`private Material sphereMaterial;`	Will be used to set the color of the sphere

Using the `simpleRender` Method

To effect changes to the sphere, the user will use function keys, the mouse wheel, and the mouse buttons. These actions will modify the application's variables such as `radius`. Usually, spatials are rendered automatically. However, for this application we need to update the spatial explicitly.

For these changes to be seen, the `updateGeometry` method needs to be executed against the sphere. As the name implies, this method should be executed whenever the scene is rendered to effect changes made to the sphere.

The `simpleRender` method is called automatically whenever the scene needs to be rendered. To effect changes to the scene, all we need to do is to call the `updateGeometry` method in the `simpleRender` method as shown here:

```
public void simpleRender(RenderManager rm) {
    sphere.updateGeometry(zSamples, radialSamples, radius);
}
```

Using Triggers

There are different types of triggers supported in JME3 are found in *Table 3 - Trigger Classes.* The names of the triggers give a good indication of their purpose. A specific trigger is declared for a specific type of input. For example, a `KeyTrigger` may be defined for the X key or a `MouseAxisTrigger` may be defined to handle mouse wheel input.

Table 3 - Trigger Classes

Trigger Class	Purpose
KeyTrigger	Handles keyboard input
MouseButtonTrigger	Handles mouse buttons
MouseAxisTrigger	Handles the mouse wheel
JoyButtonTrigger	Handles joystick buttons
JoyAxisTrigger	Handles joystick axis movement
TouchTrigger	Handles touch screen input (Android)

A trigger could conceivably be tied directly to a listener. However, a more flexible approach is to define a mapping name that describes a general action, associate one or more triggers with the mapping name, and then have the listener act on the mapping name. This makes it easier to associate one or more triggers to the same general action. For example, the up arrow key and the | (pipe) key could both result in the same behavior.

Understanding Default Trigger Mappings

The basic JME3 application uses a set of default key mappings as defined in *Table 4 - Default Trigger Mappings*. The `KeyInput` is an interface that contains constants. We will use these for the actual mapping later.

We have used these mappings in our previous applications. However, the last three table entries may be of interest when debugging an application. For example, executing any of the previous applications and pressing the C will display information about the camera as shown next:

Camera Position: (0.0, 0.0, 10.0)

Camera Rotation: (0.0, 1.0, 0.0, 0.0)

Camera Direction: (0.0, 0.0, -1.0)

cam.setLocation(new Vector3f(0.0f, 0.0f, 10.0f));

cam.setRotation(new Quaternion(0.0f, 1.0f, 0.0f, 0.0f));

The use of the M key will produce output similar to this:

Total   heap memory held: 7712kb

Only heap memory available, if you want to monitor direct memory use BufferUtils.setTrackDirectMemoryEnabled(true) during initialization

We can use the `setTrackDirectMemoryEnabled` to get additional memory usage information. The method is placed in the `simpleInitApp` method as shown here:

```
BufferUtils.setTrackDirectMemoryEnabled(true);
```

One possible output is shown here:

Existing buffers: 24129

(b: 29 f: 18071 i: 0 s: 6029 d: 0)

Total   heap memory held: 36516kb

Total direct memory held: 3531kb

(b: 3094kb f: 404kb i: 0kb s: 32kb d: 0kb)

If your application uses one of the default mappings for other purposes, then the action specified by your key mapping will affect your action and the action associated with the default mapping. For example, if you use the F5 key to increase the radius of a sphere, then the radius will be increase and the HUD statistics will be toggled. Deleting existing mappings is covered in Using Different Keyboards.

Table 4 - Default Trigger Mappings

Key	`KeyInput` **Constants**	**Effect**
W	KEY_W	Camera moves forward
S	KEY_S	Camera moves backwards
A	KEY_A	Camera moves left
D	KEY_D	Camera moves right
Q	KEY_D	Camera moves up
Y	KEY_Y	Camera moves down
Escape	KEY_ESCAPE	Terminates the game
Left Mouse Key	KEY_LEFT	Camera rotates left
Right Mouse Key	KEY_RIGHT	Camera rotates right
Up Mouse Key	KEY_UP	Camera rotates up
Down Arrow Key	KEY_DOWN	Camera rotates down
F5	KEY_F5	Hide/unhide HUD statistics
C	KEY_C	Prints camera information
M	KEY_M	Prints memory usage information

Handling Keyboard Input

In this section we will demonstrate how to bind a specific key to some action. For example, if the user presses the + key, a new opponent may appear. The process of binding a key to some action involves 4 steps:

1. Create a key trigger for the key

2. Map the trigger to a name

3. Associate the name event with a listener

4. Process the event within the listener

In this section, we will illustrate the handling of key events using the Sphere application. Declarations are placed at the beginning of the class and code sequences are placed in the `simpleInitApp` method.

Defining a Key Trigger

The `KeyTrigger` class, found in the `com.jme3.input.controls` package, supports the definition of key triggers. The `KeyTrigger` constructor is used to specify the key of interest such as the F1 key. Its constructor's single argument is an integer identifying the key.

The `KeyInput` interface, found in the `com.jme3.input` package, possesses a large number of static integer fields corresponding to the keys of the keyboard. For example, `KEY_N` is defined for the N key. When we define a trigger, it is good practice to declare them as static final variables. This makes them easier to access and encourages a more efficient implementation. In the next statement we declare a trigger, `TRIGGER_F1`, corresponding to the F1 key:

```
private final static Trigger TRIGGER_F1 =
    new KeyTrigger(KeyInput.KEY_F1);
```

Trying to figure out the correct name for a `KeyInput` field can be hard to find at times. To make this easier, we have included *Table 5- Key Event Fields*, an enumeration of triggers which has been adapted from
http://hub.jmonkeyengine.org/wiki/doku.php/jme3:advanced:input_handling.

Table 5- Key Event Fields

Event	`KeyInput` Fields
NumPad: 1, 2, 3, ...	KeyTrigger(KeyInput.KEY_NUMPAD1) ...
Keyboard: 1, 2 , 3, ...	KeyTrigger(KeyInput.KEY_1) ...
Keyboard: A, B, C, ...	KeyTrigger(KeyInput.KEY_A) ...
Keyboard: Spacebar	KeyTrigger(KeyInput.KEY_SPACE)

Keyboard: Shift	KeyTrigger(KeyInput.KEY_RSHIFT), KeyTrigger(KeyInput.KEY_LSHIFT)
Keyboard: F1, F2, ...	KeyTrigger(KeyInput.KEY_F1) ...
Keyboard: Return, Enter	KeyTrigger(KeyInput.KEY_RETURN), KeyTrigger(KeyInput.KEY_NUMPADENTER)
Keyboard: PageUp, PageDown	KeyTrigger(KeyInput.KEY_PGUP), KeyTrigger(KeyInput.KEY_PGDN)
Keyboard: Delete, Backspace	KeyTrigger(KeyInput.KEY_DELETE), KeyTrigger(KeyInput.KEY_BACK)
Keyboard: Escape	KeyTrigger(KeyInput.KEY_ESCAPE)
Keyboard: Arrows	KeyTrigger(KeyInput.KEY_DOWN), KeyTrigger(KeyInput.KEY_UP) KeyTrigger(KeyInput.KEY_LEFT), KeyTrigger(KeyInput.KEY_RIGHT)

Assigning a Trigger to a Mapping Name

When working with user input, it is common to have more than one way of affecting a command. For example, the + key or the P key could be used to increase a value. Using more than one command provides the user with more user interaction flexibility. We have already seem this with the default key mappings for the Left Arrow key and the A key. These both result in the default camera moving to the left.

To support this idea, JME3 uses a mapping name to designate a command. This mapping name is a string literal. For example, the string, "Move Left", could be used to represent the intended action of one or more events. In the next statement, we define a mapping for increasing the number of samples to use for the Z axis:

```
private final static String MAP_INCREASE_Z_SAMPLES =
    "Increase Z Samples";
```

Mapping names are case-sensitive strings, each of which needs to be unique. As the name implies, these strings are mapped to actions. It is a good idea to choose names that convey the action being performed and to make these strings final. This results in more efficient code and avoids spelling errors.

To associate a trigger with a mapping, use the inputManager's addMapping method as shown here:

```
inputManager.addMapping(
    MAP_INCREASE_Z_SAMPLES, TRIGGER_F1);
```

We can easily add a second trigger to the same mapping. In the next sequence, a new trigger is defined for the + key and then it is mapped to the same mapping name as for the F1 key. This mapping is illustrated in *Figure 2 - Key Mapping*.

```
private final static Trigger TRIGGER_ADD =
    new KeyTrigger(KeyInput.KEY_ADD);
...
inputManager.addMapping(
    MAP_INCREASE_Z_SAMPLES, TRIGGER_ADD);
```

Figure 2 - Key Mapping

Associating a Mapping Name with a Listener

Before the application will respond to the command, the mapping name needs to be associated with the listener. This is accomplished using the addListener method as illustrated next. This relationship is shown in *Figure 3 - Mapping Relationship*.

```
inputManager.addListener(
    actionListener, MAP_INCREASE_Z_SAMPLES);
```

Figure 3 - Mapping Relationship

Adding Multiple Mappings to a Listener

In the Sphere Application, several mapping names are associated with the same listener. One approach is to add each mapping individually as shown here:

```
inputManager.addListener(
    actionListener, MAP_INCREASE_Z_SAMPLES);
 inputManager.addListener(
    actionListener, MAP_DECREASE_Z_SAMPLES);
inputManager.addListener(
    actionListener, MAP_INCREASE_RADIAL_SAMPLES);
```

```
inputManager.addListener(
    actionListener, MAP_DECREASE_RADIAL_SAMPLES);
inputManager.addListener(
    actionListener, MAP_INCREASE_RADIUS);
inputManager.addListener(
    actionListener,MAP_DECREASE_RADIUS);
```

A more concise approach is to use one statement to add all of the mapping names as illustrated next. Both approaches have the same effect.

```
inputManager.addListener(actionListener,
    MAP_INCREASE_Z_SAMPLES,
    MAP_DECREASE_Z_SAMPLES,
    MAP_INCREASE_RADIAL_SAMPLES,
    MAP_DECREASE_RADIAL_SAMPLES,
    MAP_INCREASE_RADIUS,
    MAP_DECREASE_RADIUS);
```

Processing an Event with a Listener

We need to define a listener for the command to affect a command. In the next sequence an `ActionListener` object is created using an anonymous inner class. When a key is pressed, the mapping name for the action is passed to the `onAction` method as the `name` parameter. Based on the value of the parameter, the appropriate action will be taken. In this case, the `zSamples` variable is increased. This is eventually reflected in a change in the number of Z axis samples used to render a sphere.

```
private ActionListener actionListener =
        new ActionListener() {
    @Override
    public void onAction(String name,
        boolean isPressed, float tpf) {
        if (MAP_INCREASE_Z_SAMPLES.equals(name)) {
            zSamples += 5;
        }
        ...
    }
};
```

The `onAction` method is also passed a boolean, `isPressed`, variable indicating whether the key is being pressed or is being released. When a key is pressed, a key event will occur twice. First when the key is pressed and again when it is released. When the key is pressed, the `isPressed` parameter is set to true. When the key is being released, it is set to false. Sometimes, this distinction is not important. However, the `isPressed` parameter is used to differentiate between these events when necessary.

Keep in mind that two key events will be generated for every key press. This may affect the behavior of the program. For example, if the command means moving one square to the right, the two key events generated may result in the user moving two squares to the right. An `if` statement may be needed to select only one of these events.

Using Different Keyboards

Different keyboard layouts are used around the world. They are often named after the layout of the keys. For example, the QWERTY keyboard is named after the first 6 letters on the first letter row. *Table 6 - Common Keyboard Types* lists a few of the more common keyboards used for Latin scripts.

Table 6 - Common Keyboard Types

Keyboard	Usage
QWERTY	Used in most English speaking countries
QWERTZ	Used in Germany with variations in other neighboring countries
AZERTY	Used by French speakers
Dvorak	A simplified keyboard designed to increase typing rate and accuracy

If your design goal is to make the game adaptable for different cultures, then using a customized key mapping based on the user preferences is one step in this direction. The basic approach is to delete the mappings you need to replace, using the `deleteMapping` method, and then add them back with the appropriate mappings using the `addMapping` method. This method uses mapping names and not the names of input constant such as `TRIGGER_F1`.

An example of modifying the keyboard assignments will be shown in Chapter 4 using application states. We will discuss the application state that makes the default assignments and see how we can change these mappings. Application states are classes that help make a game more maintainable be providing alternatives to where game logic can be placed, such as keyboard mappings.

When configuring your application to handle different keyboards, beware that the `SimpleApplication` class defines several mappings as listed in *Table 7 - SimpleApplication Class Mapping Names*. You may need to delete these also.

Table 7 - SimpleApplication Class Mapping Names

Variable	Value
INPUT_MAPPING_CAMERA_POS	"SIMPLEAPP_CameraPos"
INPUT_MAPPING_EXIT	"SIMPLEAPP_Exit"
INPUT_MAPPING_HIDE_STATS	"SIMPLEAPP_HideStats"

Variable	Value
INPUT_MAPPING_MEMORY	"SIMPLEAPP_Memory"

We may not readily know which keys have been bound to a specific mapping such as for INPUT_MAPPING_MEMORY which is bound to the M key. The deleteMapping method, as shown next, will disassociate all of the keys with the mapping name:

```
inputManager.deleteMapping(
    SimpleApplication.INPUT_MAPPING_MEMORY );
```

Handling Mouse Input

There are two events associated with a mouse: a mouse button click and the mouse wheel scroll. In this section we will demonstrate how both events are handled. To capture mouse button events, we need to create either a MouseButtonTrigger or a MouseAxisTrigger object. We also need to setup the mappings and listeners as described earlier. Mappings for mouse events are found in *Table 8 - Mouse Event Fields*.

Table 8 - Mouse Event Fields

Event	MouseInput **Fields**
Mouse button: Left Click	MouseButtonTrigger(MouseInput.BUTTON_LEFT)
Mouse button: Right Click	MouseButtonTrigger(MouseInput.BUTTON_RIGHT)
Mouse button: Middle Click	MouseButtonTrigger(MouseInput.BUTTON_MIDDLE)
Mouse movement: Right	MouseAxisTrigger(MouseInput.AXIS_X, true)
Mouse movement: Left	MouseAxisTrigger(MouseInput.AXIS_X, false)
Mouse movement: Up	MouseAxisTrigger(MouseInput.AXIS_Y, true)
Mouse movement: Down	MouseAxisTrigger(MouseInput.AXIS_Y, false)
Mouse wheel: Up	MouseAxisTrigger(MouseInput.AXIS_WHEEL,false)
Mouse wheel: Down	MouseAxisTrigger(MouseInput.AXIS_WHEEL,true)

Using Mouse Buttons

To demonstrate mouse button events, we will use the left and right mouse buttons to change the color of the sphere. Pressing the left mouse button will render the sphere in blue. Pressing the right mouse button will render the sphere in red.

First we setup the MouseButtonTrigger and mapping variables as shown here:

```
private final static MouseButtonTrigger
```

```
      TRIGGER_MOUSE_BUTTON_RIGHT =
      new MouseButtonTrigger(MouseInput.BUTTON_RIGHT);
   private final static String MAP_MOUSE_BUTTON_RIGHT =
      "Mouse Button Right";

   private final static MouseButtonTrigger
      TRIGGER_MOUSE_BUTTON_LEFT =
      new MouseButtonTrigger(MouseInput.BUTTON_LEFT);
   private final static String MAP_MOUSE_BUTTON_LEFT =
      "Mouse Button Left";
```

Next, the mapping and assignment of the listeners occur as shown next. To illustrate the differences between an action and an analog listener, we have added the right mouse button mapping name to both an action and an analog listener.

```
   inputManager.addMapping(MAP_MOUSE_BUTTON_RIGHT,
      TRIGGER_MOUSE_BUTTON_RIGHT);
   inputManager.addMapping(MAP_MOUSE_BUTTON_LEFT,
      TRIGGER_MOUSE_BUTTON_LEFT);

   inputManager.addListener(
      actionListener, MAP_MOUSE_BUTTON_RIGHT);
   inputManager.addListener(
      analogListener, MAP_MOUSE_BUTTON_RIGHT);

   inputManager.addListener(
      actionListener, MAP_MOUSE_BUTTON_LEFT);
```

Simplified versions of the two listeners are listed next. For each button action, the values of the `onAnalog` or `onAction` methods are displayed. The `sphereMaterial` variable, which has been declared as an instance variable, is used to change the color of the sphere.

```
   private AnalogListener analogListener =
         new AnalogListener() {
      public void onAnalog(String name, float value,
         float tpf) {
      ...
        } else if (MAP_MOUSE_BUTTON_RIGHT.equals(name)) {
          System.out.println(name + " value: " +
            value + "  tpf: " + tpf);
          sphereMaterial.setColor("Color", ColorRGBA.Red);
        } else if (MAP_MOUSE_BUTTON_LEFT.equals(name)) {
          System.out.println(name + " value: " +
            value + "  tpf: " + tpf);
          sphereMaterial.setColor("Color", ColorRGBA.Blue);
        }
      }
   };
```

```
    private ActionListener actionListener =
        new ActionListener() {
      @Override
      public void onAction(String name,
          boolean isPressed, float tpf) {
        ...
        } else if (MAP_MOUSE_BUTTON_RIGHT.equals(name)) {
          System.out.println("name: " + name +
              "  isPressed: " + isPressed + "  tpf: " +
              tpf + " [" + title +"]");
          sphereMaterial.setColor("Color", ColorRGBA.Red);
        } else if (MAP_MOUSE_BUTTON_LEFT.equals(name)) {
          System.out.println("name: " + name +
              "  isPressed: " + isPressed + "  tpf: " +
              tpf + " [" + title +"]");
          sphereMaterial.setColor("Color", ColorRGBA.Blue);
        }
      }
    };
```

The output will vary depending on the order the buttons are clicked, but the next output shows a partial listing of what happens when the left mouse button is pressed followed by the right mouse button. The onAnalog method is triggered repeatedly for a single click which is not useful in this situation. This makes the action listener is a better choice for mouse button actions.

name: Mouse Button Left isPressed: true tpf: 0.003499639 [Sphere Application]

name: Mouse Button Left isPressed: false tpf: 0.002582886 [Sphere Application]

name: Mouse Button Right isPressed: true tpf: 0.00236017 [Sphere Application]

Mouse Button Right value: 0.0017134439 tpf: 0.0017134439

Mouse Button Right value: 0.002474875 tpf: 0.002474875

...

Mouse Button Right value: 0.0017607539 tpf: 0.0017607539

name: Mouse Button Right isPressed: false tpf: 0.002466841 [Sphere Application]

Using the Mouse Wheel

The MouseAxisTrigger class is used to support mouse wheel events. To handle these events, we need to define a trigger, map it to a mapping name, add the mapping name to an analog listener, and then implement the listener.

In this example, we will augment the Sphere application to use the mouse wheel to increase and decrease the radius of the Sphere. An instance of the MouseAxisTrigger class is used to capture mouse wheel events. The constructor for this class has two parameters:

90

- A mouse axis to specify the mouse wheel, and

- A boolean value to indicate whether positive or negative axis events should be captured

These positive or negative axis events reflect moving the mouse wheel forward or backwards. Positive values are those generated when the top of the wheel moves "away" from the user. A negative value is generated when the top of the wheel is rotated "backwards", that is, toward the user.

In the next statement, a `MouseAxisTrigger` object is created that captures positive changes to the mouse wheel. The `MouseInput.AXIS_WHEEL` argument specifies the mouse wheel and the false value indicates that only positive values will be captured.

```
private final static MouseAxisTrigger
    TRIGGER_SCROLL_WHEEL_POSITIVE =
        new MouseAxisTrigger(MouseInput.AXIS_WHEEL, false);
```

In the next sequence, a second `MouseAxisTrigger` object is defined for negative values and mapping names:

```
private final static MouseAxisTrigger
    TRIGGER_SCROLL_WHEEL_NEGATIVE =
        new MouseAxisTrigger(MouseInput.AXIS_WHEEL, true);

private final static String MAP_MOUSE_WHEEL_POSITIVE =
    "Mouse Wheel Positive";
private final static String MAP_MOUSE_WHEEL_NEGATIVE =
    "Mouse Wheel Negative";
```

The `addMapping` method associates the triggers with the mapping names and the `addListener` method assigns the names to an analog listener in the next statements:

```
inputManager.addMapping(MAP_MOUSE_WHEEL_NEGATIVE,
    TRIGGER_SCROLL_WHEEL_NEGATIVE);
inputManager.addMapping(MAP_MOUSE_WHEEL_POSITIVE,
    TRIGGER_SCROLL_WHEEL_POSITIVE);

inputManager.addListener(analogListener,
    MAP_MOUSE_WHEEL_NEGATIVE);
inputManager.addListener(analogListener,
    MAP_MOUSE_WHEEL_POSITIVE);
```

The analog listener is defined next. The `radius` variable is incremented or decremented by the value passed to the `onAnalog` method. Depending on the sensitivity of the mouse, the value added to, or subtracted from, `radius` may need to be adjusted.

```
private AnalogListener analogListener =
        new AnalogListener() {
    public void onAnalog(String name, float value,
            float tpf) {
```

```
            if (MAP_MOUSE_WHEEL_POSITIVE.equals(name)) {
                radius += value;
            } else if(MAP_MOUSE_WHEEL_NEGATIVE.equals(name)) {
                radius -= value;
            }
        }
    };
```

Using a Joystick

Joysticks are supported by many games. These devices can make certain types of interaction with a game easier. However, usage of a joystick is not enabled by default. To enable a joystick, use the `AppSettings` class' `setUseJoysticks` method with a value of true as shown here:

```
    settings.setUseJoysticks(true);
```

The `useJoysticks` method will return true if joysticks are in use. More than one joystick may be available on a system. The `InputManager` class' `getJoysticks` method will return an array of `JoyStick` objects, each representing a joystick. As shown next, the method is used to display a list of the joysticks available on a system, along with information about its buttons and axes:

```
    Joystick[] joysticks = inputManager.getJoysticks();
    if (joysticks != null) {
        for (Joystick joy : joysticks) {
            System.out.println(joy.toString());
            System.out.println("Buttons - " +
                joy.getButtonCount());
            for (JoystickButton button : joy.getButtons()) {
                System.out.println(button);
            }
            System.out.println("Axes - " + joy.getAxisCount());
            for (JoystickAxis axis : joy.getAxes()) {
                System.out.println(axis);
            }
        }
    }
```

One possible output follows:

Joystick[name=Microsoft Hardware USB Mouse, id=0, buttons=31, axes=1]

Buttons - 31

JoystickButton[name=Button 0, parent=Microsoft Hardware USB Mouse, id=0, logicalId=0]

JoystickButton[name=Consumer Control, parent=Microsoft Hardware USB Mouse, id=1, logicalId=1]

...

JoystickButton[name=Button 30, parent=Microsoft Hardware USB Mouse, id=30, logicalId=31]

Axes - 1

JoystickAxis[name=Axis 6, parent=Microsoft Hardware USB Mouse, id=0, logicalId=unknown, isAnalog=true, isRelative=true, deadZone=0.0]

Joystick[name=Logitech Extreme 3D Pro USB, id=1, buttons=12, axes=7]

Buttons - 12

JoystickButton[name=Button 0, parent=Logitech Extreme 3D Pro USB, id=0, logicalId=0]

...

JoystickButton[name=Button 11, parent=Logitech Extreme 3D Pro USB, id=11, logicalId=11]

Axes - 7

JoystickAxis[name=Y Axis, parent=Logitech Extreme 3D Pro USB, id=0, logicalId=y, isAnalog=true, isRelative=false, deadZone=0.0]

...

JoystickAxis[name=Slider, parent=Logitech Extreme 3D Pro USB, id=6, logicalId=slider, isAnalog=true, isRelative=false, deadZone=0.0]

In the following code sequence, mappings are made for typical joystick usage and then associated with a listener. Joystick events are listed in *Table 9 - Joystick Event Fields*.

```
// Add to simpleInitApp method
inputManager.addMapping("DPAD Left",
   new JoyAxisTrigger(0, JoyInput.AXIS_POV_X, true));
inputManager.addMapping("DPAD Right",
   new JoyAxisTrigger(0, JoyInput.AXIS_POV_X, false));
inputManager.addMapping("DPAD Down",
   new JoyAxisTrigger(0, JoyInput.AXIS_POV_Y, true));
inputManager.addMapping("DPAD Up",
   new JoyAxisTrigger(0, JoyInput.AXIS_POV_Y, false));

inputManager.addListener(this, "DPAD Left",
   "DPAD Right", "DPAD Down", "DPAD Up");
inputManager.addMapping("Joy Left",
   new JoyAxisTrigger(0, 0, true));
inputManager.addMapping("Joy Right",
   new JoyAxisTrigger(0, 0, false));
inputManager.addMapping("Joy Down",
   new JoyAxisTrigger(0, 1, true));
inputManager.addMapping("Joy Up",
```

```
        new JoyAxisTrigger(0, 1, false));
    inputManager.addListener(this, "Joy Left", "Joy Right",
        "Joy Down", "Joy Up");

    // Listener for joystick
    public void onAnalog(String name, float isPressed,
        float tpf) {
        System.out.println(name + " = " + isPressed);
    }
```

Add this code to any of the previous games to see how it works.

Table 9 - Joystick Event Fields

Event	JoyInput **Fields**
Joystick Movement: Right	JoyAxisTrigger(0, JoyInput.AXIS_POV_X, true)
Joystick Movement: Left	JoyAxisTrigger(0, JoyInput.AXIS_POV_X, false)
Joystick Movement: Forward	JoyAxisTrigger(0, JoyInput.AXIS_POV_Z, true)
Joystick Movement: Backward	JoyAxisTrigger(0, JoyInput.AXIS_POV_Z, false)

Alternatively, to map a joystick button to a mapping name use the Joystick class' assignButton method. This method assigns its mapping name argument to the button. We can use a combination of the getJoysticks and getButtons methods to return a reference to a button. This technique is demonstrated in Improving our Shades of Infinity Game.

> Not all joysticks are recognized by JME3. However, many of them are customizable which may allow a joystick button or axis movement to generate a keystroke. If your joystick is not recognized, generating keystroke(s) will achieve the same effect. For example, moving the joystick forward may be mapped to the W key which can then be processed by your game.

Using a Gamepad Controller

The XBOX 360 controller is the most widely used gamepad for PC gaming. Most modern PC games have built-in support specifically for this remote. Since it's a Microsoft product, Windows will automatically recognize it when it is plugged into the PC running Windows. It is a good idea to provide at least some support for this controller.

If you have one of these controllers you may notice that JME3 automatically works with it. The left analog stick moves the camera and the d-pad moves the player. There is no need to add code to make the controller work.

However, to add additional game play elements like attacking or jumping, you will need to map some buttons. Additionally, the d-pad may not be ideal for moving the player.

In the following application we perform a controller test which discovers how the various controls are mapped. Though it is designed with the XBOX remote in mind, this example should work on most gamepads allowing you to find the proper mapping for the controls.

The application uses a series of JoyAxisTriggers associated with mapping names. Only some of the mappings are shown here. The rest are found in *Table 10 - Gamepad Mappings*. When you run this example you should see the buttons and controls you press as output.

```java
public class GamePad extends SimpleApplication {

    public static void main(String[] args){
        GamePad app = new GamePad();
        app.start();
    }

    @Override
    public void simpleInitApp() {
        inputManager.addMapping("D-Pad Left",
            new JoyAxisTrigger(0, JoyInput.AXIS_POV_X, true));
        // Provide additional mappings

        inputManager.addListener(actionListener,
            "D-Pad Left" , … "Button LT");

    public void onAction(String name, boolean isPressed,
            float tpf) {
        System.out.println(name + " = " + isPressed);
    }
}
```

Table 10- Gamepad Mappings

Mapping Name	Trigger
"D-Pad Left"	new JoyAxisTrigger(0, JoyInput.AXIS_POV_X, true)
"D-Pad Right"	new JoyAxisTrigger(0, JoyInput.AXIS_POV_X, false)
"D-Pad Down"	new JoyAxisTrigger(0, JoyInput.AXIS_POV_Y, true)
"D-Pad Up"	new JoyAxisTrigger(0, JoyInput.AXIS_POV_Y, false)
"Axis LS Up"	new JoyAxisTrigger(0, 0, true)
"Axis LS Down"	new JoyAxisTrigger(0, 0, false)
"Axis LS Left"	new JoyAxisTrigger(0, 1, true)
"Axis LS Right"	new JoyAxisTrigger(0, 1, false)
"Axis RS Up"	new JoyAxisTrigger(0, 2, true)
"Axis RS Down"	new JoyAxisTrigger(0, 2, false)
"Axis RS Left"	new JoyAxisTrigger(0, 3, true)
"Axis RS Right"	new JoyAxisTrigger(0, 3, false)
"Button A"	new JoyButtonTrigger(0, 0)
"Button B"	new JoyButtonTrigger(0, 1)
"Button X"	new JoyButtonTrigger(0, 2)
"Button Y"	new JoyButtonTrigger(0, 3)
"Button LB"	new JoyButtonTrigger(0, 4)
"Button RB"	new JoyButtonTrigger(0, 5)
"Button BACK"	new JoyButtonTrigger(0, 6)
"Button START"	new JoyButtonTrigger(0, 7)
"Button RT"	new JoyButtonTrigger(0, 9)
"Button RT"	new JoyAxisTrigger(0, 4, true)
"Button LT"	new JoyAxisTrigger(0, 4, false)

Adding Picking

Picking is the term JME3 uses to describe a type of interaction between the player and objects in the game. This includes interactions such as opening a door, picking up an object, or firing a weapon. Picking uses several previously covered techniques, including action listeners and triggers. However, there are two new concepts we must learn before we can successfully implement picking. These new concepts are **ray casting** and **collision detection**.

Implementing Ray Casting

A **Ray** is basically just an invisible line segment that starts at an origin point and extends infinitely in a specified direction. The primary use of rays is picking. They are also used to determine if an object is in the line of sight of the player or **NPC** (Non-Player-Character) and to detect collisions. Picture the laser security systems used in every spy movie. When the laser is touched the alarms go off. In JME3, when the ray touches an object, a collision is detected.

Ray casting is how we use rays in JME3. This involves sending a ray from a point of origin out into a particular direction. Ray casting is the technique you would use if you wanted to have a player cast spells, enable an AI controlled car to avoid running into objects, or set traps that activate when a player steps on them. For our example, we will be casting a ray using the player's position as origin and the direction that the camera is facing. The camera represents out player.

The concept of a ray is supported in JME3 using the `com.jme3.math` package's `Ray` class. In the next statement, we create an instance of a ray. Its constructor takes two `Vector3f` arguments. The first argument is the origin of the ray and the second is the direction. In this example we are interested in where the default camera, `cam`, is and which way it is pointing.

```
Ray ray = new Ray(cam.getLocation(), cam.getDirection());
```

Implementing Collision Detection

As you may have already concluded from the name, collision detection is the process of detecting a collision. This usually happens in JME3 with a ray and one or more objects.

The basic steps for collision detection for picking include:

1. Create a new `Ray` object and assign it an origin and direction
2. Create a new `CollisionResults` object
3. Populate the collision results using the `collideWith` method
4. Gather the results of the collision using various `CollisionResults` methods

The `collideWith` method executes against a spatial or group of spatials. You can either call the `collideWith` method against the `rootNode` to make everything collidable, or run the method against a node that holds everything you want to allow the player to collide with.

The two arguments to this method are a `Ray` object and a `CollisionResults` object. Running this method against a spatial will allow the ray to collide with the spatials and store the result in the `CollisionResults` object. The `CollisionResults` class possesses several useful methods as listed in *Table 11 - CollisionResult Methods*. These methods are pretty self-explanatory but we will illustrate several of them so you can get a better idea as to how all these things work together.

Table 11 - CollisionResult Methods

Methods	Purpose
getClosestCollision	Returns data about the closest collision of the ray
getGeometry	Returns the geometry that collided with the ray. Running getName against this method returns the name of the geometry.
getDistance	Returns the distance from the origin to the collision
getContactPoint	Returns the world coordinates of the collision point as a Vector3f

Implementing Picking

Let's take what we have learned about picking and put it to good use. We will create an example using some of the code we have already written. Remember the AI ships from Chapter 2? These guys will make great target practice for our picking exercise. We will start by reusing this code and build upon it.

This example implements picking to target AI ships. In the simpleInitApp method the ships are created and attached to the scene graph. The initKeys method is then called. This method maps the left mouse click to shoot at targets and adds an action listener. Now when the user clicks the left mouse button we can respond to this input.

```java
public class Main extends SimpleApplication {

    public static void main(String[] args) {
        Main app = new Main();
        app.start();
    }
    Node enemies;

    @Override
    public void simpleInitApp() {
        enemies = getAIShips();
        rootNode.attachChild(enemies);
        initKeys();
    }

    private void initKeys() {
        inputManager.addMapping("Shoot",
            new MouseButtonTrigger(MouseInput.BUTTON_LEFT));
        inputManager.addListener(actionListener, "Shoot");
    }
```

An action listener is created next. Its onAction method will respond to "shoot" operations. An addCollision method is added to simplify the application. In this method we will follow the four steps for collision detection and generate some feedback about the collisions.

```
    private ActionListener actionListener =
        new ActionListener() {
    @Override
    public void onAction(String name, boolean keyPressed,
        float tpf) {
        if (name.equals("Shoot") && !keyPressed) {
            addCollision(enemies);
        }
    }
};
```

The `addCollision` method is passed a spatial variable, `spatial`, that is used to set up collision detection. First, we will create a `CollisionResults` object called `results`. Then we will create a `Ray` object called `ray`. We then run the `collideWith` method against our spatial, using `ray` and `results` as parameters.

```
    private void addCollision(Spatial spatial){
        CollisionResults results = new CollisionResults();
        Ray ray = new Ray(cam.getLocation(),
            cam.getDirection());
        spatial.collideWith(ray, results);
        ...
```

The remaining body of the method consists of a for-loop. This loop cycles through collisions and gathers various details such as the name, contact point, and distance of each object hit by our ray.

```
        for (int i = 0; i < results.size(); i++) {
            float distance =
                results.getCollision(i).getDistance();
            Vector3f contactPoint =
                results.getCollision(i).getContactPoint();
            String who =
                results.getCollision(i).getGeometry().getName();
            System.out.println("* Collision #" + i);
            System.out.println("  You hit " + who + " at " +
                contactPoint + ", " + distance + " WU away.");
        }
    }
}
```

Run the application, center a ship on the screen, and then shoot at the AI ships using the left mouse button. The details from each successful shot will be printed as output. These details should be similar to the results seen here:

Collision #0

　You hit Alien Ship 1 at (1.4420315, 0.25761244, 1.0), 8.66248 WU away.

Collision #1

　You hit Alien Ship 1 at (1.7651113, 0.3150024, -1.000001), 10.689221 WU away.

You probably noticed that there are usually two collisions on the same object every time you cast a ray. This is because the ray passes through the front facing side of an object and then through the back side as well. For most games this behavior is probably not ideal. The good news is there is another method to deal with this issue. Let's rework some of the code from the picking example to account for the extra collision(s), and add some additional effects so we can see exactly where the ray hits.

We will do this by modifying the existing code to determine the closest object we collided with. We will create a geometry that represents a hit, and then attach the new geometry to the object at the collision point. This way we will have instant visual feedback when we successfully hit one of the AI ships.

First, let's add a new method that creates a new geometry at a specified location (as shown next). We will call this method addHit, with a Vector3f location as the single parameter. In this method we go through the usual steps of creating a new geometry. We will use the usual wireframe material with an orange color. The method returns a geometry with the location set using the setLocalTranslation method and the location parameter.

```
private Geometry addHit(Vector3f location){
    Sphere sphere = new Sphere(32,32,0.3f);
    Geometry hit = new Geometry("Sphere", sphere);
    Material mat = new Material(assetManager,
    "Common/MatDefs/Misc/Unshaded.j3md");
    mat.setColor("Color", ColorRGBA.Orange);
    mat.getAdditionalRenderState().setWireframe(true);
    hit.setMaterial(mat);
    hit.setLocalTranslation(location);
    return hit;
}
```

Next, remove the for-loop from addCollision, unless you would like to keep it for further testing. Replace it with an if-statement with the logical test condition results.size() > 0 as shown next. Inside the if-statement create a CollisionResult object called closest. Assign the result of the getClosestCollision method to closest. We can now use closest to get the closest contact point and create a hit image to attach to the scene graph.

```
private void addCollision(Spatial s){
    CollisionResults results = new CollisionResults();
    Ray ray = new Ray(cam.getLocation(), cam.getDirection());
    s.collideWith(ray, results);
```

```
    if (results.size() > 0){
        CollisionResult closest = results.getClosestCollision();
        Geometry hit = addHit(closest.getContactPoint());
        rootNode.attachChild(hit);
    }
}
```

When you run the revised game you should be able to see where the AI ships are hit. Your result should be similar to *Figure 4 - Picking Example*. In this example, both AI ships were hit twice.

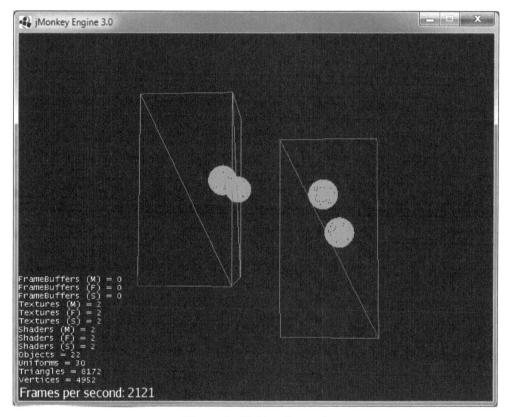

Figure 4 - Picking Example

At this point you should be familiar with rays, collision detection, and the basics of picking. This means that you now have the foundation to create an endless variety of interactions between the user and the game world. These techniques are used for attacking enemies, opening doors, picking up objects, navigation, environmental snares, and many more game-world concepts.

The picking technique presented here is the typical approach used in most tutorials and books. However, it may not always be a satisfactory approach for many applications. The marks are not attached to the boxes. If the boxes move, the marks will not. If the boxes are removed from the scene, the marks are not automatically removed. An alternative that builds on the technique used in this section and which addresses these concerns is found in Improving our Shades of Infinity Game.

Adding Situational Sound

Situational sounds are pretty similar to the ambient sounds we covered in Chapter 1. The main differences are:

- Situational sounds are usually triggered by some event

- They use the `playInstance` method rather than the `play` method

- Looping is set to `false`

Let's add some sound to our previous picking example. Since our game uses a space ship, we will use a laser sound effect, triggered when the player shoots. The laser sound effect are downloaded from the publisher's website.

The audio node needs to be created and associated with the appropriate sound file. We will do this in a method called `initAudio`. You will want to make the audio node variable, `laser`, an instance variable so it is available throughout the game as shown next. It is initialized in the `initAudio` method. The `simpleInitApp` sets up the AI ships, keys, and calls the `initAudio` method as shown here.

```
AudioNode laser;

@Override
public void simpleInitApp() {
    enemies = getAIShips();
    rootNode.attachChild(enemies);
    initKeys();
    initAudio();
}
```

As you may recall from Chapter 1, the arguments to the audio node are the `assetManager` and the location of the sound file. Because we do not want our sound to repeat, we will call the `setLooping` method with `false` as the parameter in the `initAudio` method as shown next. Additionally, we can call the `setVolume` method if we want to change the volume of the sound. The last thing we want to be sure to do in `initAudio` is attach `laser` to the `rootNode`. This node is not visible.

```
private void initAudio(){
    laser = new AudioNode(assetManager, "Sounds/laser.wav");
    laser.setLooping(false);
    laser.setVolume(3);
    rootNode.attachChild(laser);
}
```

> Volume can be a little tricky in JME3. It may vary between computers and sound files. The default volume is 1, and 2 is twice as loud, etc.

At this point we have our sound ready to go. We just need to add one final line of code to the onAction method we created in Implementing Picking. Call the playInstance method against laser, right next where we call addCollision. The updated onAction method is shown here:

```
public void onAction(String name, boolean keyPressed,
        float tpf) {
    if (name.equals("Shoot") && !keyPressed) {
        addCollision(enemies);
        laser.playInstance();
    }
}
```

Now, when we run the game, we should be able to hear the situational sound effect of the laser every time we left-click, or shoot.

Improving our Shades of Infinity Game

In this section we will incorporate many of the techniques discussed in this chapter to improve our game.

Specifically, we will:

- Add joystick and gamepad support
- Add a sound when the laser is fired

Due to the length of the code, only code snippets will be listed here. The complete source can be downloaded from the publisher's website. When the game executes it will appear as shown in *Figure 5 - Shades of Infinity - 3*. Go ahead and play with the game to get a feel for how it works.

The user is able to use the F key, joystick trigger, or left mouse button to fire the laser. The joystick can also be used to navigate the scene graph. Sounds have been added to enhance the game feel.

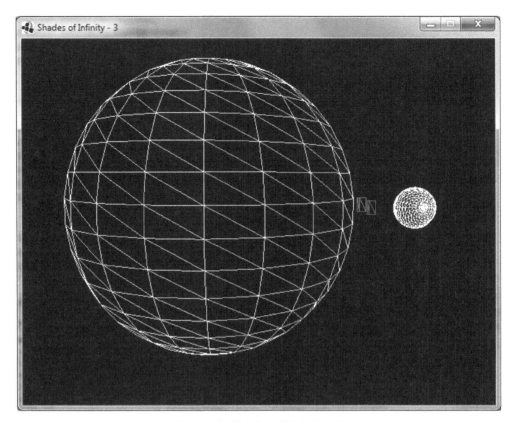

Figure 5 - Shades of Infinity - 3

Let's start with a set of instance variable declarations as shown next. They are used to setup variables that need to be used in multiple methods.

```
private AudioNode laser;
private static String title = "Shades of Infinity - 3";
private Node enemies;
private final static Trigger TRIGGER_F =
    new KeyTrigger(KeyInput.KEY_F);
private final static MouseButtonTrigger
    TRIGGER_MOUSE_BUTTON_LEFT =
        new MouseButtonTrigger(MouseInput.BUTTON_LEFT);
private final static String MAP_SHOOT = "Shoot";
```

In the `simpleInitApp` method several methods are called to initialize the game:

```
initKeys();
initJoystick();
initAudio();
buildPlanetarySystem();
```

The `initKeys` method maps the F key and left mouse click events:

```
private void initKeys() {
    inputManager.addMapping(MAP_SHOOT, TRIGGER_F);
    inputManager.addMapping(MAP_SHOOT,
        TRIGGER_MOUSE_BUTTON_LEFT);
    inputManager.addListener(actionListener, MAP_SHOOT);
}
```

The `initJoystick` method uses the second joystick on the test system. It maps the first button to the `MAP_SHOOT` mapping name. This button corresponds to the joystick's trigger.

```
private void initJoystick() {
    Joystick[] joysticks = inputManager.getJoysticks();
    Joystick joystick = joysticks[1];
    List<JoystickButton> buttons = joystick.getButtons();
    JoystickButton b = buttons.get(0);
    b.assignButton(MAP_SHOOT);
}
```

The remainder of the code is almost identical to the previous version of the game. Methods such as the `addHit` and `handleCollision` that we developed earlier in this chapter have been added with a few minor adjustments. For example, in the `addHit` method the size of the hit has been reduced to match the size of the target ships. Also, the AI ships have been assigned to the `enemies` variable.

Conclusion

We showed how to tie user input to specific game actions. The approach used by JME3 is to define a trigger, associate it with a mapping name, and then (when an input event occurs) send the mapping name and other relevant information to a listener.

JME3 supports both action and analog listeners. Discrete events, such as a button clicks are best used with action listeners. Continuous events such as joystick movements are best used with analog listeners. We illustrated them using the mouse, keyboard, joystick, and game pad.

The concept of picking, and how JME3 implements picking, was demonstrated using ray casting and collision detection. This permits a player to interact with a game by shooting or otherwise selecting elements of a game. We also discussed an updated version of the Shades of Infinity game and integrated many of this chapter's topics into the game.

In the next chapter, we will demonstrate various ways by which we can use input events to update the game state.

4

Game Logic

Introduction

In this chapter, we will build upon Chapter 3 and demonstrate various ways we can use input events to update the game state. We will use the `SimpleApplication` class' `simpleUpdate` method to update the game state which includes the control of **Non-Player Characters (NPCs)**, character statistics, checking for game state changes, and (of course) user input. Everything in the method should be executed as rapidly as possible. In addition, this is where you would place conditional statements, triggers, and updates to the HUD.

However, this method can quickly become large and unwieldy. What we need to do is move the code that updates the game state to different places in a logical and convenient manner. This is where application states and custom controls become useful.

Application States are concerned with the global game logic and will help simplify the organization of code. Application states are used for modularizing the code that controls the execution flow of a game. In a similar fashion, custom controls are focused on the behaviour of a single spatial. Application states, custom controls, and `simpleUpdate` provide variations on how the state of the game is controlled.

> Keep in mind that because the `simpleUpdate` method is always running, it can be easy to bog your game down here. If you have a lot going on in `simpleUpdate` it might be a good idea to create an `AppState` to take care of global activities such as switching between game modes and scenes.

In the last section of this chapter we will demonstrate how many of this chapter's techniques can be applied to the Shades of Infinity game. Of particular focus is how to incorporate the object oriented nature of Java development with the game and graphic support provided by JME3. For example, a `SpaceShip` class may contain data and methods related to an object in our game. We will demonstrate how this class can be integrated with JME3.

Understanding Application States

The `Appstate` interface is found in the `com.jme3.app.state` package. It allows us to control the logic of the game on a global scale. Application states are used to handle a wide variety of different situations and to simplify the `simpleUpdate` method. Let's look at a few different examples of how application states are used. We can do this by moving code from `simpleUpdate` to an `AppState` object's `update` method.

An `AppState` class is an extension of your application. `AppState`s have access to every field in your application. Each `AppState` calls an `initialize` and `cleanup` method when added and removed from the game, respectively. It also has its own `update` method that connects to `simpleUpdate`. You can specify exactly what happens when an `AppState` is paused and resumed. You can also use one `AppState` to switch between other sets of `AppState`s.

Once an application state is attached to a game, every time the `simpleUpdate` method executes, the application state's `update` method is executed. This permits moving game logic to the appropriate method.

There are 5 steps to follow when creating and using an `AppState`:

1. Create a new class extending `AbstractAppState`

2. Implement its abstract methods

3. Add game behaviour to the `AppState`'s `update` method

4. Attach the `AppState` to the `AppStateManager`

5. Detach the `AppState` when you are done with it

Creating an `AppState` Object

To illustrate this process, we will demonstrate an `AppState` that will create and add a rotating effect to the planetary system we created in Chapter 2. To create a new Java class for our new `AppState`:

1. Right click on the package in the project window and select New > Java Class…

2. Name the class `PlanetsAppState`

3. Click Finish

We will use the same `getPlanets` and `getSphere` methods that we used in Chapter 2. These methods you can just drop into the class. The only change we are making to the `getPlanets` method is making the `baseNode` an instance variable so that we can access it from other methods in the class. Now let's jump into the new code.

Starting at the class declaration you will notice that `AppState`s must extend the `AbstractAppState` interface. There are four methods you need to implement: `initialize`, `cleanup`, `setEnabled`, and `update`. We will need an instance of `SimpleApplication` to use throughout our class, so we will declare it as a global variable called `app`.

```
public class PlanetsAppState extends AbstractAppState {

    private SimpleApplication app;
    private Node baseNode = new Node("Base Node");
```

Overriding the Base Class Methods

Now let's start overriding the base class methods. The `initialize` method takes two arguments, an `AppStateManager` and an `Application`. The `initialize` method, shown next, has three lines. The first line invokes the base class' `initialize` method. The second line assigns this class' instance of `SimpleApplication` to the instance in `Main`, This makes it easy to access the `SimpleApplication` variables such as `rootNode`. The third line attaches the `baseNode` to the `rootNode` from the `Main` class.

```
    @Override
    public void initialize(AppStateManager stateManager,
            Application app) {
        super.initialize(stateManager, app);
        this.app = (SimpleApplication) app;
        this.app.getRootNode().attachChild(getPlanets());
    }
```

The `cleanup` method is used to get rid of anything we no longer need if we stop using our `AppState`. First we call the base class method using `super.cleanup`. This will run the code in the base class' `cleanup` method. The only thing we need to do is to detach the `baseNode`, since we no longer need it.

```
    @Override
    public void cleanup() {
        super.cleanup();
        this.app.getRootNode().detachChild(baseNode);
    }
```

The `setEnabled` method is used to pause and resume the `AppState`. The only argument to this method is a boolean value that controls whether or not the `AppState` is paused. The first line of this method calls the base class' `setEnabled` method. The remainder of the method body is simply a conditional block that handles what to do if the state is paused or enabled. We won't be using it in this example, but it is necessary to implement all the abstract methods of a base class. Typically, application state-specific spatials are attached and detached in this method.

```
    @Override
    public void setEnabled(boolean enabled) {
        super.setEnabled(enabled);
        if (enabled) {
            this.app.getRootNode().attachChild(baseNode);
        } else {
            this.app.getRootNode().detachChild(baseNode);
        }
    }
```

The final method we are inheriting from `AbstractAppState` is the `update` method. This method will be called repeatedly as long as the `AppState` is active. This is where we apply a constant rotation to our planetary system.

Let's add some rotation to our planetary system use the `rotate` method, as discussed in Chapter 2. Notice the value we will be using: `(0, .01f * FastMath.DEG_TO_RAD, 0)`. This means that we will be applying a .01 degree rotation around the y axis, once per frame. So, if the game is running at 300 frames per second, the planetary system will rotate at 3 degrees per second. Alternatively we could use the `tpf` parameter to control the rotation such as: `(0, 2 * tpf, 0)`.

```java
@Override
public void update(float tpf) {
    baseNode.rotate(0, .01f * FastMath.DEG_TO_RAD, 0);
}
```

The `getPlanets` and `getSphere` methods are shown here:

```java
public Node getPlanets() {
    //Create Planet
    Geometry centerSphere = getSphere(20, 20, 2f);
    centerSphere.setLocalTranslation(0, 0, 0);
    Material sphereMaterial =
        new Material(app.getAssetManager(),
        "Common/MatDefs/Misc/Unshaded.j3md");
    centerSphere.setMaterial(sphereMaterial);
    sphereMaterial.getAdditionalRenderState().
        setWireframe(true);
    baseNode.attachChild(centerSphere);

    //Create Moon
    Geometry moon = getSphere(20, 20, 0.3f);
    moon.setLocalTranslation(3f, 0, 0);
    moon.setMaterial(sphereMaterial);
    baseNode.attachChild(moon);

    return baseNode;
}

public Geometry getSphere(int y, int z, float radius) {
    Sphere sphere1 = new Sphere(y, z, radius);
    Geometry sphere = new Geometry("Sphere", sphere1);
    return sphere;
}
}
```

Our `PlanetsAppState` class is complete and ready to use. In the following section we will add the class to the application and our planets will appear in the scene.

Using an `AppState`

Once we have created `PlanetsAppState`, we can use it in our `Main` class. We will create an instance of the state and attach it to the `stateManager`. The `stateManager` is responsible for calling the various methods of the `AppState`, so we do not worry about calling them explicitly. As soon as the state is attached, the `stateManager` handles the rest. As you can see next, we only need to add two lines to the `simpleInitApp` method of our `Main` class.

```
public void simpleInitApp() {
    ...
    PlanetsAppState planets = new PlanetsAppState();
    stateManager.attach(planets);
}
```

When you run the game you should see the moon rotating around the planet, similar to *Figure 1 - PlanetsAppState*.

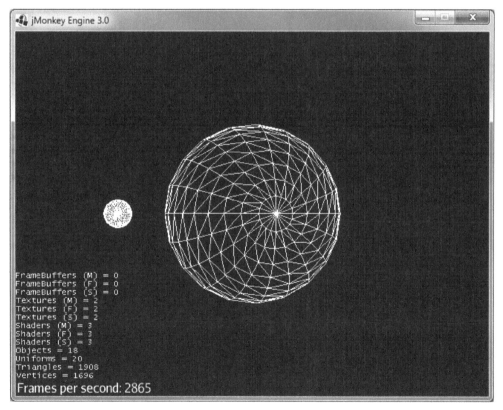

Figure 1 - PlanetsAppState

In the application's `simpleUpdate` method, we can enable or disable the state based on some condition.

```
public void simpleUpdate(float tpf) {
    if (someCondition) {
        planetsAppState.setEnabled(true);
        ...
        }
    } else {
        planetsAppState.setEnabled(false);
        ...
    }
}
```

The `SimpleApplication` Class' `AppState`s

When a game derived from `SimpleApplication` is created, the `SimpleApplication` constructor is called, which then calls a second constructor. The source code for these constructors is as follows:

```
public SimpleApplication() {
    this( new StatsAppState(), new FlyCamAppState(),
        new DebugKeysAppState() );
}

public SimpleApplication( AppState... initialStates ) {
    super();

    if (initialStates != null) {
        for (AppState a : initialStates) {
            if (a != null) {
                stateManager.attach(a);
            }
        }
    }
}
```

The result is three application states associated with the game that are listed in *Table 1-SimpleApplication Initial Application States*.

The `FlyCamAppState` is used to map input for the camera and provides a good example of an application state as detailed in the next section. The other two applications states are not discussed here because they are more specialized and deal with debugging and the display of statistics in the HUD.

Table 1- SimpleApplication Initial Application States

AppState	Purpose
DebugKeysAppState	Setups the C and M keys to display camera and memory statistics
FlyCamAppState	Setups up keys for controlling camera
StatsAppState	Setups up stats view in the HUD

> If you need to see what the source code looks like for a JME3 class, right click on the class name in the editor and choose Navigate - Go To Source. This will bring up the source code in a separate window. Source code for JME3 is available on the internet but it does not always match what is used in the JDK.

Understanding the `FlyCamAppState`

The `FlyCamAppState` is a good example of how application states can be written. The code shown next is adapted from the JME3 source code. The application state is associated with a game in the `SimpleAppplication` class' constructor.

The `FlyByCamera` class is the camera associated with the default camera used by a game. Its `registerWithInput` method initializes the keys used to control the movement of the camera. In the `setEnabled` method, the camera is enabled or disabled depending on the method's argument. When the application state is removed, then the `cleanup` method is called, which unregisters the camera.

```java
public class FlyCamAppState extends AbstractAppState {

    private Application app;
    private FlyByCamera flyCam;

    public FlyCamAppState() { }

    void setCamera( FlyByCamera cam ) {
        this.flyCam = cam;
    }

    public FlyByCamera getCamera() {
        return flyCam;
    }

    @Override
    public void initialize(AppStateManager stateManager,
            Application app) {
        super.initialize(stateManager, app);
        this.app = app;
```

```
            if (app.getInputManager() != null) {
                if (flyCam == null) {
                    flyCam = new FlyByCamera(app.getCamera());
                }
                flyCam.registerWithInput(app.getInputManager());
            }
        }

        @Override
        public void setEnabled(boolean enabled) {
            super.setEnabled(enabled);
            flyCam.setEnabled(enabled);
        }

        @Override
        public void cleanup() {
            super.cleanup();
            flyCam.unregisterInput();
        }
    }
```

Creating Custom Input Settings Using an Application State

The default keyboard mapping was discussed in Chapter 3 but is not always applicable to other games. When it is not, the mapping needs to be changed. A good place to perform this alternate mapping is in an application state.

The best approach for remapping input is by:

1. Removing the FlyCamAppState

2. Creating a new application state

3. Adding this new application state to the game

To remove an application state, use the stateManager class' detach method as shown next. The getState method is called first to get a reference to the FlyCamAppState object. It is then used as an argument to the detach method removing it from the game. At this point, the mappings used to move the camera will no longer work.

```
        stateManager.detach(stateManager.getState(
            FlyCamAppState.class));
```

We could have used the following statement to disable the camera's mappings but it does not get rid of them. Sometimes this method is useful for temporarily disabling the flycam so that the player may appear "frozen". It would later become enabled.

```
        flyCam.setEnabled(false);
```

To create a new set of bindings, create a new application state that is derived from `AbstractAppState`. Override the necessary methods including the `initialize` method. In this method, replace the `FlyByCamera` constructor call with your own camera class as shown here. In this case, we use a class called `MyFlyByCamera`.

```
public void initialize(AppStateManager stateManager,
        Application app) {
    super.initialize(stateManager, app);
    this.app = app;
    if (app.getInputManager() != null) {
        if (flyCam == null) {
            flyCam = new MyFlyByCamera(app.getCamera());
        }
        flyCam.registerWithInput(app.getInputManager());
    }
}
```

Create your `MyFlyByCamera` class by extending the `FlyByCamera` class. Override the `registerWithInput` method and provide your own input mappings. Override the `unregisterInput` method to remove the mappings if your application state is removed.

In this section we have illustrated how to create and use an application state. From a functional point of view, it is not that different from previous applications. However, the approach does simplify the `simpleUpdate` method. In the Improving our Shades of Infinity Game section, we will reuse `PlanetsAppState` and add a new one to fully demonstrate the utility of this technique.

Understanding Custom Controls

A **Custom Control** is used to control the behavior of a particular spatial. Similar to how application states affect global game behavior, custom controls affect a single spatial's behavior. These controls are excellent for handling NPCs, doors, and anything that you want to behave a specific way. It helps organize the application by moving spatial's control logic out of the `simpleUpdate` method and tying it directly to the spatial.

A good approach is to add one control for each type of behavior you want a spatial to perform. For example, you might have one control that makes a spatial walk around, one control that makes a spatial respond to a collision, and another that removes a spatial from the scene when destroyed. One spatial could use all three of these controls. The spatial will act on these controls in the order they are attached. As we will see, each custom control has its own update loop that functions the same way as `simpleUpdate`.

The steps for creating a custom control are very similar to those for creating an application state. The main difference here is that a custom control focuses on a single spatial:

1. Create a new class extending `AbstractControl`

2. Implement the abstract methods

3. Add the desired behaviour to the custom control's `update` method

4. Attach the control to a spatial

Let's use these steps to create a control for the AI ships.

Creating a Custom Control

We will create a control to keep track of the AI ships' health points and remove the ships from the scene when they run out of points. To start this process we will need to create a new Java class with the name `AIControl`. Of course, you can use any name you like for this class.

First, inherit from the `com.jme3.scene.control` package's `AbstractControl` class and implement its abstract methods as shown next. Create two instance variables. The first is an integer called `health`, and the second is a `Node` called `baseNode`.

```
public class AIControl extends AbstractControl {
    int health;
    Node baseNode;
```

Add a constructor so we can set the number of health points for the ship and get access to the AI ship's `baseNode`. Our constructor will need two lines. The first line assigns the global variable `health` using the constructor's parameter. The second line does the same thing with the global variable `baseNode`.

```
public AIControl(int health, Node rootNode){
    this.health = health;
    this.baseNode = rootNode;
}
```

Overriding the Base Class Methods

The `spatial` variable is inherited from the `AbstractControl` class and references the spatial that is attached to the control. The two methods that must be implemented are the `controlUpdate` and the `controlRender` methods.

The `controlUpdate` method works in exactly the same way as `simpleUpdate` and the `update` method from the `AppState` class. It has the `tpf` parameter that represents the time per frame. We will use this method to remove the spatial, the AI ship, when the ship's health points are reduced to 0. To do this we will use an if-statement that makes sure the spatial is not null and a nested if-statement that checks the health value. If health falls below 0, we will detach the AI ship from the `baseNode`.

```
@Override
protected void controlUpdate(float tpf) {
    if(spatial != null){
        if(health<=0){
            baseNode.detachChild(spatial);
        }
    }
}
```

The `decrementHealth` method is used to decrease the health of a ship as shown here:

```
public void decrementHealth(int healthLoss){
    this.health -= healthLoss;
}
```

The `controlRender` method is used for special rendering operations. For this application, there is nothing special that needs to be done so we will leave it empty.

```
@Override
protected void controlRender(RenderManager rm,
    ViewPort vp) {
    //Not Used Right Now
}
```

Using a Custom Control

At this point our `AIControl` is ready to use in our `Main` class. First, declare global `AIControl` variables for `ship1Control` and a `ship2Control`. We can instantiate both of these controls within the `getAIShips` method as shown next. We then attach `ship1Control` and `ship2Control` to the Alien Ship 1 and Alien Ship 2 geometries, respectively.

```
private Node getAIShips() {
    Geometry geom = createAIShip(
    "Alien Ship 1", 1, 0, 0, ColorRGBA.Blue);
    Geometry geom2 = createAIShip(
    "Alien Ship 2", -2, 1, 0, ColorRGBA.Red);

    Node baseNode = new Node("base node");
    Node node1 = new Node("node 1");
    Node node2 = new Node("node 2");

    baseNode.attachChild(node1);
    node1.attachChild(geom);
    node1.attachChild(geom2);
    baseNode.attachChild(node2);

    ship1Control = new AIControl(20, node1);
    geom.addControl(ship1Control);
```

```
        ship2Control = new AIControl(15, node1);
        geom2.addControl(ship2Control);

        return baseNode;
    }
```

When the ships are hit, we need to call the decrementHealth method. To do this, add if-statements to the addCollision method to determine which ship was hit and then call the decrementHealth method. The updated addCollision method is displayed in the following code:

```
private void addCollision(Spatial s){
    CollisionResults results = new CollisionResults();
    Ray ray = new Ray(cam.getLocation(), cam.getDirection());
    s.collideWith(ray, results);

    if (results.size() > 0){
        score++;
        CollisionResult closest =
          results.getClosestCollision();
        if(closest.getGeometry().getName().equals(
            "Alien Ship 1")){
          ship1Control.decrementHealth(5);
        }
        if(closest.getGeometry().getName().equals(
            "Alien Ship 2")){
          ship2Control.decrementHealth(5);
        }
        boom = addHit(closest.getContactPoint());
        rootNode.attachChild(boom);
    }
}
```

Now, when you run the game the AI ships will disappear when their health points reach zero.

Improving our Shades of Infinity Game

In this section we will incorporate many of the techniques discussed in this chapter to improve our game. Java should be used in an object oriented manner to take full advantage of the language. We will use and expand upon our SpaceShip class to illustrate how you can do this with JME3.

Specifically, we will:

- Modify the `Main` class

- Create a new application state, `CombatAppState`, to handle combat

- Create a new derived class, `AISpaceShip`, for our AI ships

Due to the length of the code, only code snippets will be listed here. The complete source is found on the publisher's website. When the game executes it will appear as shown in *Figure 2 - Shades of Infinity GUI*. Execute the game to get a feel for how it works.

The user is able to use the F key or left mouse button to fire the laser. A joystick can be used to navigate the scene graph. Sounds have been added to enhance the game feel. Both of the AI ships are independent of each other though, in this implementation, they move together. In addition, any hits are attached directly to the ship. When a ship is destroyed, the hit images will go away automatically. Also, the player cannot fire on a target until it is in range. Axes have been drawn to make it easier to see how the objects are positioned in the game.

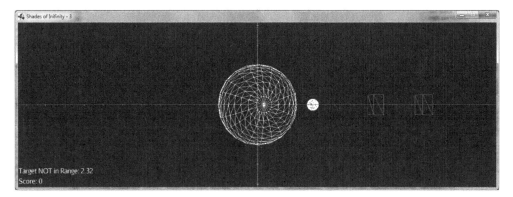

Figure 2 - Shades of Infinity GUI

Modifying the `Main` Class

This class is concerned with initializing the scene graph using two `AppState` objects. Initialization of the HUD, joystick, and sounds are performed here. The `simpleUpdate` method controls whether combat can occur.

The `simpleInitApp` Method

This version of the game will use two application states. The first one is the `PlanetsAppState` developed in the *Creating an AppState Object* section. It will always be enabled. The second one is the `CombatAppState` to be detailed in the *Creating the CombatAppState Class* section. These are added to game in the `simpleInitApp` method:

```
        stateManager.attach(planetsAppState);
        stateManager.attach(combatAppState);
```

We also adjust the frustum to permit us to get closer to objects than is possible using the default frustum settings (as shown next). We changed the third argument from `1.0f` to `0.1f`.

```
        cam.setFrustumPerspective(45, settings.getWidth() /
            settings.getHeight(), 0.1f, 1000);
```

One of our goals is to integrate Java classes such as our `SpaceShip` class into the game. We start by creating an instance of `SpaceShip` where `player` is a static variable. We also initialize our HUD.

```
        player = new SpaceShip("Player", cam.getLocation(),
            100, 100, 20, 50, 0);
        initHUD();
```

The `initHUD` method should be simple enough to follow. Two fields are created. One is used to display the score and the other is used to indicate whether the target ships are in range or not.

In the remainder of the method, we create two `AISpaceShips` that are independent of each other. They are attached to a base node and made part of the `shootable` node that we will use with picking later.

The `simpleUpdate` Method

In this method we make our enemy ships move using the `move` method as shown next. The ships simply move along the X axis. In Chapter 7 we will demonstrate how to move the ships in a more interesting fashion.

```
        shootables.move(0.1f * tpf, 0, 0);
```

The next part of the method determines whether the enemy ships are in range and then updates the HUD to reflect their state. In calculating the distance, the world coordinates of the ships are used and not their local coordinates. This is important. Using the `getLocalTranslation` for a ship will provide its location relative to its parent node. We need its world coordinates otherwise the relative distance will not be calculated correctly. The camera location is given in world coordinates.

```
        float d = cam.getLocation().distance(
            spatial.getWorldTranslation());
```

In the next outer if-statement, we use the distance to update the HUD and to enable or disable the `combatAppState` object. This state is enabled if the ships are within `2.0f` world units. Otherwise it is disabled. When it is enabled, the user is able to fire at the ships.

```
    if (distance > 2.0f) {
        targetInRange = false;
        combatAppState.setEnabled(false);
        if (distance >= Float.MAX_VALUE) {
            hudTargetRange.setText("No targets present");
        } else {
            hudTargetRange.setText("Target NOT in Range: " +
                formatter.format(distance));
        }
    } else {
            // At least one target is in range
            targetInRange = true;
            // If statment used to avoid attempt to add
            // Fire mapping multiple times
            if (!combatAppState.isEnabled()) {
                combatAppState.setEnabled(true);
            }
            hudTargetRange.setText("Target in Range!: " +
                formatter.format(distance));
    }
```

Creating the CombatAppState Class

This class is responsible for managing the state of an enemy ship. It needs to initialize keys, the cross hairs, and sound. Most of the work is performed in the setEnabled and addCollision method.

The initialize Method

The initialize method assigns values to several instance variables. This will simplify access to values in the game. It also initializes the keys, cross hairs, and audio.

```
    public void initialize(AppStateManager stateManager,
            Application app) {
        super.initialize(stateManager, app);
        this.app = (SimpleApplication) app;
        this.settings = Main.settings;
        …
        this.shootables = Main.shootables;

        initKeys();
        initCrossHairs();
        initLaserAudio();
    }
```

The `setEnabled` Method

When this application state is enabled, mappings are made to enable the F key and left mouse buttons to fire a laser. We also need to attach the cross hairs to the HUD. When the state is disabled, these mappings need to be removed.

```
public void setEnabled(boolean enabled) {
    super.setEnabled(enabled);
    if (enabled) {
        this.inputManager.addMapping(MAP_FIRE, TRIGGER_F);
        this.inputManager.addMapping(
            MAP_FIRE, TRIGGER_LEFT_MOUSE_BUTTON);
        guiNode.attachChild(crossHairs);
    } else {
        inputManager.deleteTrigger(MAP_FIRE, TRIGGER_F);
        this.inputManager.deleteTrigger(
            MAP_FIRE, TRIGGER_LEFT_MOUSE_BUTTON);
        guiNode.detachChild(crossHairs);
    }
}
```

The `onAction` Method

This method is similar to the one used in the earlier collision example. The `addCollision` method is called and the laser sound is played:

```
public void onAction(String name, boolean keyPressed,
        float tpf) {
    if (name.equals(MAP_FIRE) && !keyPressed) {
        addCollision(shootables);
        laser.playInstance();
    }
}
```

The `addCollision` Method

Since there are two targets, we need to verify that the one we have collided with is in range. The details of this process are not shown here. The important concern is how we get a reference to the `AISpaceShip` class' object. Since there are two possible ships, and we want to maintain independent health values for each of them, we need a reference to the right ship.

In the `AISpaceShip` class, a reference to the current AI ship instance is attached to the ship's node as discussed in the *Creating the AISpaceShip Class* section. In the following sequence, `getUserData` is used to return this reference. The ship's `handleCollision` method is then called to process the hit.

```
AISpaceShip ship = (AISpaceShip)
    closest.getGeometry().getParent().
        getUserData("AINodeEnclosingObject");
ship.handleCollision(spatial, closest);
```

The `closest` variable references a `CollisionResult` object. The `getGeometry` call returns a reference to the geometry and a call to the `getParent` returns its enclosing node. Applying the `getUserData` method against the node returns the reference. This is illustrated in *Figure 3 - Class Connection Diagram*.

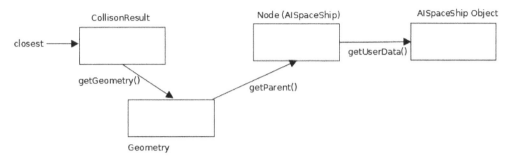

Figure 3 - Class Connection Diagram

This technique, while round about, allows us to connect Java game objects to JME3 graphic elements.

Creating the `AISpaceShip` Class

The `SpaceShip` class has been modified to add a `score` variable and an `incrementScore` method. An `AISpaceShip` class has been derived from `SpaceShip` to support any enemy-specific needs. This class will:

- Return a node and geometry for the ship

- Handle collisions

- Host a custom control object

Most of the code in this class has been adapted from previous examples. Many of these methods will be moved to the base class later. Here we will focus on how collisions are handled and the custom control class.

In the `getAIShip` method, a node and geometry are created as shown next. The `setUserData` method will attach a reference to the current object to the node. This method works fine for primitive data types but if an object is attached, the class must implement the `com.jme3.export.Savable` interface. In this version of our class we provided empty `read` and `write` methods that are needed to implement the interface. For our needs, this will work.

```
public Node getAIShip() {
    Geometry AIShipGeometry = createAIShip(
        "AIShipGeometry", 1, 0, 0, ColorRGBA.Blue);
    Node AIShipNode = new Node(name + " Node");
    AIShipNode.attachChild(AIShipGeometry);
    AIShipNode.scale(0.05f);
```

```
        AIShipNode.setUserData("AINodeEnclosingObject", this);

        AIControl control = new AIControl(5, AIShipNode);
        AIShipGeometry.addControl(control);
        System.out.println("Ship returned: " + AIShipNode);
        return AIShipNode;
    }
```

In the `handleCollision` method, the control class decrements the health and the location of the hit image, `boom`. World coordinates are needed instead of local coordinates. Otherwise the `boom` will not be positioned correctly.

```
    public void handleCollision(Spatial spatial,
            CollisionResult closest) {
        control.decrementHealth(5);
        Vector3f localPoint = closest.getContactPoint().
            subtract(AIShipNode.getWorldTranslation());
        Geometry boom = addHit(localPoint);
        AIShipNode.attachChild(boom);
    }
```

The `AIControl` class' `controlUpdate` method is similar to our earlier control class version. Its purpose is to detach the AI ship and hits from the scene graph when destruction is complete. This is accomplished using the following statement. The `spatial.getParent().getParent()` call returns a reference to the base node. The child being detached is the `AIShipNode` as obtained using `spatial.getParent()`. This relationship is depicted in *Figure 4 - Scene Graph Ship Hierarchy*.

```
    spatial.getParent().getParent().detachChild(
        spatial.getParent());
```

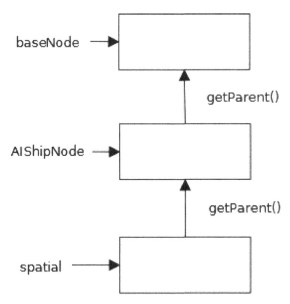

Figure 4 - Scene Graph Ship Hierarchy

Conclusion

In this chapter, we learned about application states and custom controls in detail. They provide a convenient way of partitioning control logic in different places as opposed to placing it all in the simpleUpdate method. This will result in more maintainable and readable code.

We examined how the SimpleApplication class uses application states and how the FlyCamAppState works. We illustrated the general approach for creating new input mappings for an application using an application state. How a custom control can be developed was illustrated.

We also discussed an updated version of the Shades of Infinity game and integrated many of this chapter's topics into the game. We showed how other Java classes, such as SpaceShip, can be integrated with the JME3's graphics elements. In addition, the picking technique was enhanced to attach a hit image directly to a target and have the hit images and target disappear at the same time when a ship is destroyed.

In the next chapter we will learn how to use materials to give our game objects a more pleasing appearance. The use of lighting to achieve effects such as shininess will be covered along with how to add prebuilt models to a game.

5
Materials

Introduction

To make a geometry visible, you need to apply either a color or a material to it. This provides information to the renderer about its surface properties. Materials, which are represented by the JME3 `Material` class, are defined in a material definition file that has the `.j3md` extension. Materials and their use is a complex topic.

There are two commonly used materials in JME3: unshaded and lighted. Unshaded materials are easier to render but do not take advantage of any light source that is present in a scene such as a lamp or sun. Lighted materials reflect light providing more opportunities for interesting effects but are more complex to work with. With lighted materials we have a broader range of appearance possibilities including: shininess, bumpiness, and transparency.

A **Texture** is an image that can be applied and wrapped around an object. It is frequently stored in a `.jpg` or `.png` file. When a texture is associated with a material, it provides additional ways of controlling how an object is rendered. Textures can be thought of as having layers that support different behaviors such as shininess or transparency.

Textures cannot be created within JME3 but are created with an external editor. However, JME3 does have a texture editor that provides limited modification of a texture. There are also a number of sources where free textures can be found including http://opengameart.org/

There are a few material-related topics that will be postponed until later. Height maps and texture splatting are techniques used to generate terrains. We will discuss this topic in Chapter 8 along with tiling.

In this chapter we will also examine asset management more closely. Understanding how JME3 manages assets will make writing code in the JME3 SDK easier.

Understanding Materials

While there are many different types of materials, we will focus on unshaded and lighted materials as defined by the `Unshaded.j3md` and `Lighting.j3md` material definition files. The next few examples illustrate the basics of how materials are used. Details of these techniques will follow in Using Unshaded Materials and Using Lighted Materials.

We can either set a color to a material or use combinations of textures with a material. To set a color, the `setColor` method is used with unshaded material as illustrated here:

```
Material mat = new Material(assetManager,
    "Common/MatDefs/Misc/Unshaded.j3md");
mat.setColor("Color", ColorRGBA.Blue);
someGeometry.setMaterial(mat);
```

To use a texture, a `Texture` object is created from an image and then applied to a material using the `loadTexture` method as shown here:

```
Texture cubeTexture = assetManager.loadTexture(
    "Interface/Logo/Monkey.jpg");
mat.setTexture("ColorMap",cubeTexture);
```

We can also control how light behaves with a lighted material using the `setColor` method with different properties as specified by its first argument:

```
Material mat = new Material(assetManager,
    "Common/MatDefs/Light/Lighting.j3md");
mat.setColor("Diffuse", ColorRGBA.Red);
someGeometry.setMaterial(mat);
```

We will explain these examples in more detail in later sections.

Demystifying Material Terms and Concepts

There are many terms describing materials and how materials can be applied to a geometry. In this section we will introduce a few of the more commonly used terms you may encounter. Understanding these terms provides a context for working with materials. Unfortunately, it can be difficult to understand what they mean. For many terms, there are multiple words used to describe the same concept. In other cases, a graphics/game engine such as JME3 may only provide partial support of a concept or they may have a slightly different use for the term. For example, the difference between materials and textures has tended to blur.

The intention of this section is simply to introduce many of these terms. As with most definitions, it may not always be clear what they mean without a concrete example. Consider these definitions to be your first exposure to a term. Later, we will see how they are applied within the context of JME3.

Common Graphics Terms

Aliasing is a distortion effect that commonly occurs in digital images. This is usually caused by the rate at which images are redrawn or reconstructed. One of the most common examples of aliasing that you might recognize is the wagon-wheel effect, where a spoke on a wheel, or a blade on a propeller, appears to begin spinning backwards or more slowly than it actually is. There are various types of aliasing that can occur in video games. Most modern computer games have an anti-aliasing feature that can be activated if the user has sufficient hardware to support it. Anti-aliasing features make games appear smoother and reduce the pixelated effects that occur when round objects are created with square pixels.

Shaders are sequences of code executed on a **Graphics Processing Unit (GPU)**. They take advantage of the hardware acceleration provided by GPUs. The processing is offloaded to a GPU.

JME3 supports shaders written in OpenGL Shading Language (GLSL):

- **Vertex shaders** - Modify existing shapes and are used by JME3 to animate objects like water and flags

- **Fragment shaders** (pixel shaders) - Used for color effects such as reflections and glowing objects

Shader features are made accessible using material definitions such as `Unshaded.j3md`. The `setTexture` method sets parameters for the material. JME3 handles all of the processing internally. As a developer, we need not worry about the details.

MIPmaps use one texture with varying resolutions in one file. They are used to:

- Speed up rendering

- Improve optimization

- Provide realistic viewing

MIP actually means "multem in parvo" or many in one. JME3 renders the texture differently depending on the proximity of the viewer. The further away the viewer is the lower the resolution used. If custom MIPmaps are not provided, then JME3 will create basic ones automatically to improve optimization.

Seamless Tiled Textures are used when you want to use a repeating image across an object rather than stretching a single image across the entire object. A seamless texture is designed to be used as tiles. The right and left edges match, as well as the top and bottom edges. The idea is that the viewer will not be able to tell where one tile begins and the next begins.

Procedural Textures are most commonly used on spheres. This type of texture uses a combination of one small repeating image and some random gradient variations. It is typically better to use this type of texture on a larger mesh, where the repeating image is less noticeable. This texture is common for grass, soil, rust, and rock.

Texture Splatting is a technique that allows you to basically paint a texture onto a mesh with a pseudo paint brush. This is typically used for terrain like grass and dirt. This is usually done in layers.

Texture Mapping Terms

Sometimes you will hear the term, mapping, which applies a texture to a geometry. Mapping techniques apply various effects to a material. Here we will discuss a few of the more common ones.

Texture Mapping adds a color or an image to a 3D object. When we map an image, a common wrapping technique uses **UV Mapping**. The letters U and V designate the X and Y axes of a 2D texture. Since X, Y, and Z are already used in the 3D world, these letters were adopted.

UV Mapping is usually created in modeling software like Blender. For complex objects, a texture is saved as several different pieces that are designed to fit a specific mesh. As you can see in *Figure 1 - Sinbad Body* and *Figure 2 - Sinbad Clothes*, the Sinbad model included with JME3 (`Models.Sinbad` in the `jME3-testdata.jar` file) is saved as several different pieces. When these maps are applied to the mesh the result is the model in *Figure 3 - Sinbad Model*.

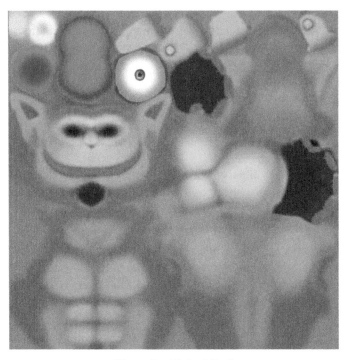

Figure 1 - Sinbad Body

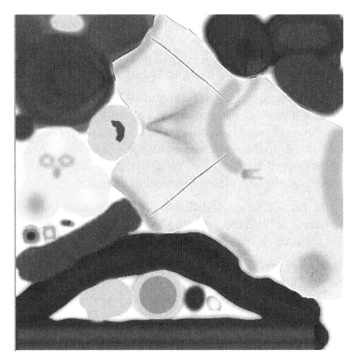

Figure 2 - Sinbad Clothes

Figure 3 - Sinbad Model

Diffuse Mapping – This is a texture mapping method that is sometimes called **Color Mapping**. It wraps the bitmap image to a geometry and uses the original colors. Diffuse is actually the property of a shader which we will discuss in Using Lighted Materials. A shader is applied to an object to give it a surface. Most shaders have a diffuse property.

Bump Mapping – Was introduced by Jim Blinn in 1978. Blinn's method creates the appearance of bumps and grooves without actually altering the geometric object. This method alters the surface normal which affects the way light is reflected. A **Normal** is a vector drawn perpendicular to the surface of an object. For a simple plane, this can be visualized as a line pointing directly up (or down) to the surface. For a curve object, such as a sphere, it is perpendicular to a plane tangential to the point.

In bump mapping, the surface is not modified; it is given the appearance of being modified. A bump map is applied to a smooth surface. This makes it easier to create surface that mimics textures such as bark or rocky surfaces.

Phong Illumination was introduced in 1973 by Bui Tuing Phong. This is a local illumination model which takes into account only direct light reflections. This means light reflected off more than one object is not computed. It allows for more efficient computing when dealing with computer generated images. The details of the model are very mathematical, but the important thing to note about this style of illumination is that it only captures direct light reflections. This the default illumination used by JME3 and standard OpenGL.

Opacity Mapping – Uses a gray scale image to create a cut-out effect. It is also called **Transparency Mapping**.

Specular Mapping – Permits certain areas of a geometry to have a specular effect commonly referred to as shininess.

Glow Mapping – A texture mapping technique where a glow can be controlled (shape, color, and strength).

Reflection Mapping – Used for reflections and sometimes called an **Environment Map**.

Using Unshaded Materials

Unshaded materials come standard with JME3 and do not require a light source. If a light source is present, the material is unaffected by the light source. Unshaded materials do not have bright or dark sides even with a light source.

The `Material` class is found in the `com.jme3.material` package. In the `Material` constructor the first parameter is `assetManager`. This object loads the material specified by the second parameter. Managing Assets discusses the management of project assets. If the `setColor` method is not used, then the cube is rendered in white.

There are three textures that we will discuss here and are defined in *Table 1 - Unshaded.j3md Textures*.

Table 1 - Unshaded.j3md Textures

Texture Type	Data Type
"Color"	ColorRGBA
"ColorMap"	Texture
"Lightmap"	Texture

Advantages of Unshaded.j3md include:

- Faster rendering than using lighted materials

- Does not need a light source

- Useful in situations where shading is not important

Using the color Property

The next example illustrates the use of the Unshaded.j3md material. In this example, a cube's color is set to blue. If only its wireframe is displayed, it will be displayed in blue. The cube is shown in *Figure 4 - Blue Cube*.

```
Box b = new Box(1, 1, 1);
Geometry geom = new Geometry("Box", b);
Material mat = new Material(assetManager,
    "Common/MatDefs/Misc/Unshaded.j3md");
mat.setColor("Color", ColorRGBA.Blue);
geom.setMaterial(mat);
rootNode.attachChild(geom);
```

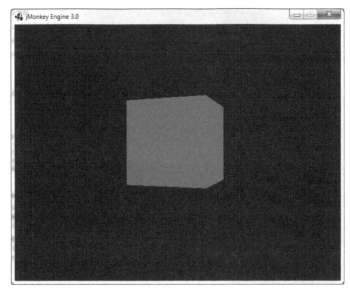

Figure 4 - Blue Cube

Using the `ColorMap` Property

The `ColorMap` property is used to load an image onto an unshaded material using the `setMaterial` method. To illustrate this, copy the `Monkey.jpg` file from `Interface/Logo/` in the `jme3-test-data` library to your Project Assets Interface folder.

Replace the call to `setColor` with the following statements. A `Texture` object is created and used as the second argument of the `setTexture` method. The effect of this is to map the monkey image onto each face of the cube as seen in *Figure 5 - Unshaded Material Example*.

```
Texture cubeTexture = assetManager.loadTexture(
    "Interface/Logo/Monkey.jpg");
mat.setTexture("ColorMap",cubeTexture);
```

Figure 5 - Unshaded Material Example

The `setTexture` method uses two arguments. The first one specifies the texture to use as defined in the material definition for `Unshaded.j3md`. We will dig into material definition later in *Creating Materials*. The second argument is the image to map as the texture.

Using the LightMap Technique

A **LightMap** is a technique where the lighting has been pre-computed for an image. It is said to be "baked in" as it cannot be changed. For some scenes, such as the internal room of a building, the light may not change. By computing the lighting effects when creating the image, a more realistic image can often be generated. In addition, it reduces the amount of processing time needed by a GPU to render the image.

The process of light mapping is done outside JME3 using software like Blender. The process of creating a LightMap is involved and is not discussed here. An example of a light map in Blender is shown in *Figure 6 - LightMap Example*.

Figure 6 - LightMap Example

Editing Textures

While it is not possible to create a texture in JME3, we can perform limited editing using the JME3 texture editor. To edit an image, right click on an image in one of the Project Assets folder such as the `Monkey.jpg`. This displays a context menu with the Edit Texture menu option. Select this option and the texture editor will appear as shown in

Figure 7 - Texture Editor. While it has limited editing capabilities, it is easy to perform simple operations such as flipping an image or resizing it using the buttons at the top of the editor.

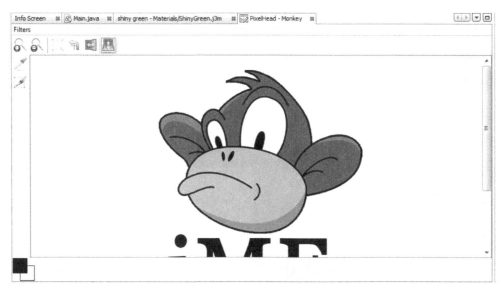

Figure 7 - Texture Editor

Using Lighted Materials

Lighted materials are those materials whose appearance is affected by a light source. We will be using the Lighting.j3md material in this section. To use illuminated materials, a light source must be added to a scene. Lighted materials use layers which can affect a material's property such as its shininess and transparency. Using lighted materials will require more processing power than unshaded materials. This can potentially affect overall game performance.

Using Simple Lights

In order to use unshaded materials, there needs to be a light source. JME3 provides this in a number of ways. Here, we will discuss two sources: directional light and ambient light. Other light sources are discussed in Chapter 6.

Directional Light

A directional light is one that comes from a long distance away and points in one direction. JME3 provides a DirectionalLight class to support this type of light. In the following code sequence, a DirectionalLight object is created that will emanate from the right side of the screen. The setDirection method uses a Vector3f object to specify the direction the light is going. This is a directional vector whose origin is (0, 0, 0). The color is set to white which happens to be the color of our sun. The `DirectionalLight` object needs to be added to the scene graph. This is done using the `addLight` method.

```
DirectionalLight sun = new DirectionalLight();
sun.setDirection(new Vector3f(-1, 0, 0));
sun.setColor(ColorRGBA.White);
rootNode.addLight(sun);
```

> Notice that we add light to the `rootNode` via the `addLight` method rather than the `attachChild` method we are used to seeing.

The light from a directional source is often referred to an emissive color, as in "it is emitted" by the source. Using white is useful in reflecting different colors. For example, if we had used a pure red light and a pure blue object, then the object would not be visible. This is because only red light is available and the object only reflects blue light. Hence, no light is reflected.

Ambient Light

Ambient light is a type of light that does not have a direction and is assumed to be always present. In some situations, it may not be obvious how an object is lighted such as a chair in a room. We can see it, but the light comes from many different directions. This is ambient light.

JME3 uses an `AmbientLight` class to support this type of light. In the following sequence, an ambient light source is created with a color of white. Like directional light, it needs to be added to the scene. However, since this light does not come from any particular direction, there is no need to use a directional vector.

```
AmbientLight ambient = new AmbientLight();
ambient.setColor(ColorRGBA.White);
rootNode.addLight(ambient);
```

We will use these settings for our lighting examples that follow.

Controlling the Brightness of a Light

The brightness of a simple light can be controlled using the `mult` method when setting the color of a light source. For example, in the following statement the brightness of the reflected ambient light is set to a tenth of its normal intensity

```
mat.setColor("Ambient", ColorRGBA.Gray.mult(0.1f));
```

Using Diffuse Light

A **Diffuse Light** is the light that will be reflected off a material. If a sphere is given a red diffuse color, then red will be reflected from a white light source. If there is no ambient color used, then the backside of the sphere will be black.

The following example creates a sphere that uses diffuse light. A sphere is created and the Lighting.j3md material is used. The setBoolean method allows the sphere's color to be used. The sphere's color is set to red using the setColor method.

```
Sphere sphere = new Sphere(32,32,1);
Geometry sphereGeometry =
    new Geometry("Unshaded sphere", sphere);
Material mat = new Material(assetManager,
    "Common/MatDefs/Light/Lighting.j3md");
mat.setBoolean("UseMaterialColors", true);
mat.setColor("Diffuse", ColorRGBA.Red);
sphereGeometry.setMaterial(mat);
rootNode.attachChild(sphereGeometry);
```

When executed, the sphere will appear as shown in *Figure 8 - Diffuse Example*. Since the sun is to the right of the sphere, the backside is black.

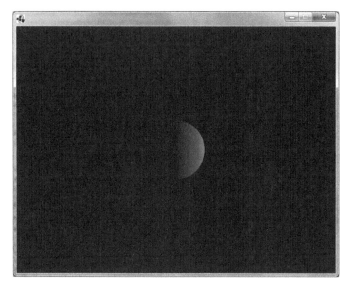

Figure 8 - Diffuse Example

Using Ambient Light

Ambient light will be reflected off an object even if there is no directional light source present. However, an ambient light source must be present. Using the previous example, if you remove the directional light from the scene, the sphere will not be visible.

However, with the directional light gone, we can add ambient light to our sphere by adding the following statement after we set our diffuse color:

```
mat.setColor("Ambient", ColorRGBA.Gray);
```

When the code is executed, we get the sphere as shown in *Figure 9 - Ambient Light Without Directional Light*. The sphere is a plain gray with no variation in the intensity of the light. This is because there is no directional light.

Figure 9 - Ambient Light Without Directional Light

If we add back the directional light, the sphere will appear as shown in *Figure 10 - Ambient Light With Directional Light*. The right side is brighter because it faces the directional light. The left side is dimly lit because there is an ambient light source. The contrast of the scene can be adjusted by changing the intensity of the light sources.

Figure 10 - Ambient Light With Directional Light

Making an Object Shiny

The term, **Specular**, refers to the shininess of an object. This is an additional property of a lighting material. The shininess is affected using the setColor method using "Specular" as the first argument. The color reflected is normally the same color as the directional light source. The setFloat method sets the shininess of the material. This value ranges from 0 to 128 with 0 being not very reflective, and 128 being very shiny.

In the next sequence the specular color is set to white. This means that the shine will be white. We removed the ambient light source to highlight shininess in this example.

```
mat.setBoolean("UseMaterialColors", true);
mat.setColor("Diffuse", ColorRGBA.Red);
mat.setColor("Specular", ColorRGBA.White);
mat.setFloat("Shininess", 128f);
```

The resultant sphere will be rendered as shown in *Figure 11 - Specular Light Example*.

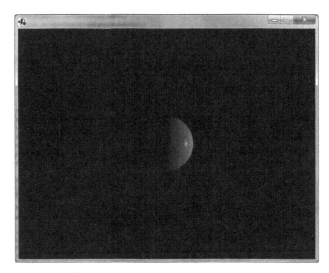

Figure 11 - Specular Light Example

In *Figure 12 - Two Sphere Example*, we have added a second sphere and positioned it a bit to the left and in front of the original sphere. Notice that there is no light reflected from the second sphere onto the original sphere. Reflection is a bit more difficult to handle in JME3. We will discuss this topic in Chapter 8 when we discuss water.

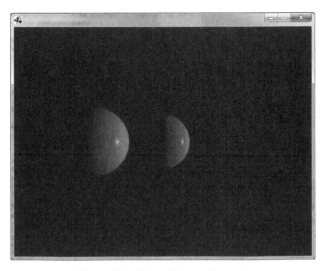

Figure 12 - Two Sphere Example

The specular property is useful for shiny objects like glass and water. Materials such as stone and paper are not as shiny. In this case the `setFloat` method should use a value like `64f`. Paper and cloth is not normally shiny. Values close to, or at, zero can be used for these types of materials.

Using a DiffuseMap

A **DiffuseMap** is a property used with the `setTexture` method to map an image to an object. In this example we will create a texture for a brick wall and map it to a `Box` object:

```
Box b = new Box(2, 1, 0.5f);
Geometry geom = new Geometry("Box", b);
Material mat = new Material(assetManager,
    "Common/MatDefs/Light/Lighting.j3md");
mat.setTexture("DiffuseMap", assetManager.loadTexture(
    "Textures/Terrain/BrickWall/BrickWall.jpg"));
mat.setBoolean("UseMaterialColors", true);
mat.setColor("Diffuse", ColorRGBA.White);
mat.setColor("Specular", ColorRGBA.White);
mat.setFloat("Shininess", 128f);
geom.setMaterial(mat);
rootNode.attachChild(geom);
```

When this sequence is executed the brick wall will appear as shown in *Figure 13 - DiffuseMap Example*. The wall is fairly plain looking. We would like to see some roughness since this is a stone wall. We will address this issue in the next section.

Figure 13 - DiffuseMap Example

Using a NormalMap

The `NormalMap` property accesses the normal map layer of a material. It is used to create more realistic appearances by apparently adding bumps, depressions, or cracks to a surface. In reality, the normals of the surface are adjusted to provide this illusion.

> The term "normal" is used to describe a line at right angles to a given surface.

In the following example, we build upon the diffuse map example in the previous section. The `setTexture` method is used, again, to create a `Texture` object based on a brick wall. In this case, the texture is created from the BrickWall_normal.jpg file. This file was created by an image editor to allow the render to provide the illusion of roughness. However, for the image to be processed correctly, the `TangentBinormalGenerator` class' static method `generate` must be executed first.

```
TangentBinormalGenerator.generate(sphereGeometry);
...
```

```
mat.setTexture("DiffuseMap", assetManager.loadTexture(
    "Textures/Terrain/BrickWall/BrickWall.jpg"));
mat.setTexture("NormalMap", assetManager.loadTexture(
    "Textures/Terrain/BrickWall/BrickWall_normal.jpg"));
```

When this sequence is executed the brick wall will appear as shown in *Figure 14 - NormalMap Example*. The actual appearance will depend on several factors including how the light sources are configured and the quality of the graphical processing units.

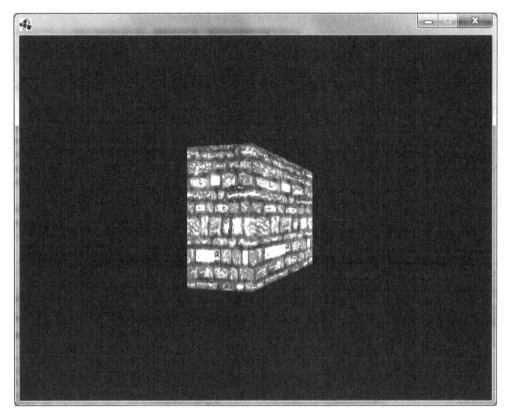

Figure 14 - NormalMap Example

Making an Object Transparent

Transparency is the condition where part, or all, of an object placed behind another object is visible. This is like a window that we see through. When a transparent material is created, its transparency can be specified to range from transparent to opaque.

The `Texture` class has an alpha channel that permits transparency. For example, the `Monkey.png` image, while the same as the `Monkey.jpg` image, has an alpha channel. This channel specifies that certain areas of the image will be transparent.

What is transparent and the degree to which it is transparent is set by an image editor. In general:

- Black areas (of the channel) are opaque

- Gray areas are translucent

- White areas are transparent

When working with transparent materials:

- Its texture must have an alpha channel

- The blend mode of the texture must be set to `BlendMode.Alpha`

- The geometry associated with it must be used with a render bucket

A render bucket makes sure that objects are rendered on top of objects appearing behind them and that they are rendered correctly based on alpha channel settings.

To demonstrate this technique, we will use a `Window.png` file whose alpha value has been set to 128. This will let half of the light through it. This image is like a pane of tinted glass. We will place a blue cube behind it to demonstrate that it is transparent.

We will start by creating our window. Copy the `Window.png` file from the code download resource and place it in the `Textures` folder under `Project Assets`. Then add the following code to your project. We create a simple cube, assign it the unshaded material, and use the `setTexture` method to load the texture for the window.

```
Box cube2Mesh = new Box(1f, 1f, 0.01f);
Geometry cube2Geo = new Geometry("Window", cube2Mesh);
Material cube2Mat = new Material(assetManager,
    "Common/MatDefs/Misc/Unshaded.j3md");
cube2Mat.setColor("Color", ColorRGBA.Red);
cube2Mat.setTexture("ColorMap", assetManager.loadTexture(
    "Textures/Window.png"));
```

To enable the texture's transparency to work, we need to set the `BlendMode` to `Alpha` as shown next. The next step is to associate a `QueueBucket` with the geometry using a value of `Bucket.Transparent`. The order in which the objects are rendered is important. The bucket will render the transparent objects on top of the other objects and ensure that the transparent parts are indeed transparent.

```
cube2Mat.getAdditionalRenderState().setBlendMode(
    BlendMode.Alpha);
cube2Geo.setQueueBucket(Bucket.Transparent);
cube2Geo.setMaterial(cube2Mat);
rootNode.attachChild(cube2Geo);
```

The cube is created next. It is scaled and then moved behind and a little to the left of the window. The diffuse and ambient colors are set to blue and gray respectively as shown next. It is also rotated a bit to make the sides more visible.

```
Box b = new Box(1, 1, 1);
Geometry geom = new Geometry("Box", b);
geom.scale(0.5f);
geom.setLocalTranslation(-2, 0, -2.0f);
Material mat = new Material(assetManager,
    "Common/MatDefs/Light/Lighting.j3md");
mat.setBoolean("UseMaterialColors", true);
mat.setColor("Diffuse", ColorRGBA.Blue);
mat.setColor("Ambient", ColorRGBA.Gray);
geom.setMaterial(mat);
geom.rotate(0, FastMath.DEG_TO_RAD * 45, 0);
rootNode.attachChild(geom);
```

To enhance the cube's color we tone down the ambient color as shown here:

```
ambient.setColor(ColorRGBA.White.mult(0.2f));
```

When the code is executed, it will appear as shown in *Figure 15 - Transparency Example*. The window had a red tint added to make it visible. Since it is partially opaque some of the red appears in front of the cube. If it had been completely transparent, there would be no red visible on the cube.

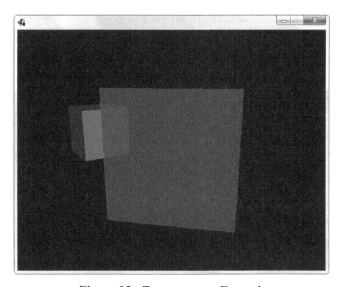

Figure 15 - Transparency Example

A summary of the common lighting properties is found in *Table 2 - Lighting.j3md Properties*.

Table 2 - Lighting.j3md Properties

Property	Method	Data Type
"UseMaterialColors"	setBoolean	boolean
"Diffuse"	setColor	ColorRGBA
"Ambient"	setColor	ColorRGBA
"Specular"	setColor	ColorRGBA
"Shininess"	setFloat	Float
"DiffuseMap"	setTexture	Texture

Creating Materials

Materials can be created using any of several tools. They can be created by using a text editor or by using JME3's Material Editor. There are two types of files that support the definition of materials: j3md and j3m. The j3md files are Material Definition files and provide a high level of control over the material definition. They are concerned with specifying, in detail, how a material is rendered. This can include the shader used. A j3m file is used for material instances that are simpler than for j3md. j3M supports the definition of the material's parameters such as ambient color or which normal map to use (if any).

If you have material configurations that never change and you use them repeatedly, then creating a material based on those configurations is a good idea. This can make your code more readable, avoid copy-and-paste type errors, and modularize your code.

The complete specification for material definitions is found at http://hub.jmonkeyengine.org/wiki/doku.php/jme3:advanced:material_specification. Here, we will cover only the basic elements of a j3md file. The format of j3m files are covered in the next section.

A j3md file consists of a root block containing nested sub-blocks. Blocks are defined using open and close curly braces. These blocks are used to define various aspects of a material. The first line of a j3md file starts with the word MaterialDef followed by the name of the material. Within the root block, sub-blocks are used to define properties of materials, techniques that use shaders, and other properties such as how the material should be rendered.

We can create a new j3md file by right clicking on the Materials folder, then selecting New and Other. This brings up the New File dialog box. Select the Material category and then Material Definition Template. Provide a file name and then select Finish. This will create a new j3md file with several default sub-blocks provided. This is illustrated in Using the Material Editor

Using a Text Editor to Create a Material

A text editor is sufficient to create and maintain material definitions and instances. In the following sequence we create a simple material instance, the file `ShinyGreen.jm3`, where the material shines in green. A material instance only uses a `MaterialParameters` section. In this example, the ambient color is set to red and the secular color is set to green. The four numbers for the color types represent the red, green, blue, and alpha values for the color.

```
Material shiny green : Common/MatDefs/Light/Lighting.j3md {

    MaterialParameters {

        Shininess: 4.0

        UseMaterialColors : true

        Ambient  : 1.0 0.0 0.0 1.0

        Diffuse  : 1.0 1.0 1.0 1.0

        Specular : 0.0 1.0 0.0 1.0

    }

}
```

We can use this material for the surface of a sphere as shown next:

```
addLights();
Sphere sphereMesh = new Sphere(32, 32, 2f);
Geometry sphereGeo = new Geometry("sphere", sphereMesh);
sphereGeo.setMaterial(assetManager.loadMaterial(
    "Materials/ShinyGreen.j3m"));
rootNode.attachChild(sphereGeo);
```

Using this material avoids having to add statements to set these colors. It makes the code more concise and readable. When this sequence is executed, the sphere will appear as shown in *Figure 16 - ShinyGreen Material Example With Ambient Light*. The reflection appears yellow because of the red ambient color and green shininess settings. If we remove the ambient light we can more clearly see the green as shown in *Figure 17 - ShinyGreen Material Example Without Ambient Light*. Using white as the ambient color will also work.

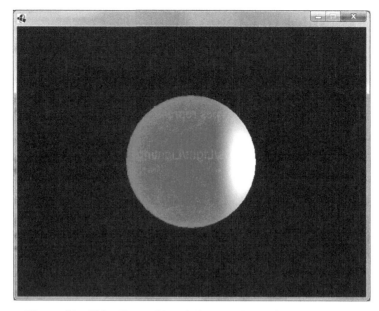

Figure 16 - ShinyGreen Material Example With Ambient Light

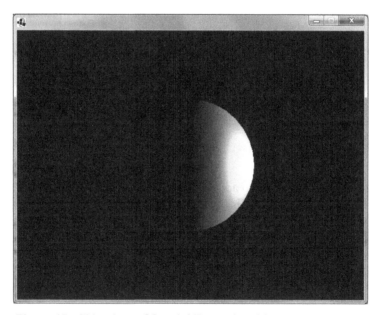

Figure 17 - ShinyGreen Material Example Without Ambient Light

Using the Material Editor

JME3 has a built-in editor that edits j3m and j3md files. To bring the editor up, right click on the material and select Open. We can also create a new j3m file by right clicking on the Materials folder then selecting New and Other. This brings up the New File dialog box. Select the Material category and then Empty Material file. Provide a file name and then select Finish.

Either editing an existing file or creating a new one will bring up the editor as shown in *Figure 18 - Material Editor*. If you scroll down to the bottom of the Textures & Colors window you will see the settings for the ShinyGreen material instance.

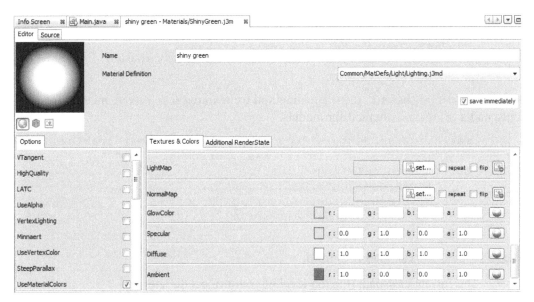

Figure 18 - Material Editor

You can easily change many of the properties of the material using the editor. A preview window is found in the upper left-hand corner of the editor. Any changes you make are saved immediately unless the save immediately checkbox is unchecked. More details regarding the use of the editor and a material instance can be found at http://hub.jmonkeyengine.org/wiki/doku.php/jme3:advanced:j3m_material_files.

Managing Assets

Assets are the multi-media files for the game. These include 3D models, materials, textures, scenes, custom shaders, sounds, and even fonts. Assets are stored in the assets directory of the JME3 Project. As described in Chapter 1, JME3 provides an integrated assetManager that is designed to keep assets organized. There are several useful features to the assetManager:

- It automatically optimizes the use of OpenGL objects.

- The paths are the same on all operating system platforms.

- Automatically bundles assets into the executable.

- Advanced users can register custom paths to the `assetManager`.

The `assetManager` is located in the `com.jme3.asset` package and every application can access it. By default you can load any object that is at the top level of the project directory. If you look in the `Libraries` folder of your project you will find a number of jar files. The following example loads a default material from the `Common` directory found in `jME3-core.jar`.

```
Material mat_brick = new Material(
    assetManager, "Common/MatDefs/Misc/Unshaded.j3md");
```

The `assetManager` has a `loadTexture` method for textures, a `loadFont` method for fonts, and a `loadModel` method for models.

```
mat_brick.setTexture("ColorMap", assetManager.loadTexture(
    "Textures/Terrain/BrickWall/BrickWall.jpg"));
guiFont = assetManager.loadFont(
    "Interface/Fonts/Default.fnt");
Spatial ninja = assetManager.loadModel(
    "Models/Ninja/Ninja.mesh.xml");
```

The `AssetManager` can load files from:

- The current classpath (the top level of your project directory),

- The assets directory of your project, and

- Optionally, custom paths that you register.

The following is the recommended directory structure for storing assets in your project directory:

MyGame/assets/	
MyGame/assets/Interface/	
MyGame/assets/MatDefs/	
MyGame/assets/Materials/	
MyGame/assets/Models/	[your .j3o models go here]
MyGame/assets/Scenes/	
MyGame/assets/Shaders/	
MyGame/assets/Sounds/	[your audio files go here]
MyGame/assets/Textures/	[your textures go here]
MyGame/build.xml	[Default Ant build script]

MyGame/src/...   [your Java sources go here]

MyGame/...

This is just a suggested best practice, and it's what you get by default when creating a new Java project in the JME3 SDK. You can create an assets directory and technically name the subdirectories to whatever you like.

Models

Models are similar to geometries. They are created from intricate meshes. While meshes for geometries are built into JME3, 3D models are created externally using graphics and animation software like Blender.

Working With Blender Models

JME3 has built-in functionality and support for the open-source Blender software. The `assetManager` has a `BlenderModelLoader` registered to it. What this means is that, by default, you can load and convert `.blend` (Blender model) files to `.j3o`. We will use the `spaceship.blend` Blender model found as part of this book's download.

When converting a Blender model to JME3:

1. Create a new folder for each model in the Project Assets/Models folder

2. Save the Blender model in the newly created folder. Models can also be dragged and dropped into the new folder.

3. Right click the model and select Convert to JME binary as shown in *Figure 19 - Blend To j30*

If the conversion process has succeeded you should be able to double click on the newly created .j3o file, opening it in the **SceneViewer** as shown in *Figure 20 - SceneViewer*. Notice the light bulb icon is in the top left of the screen. Click on the light bulb icon to illuminate the model.

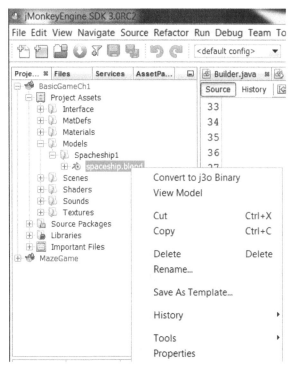

Figure 19 - Blend To j30

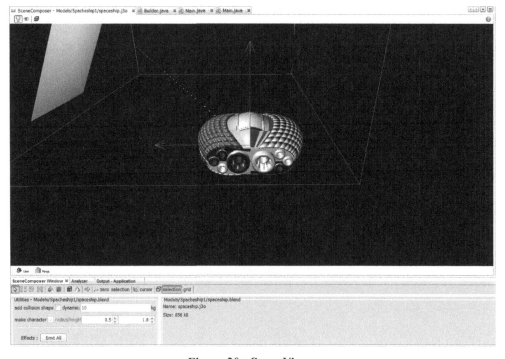

Figure 20 - SceneViewer

Loading Models

Once the model has been successfully converted to j30 format we can use it in the game. Keep in mind that models with light maps will require lighting or unshaded material to be visible in the scene. To load a model into the scene there are a few simple steps to follow:

1. Create a new `Spatial` object and assign it to a model using `assetManager`

2. If necessary, apply a material and texture

3. Attach the `Spatial` to the `rootNode`

To assign the model to a `Spatial` object we will use the `assetManager`'s `loadModel` method with the parameter of the model's location as illustrated here:

```
Spatial ship = assetManager.loadModel(
    "Models/Spaceship1/spaceship.j3o");
rootNode.attachChild(ship);
```

This model is available for download. Notice that it is visible without additional light sources or materials. This is because the model is light mapped. You can see how it appears in the scene in *Figure 21 - Spaceship Model*.

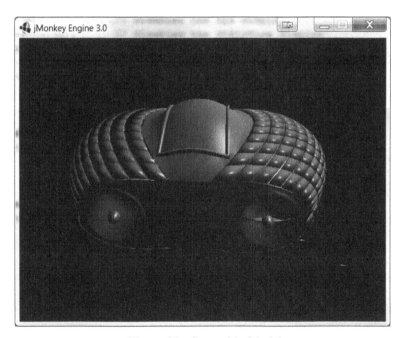

Figure 21 - Spaceship Model

Shades of Infinity – 5

A new version of the AI Ship has been created. This one is more sophisticated and uses a number of textures. The ship has been created using a combination of `Box` and `Dome` shapes.

In this section we will discuss a few of the more interesting aspects to the ship's construction. The complete source code for the ship can be found on the publisher's website. In the following figures, the ship is shown from various angles:

- *Figure 22 - AIShip View 1* – The main features of the ship is shown where the light emanates from the right

- *Figure 23 - AIShip View 2* – A view from the opposite side showing a large shiny spot

- *Figure 24 - AIShip View 3* – Viewed from the top

The ship consists of a body with two engines mounted on each side. A `Dome` shape is used to create nozzles for the engines. A cockpit appears in the front of the ship with another dome mounted in front of the cockpit. Three probes emerge from the front of the ship. The different sections of the ship have been given different textures and colors.

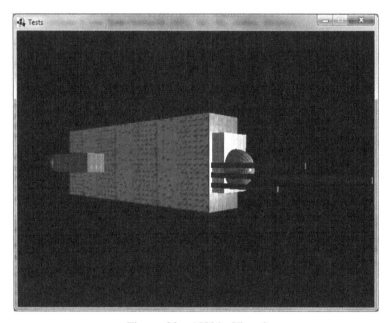

Figure 22 - AIShip View 1

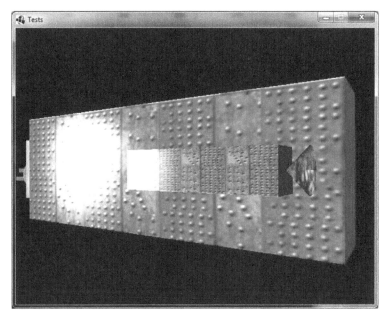

Figure 23 - AIShip View 2

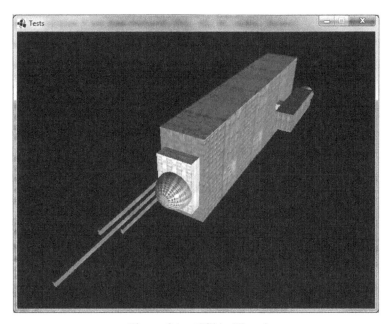

Figure 24 - AIShip View 3

To illustrate how the ship was created we will examine the code used to generate the cockpit as shown in the next code sequence. The rest of the ship was constructed in a similar manner. A `Box` was used for the body of the cockpit using a `getBox` method. This utility method is used for other parts of the ship to avoid duplicating code. A `Dome` shape was used to create the dome. We used lighted material and a `tiletopred.jpg` image loaded from http://opengameart.org/. For this material, the diffuse and specular colors are set to white and the ambient color is set to green. It was given a high level of shininess. It was also necessary rotate and move the dome into position in front of the cockpit.

```java
private Node getCockpit(String name, float width,
        float height, float depth, ColorRGBA color) {
    Node cockpitNode = getBox(
        name, width, height, depth, color);
    Dome cockpitDome = new Dome(
        Vector3f.ZERO, 32, 32, width, false);

    Geometry cockpitDomeGeometry = new Geometry(
        "Cockpit Dome Geometry", cockpitDome);

    Material mat = new Material(assetManager,
        "Common/MatDefs/Light/Lighting.j3md");
    mat.setTexture("DiffuseMap", assetManager.loadTexture(
        "Textures/tiletopred.jpg"));
    mat.setBoolean("UseMaterialColors", true);
    mat.setColor("Diffuse", ColorRGBA.White);
    mat.setColor("Ambient", ColorRGBA.Green);
    mat.setColor("Specular", ColorRGBA.White);
    mat.setFloat("Shininess", 128f);
    cockpitDomeGeometry.setMaterial(mat);
    cockpitDomeGeometry.setLocalTranslation(
        0, -height * 0.2f, depth);
    cockpitDomeGeometry.rotate(
        90 * FastMath.DEG_TO_RAD, 0, 0);
    cockpitNode.attachChild(cockpitDomeGeometry);

    return cockpitNode;
}
```

The ship is then added to the game as illustrated in *Figure 25 - Shades of Infinity*.

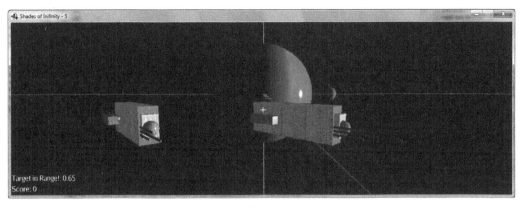

Figure 25 - Shades of Infinity

Handling Collisions

When a ship is hit, the sphere used to represent the hit needs to be placed correctly on the ship. With the various components that make up the ship, this makes the process a bit more difficult. This is further compounded by any transformations performed on the ship.

The `CollisionResult` class' `getContactPoint` method returns the point of collision. However, this point is defined in world coordinates. If we attach the sphere at this point it will remain at that point, even if the ship moves. To avoid this problem we need to attach the sphere to the appropriate component with a coordinate point local to that component.

This is accomplished using the `worldToLocal` method to perform the conversion from world to local space. This method needs to execute against a node so that it knows which local coordinate system to use. The first parameter is the world coordinate for a point and the second parameter assigns the corresponding local coordinate point.

In the following `visit` method this conversion is used to get the correct contact point. Otherwise the sphere is attached as in previous versions of the game.

```
public void visit(Spatial spatial) {
    if (closest.getGeometry().getName().
                equals(spatial.getName())) {
        Geometry boom = getHit();
        Vector3f contactPoint = new Vector3f();
        closest.getGeometry().getParent().worldToLocal(
            closest.getContactPoint(), contactPoint);
        boom.setLocalTranslation(contactPoint);
        closest.getGeometry().getParent().
            attachChild(boom);
    }
}
```

An example of what the ship hits look like is found in *Figure 26 - Ship Hits*.

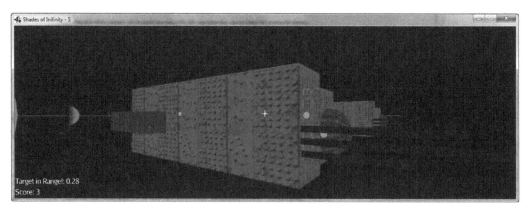

Figure 26 - Ship Hits

Conclusion

As we have seen, materials are a fairly complex yet very important aspect of 3D graphics. We introduced a number of basic terms to help provide a perspective on materials and how they are rendered.

The basics of materials have been covered using both unshaded and lighted materials. Unshaded materials are easier to use and do not require a light source. They are more efficient but they do not appear as realistic as lighted materials.

Lighted materials require a light source and we introduced a directional and an ambient light source to use with our lighted material examples. We showed how to load various textures to achieve various effects such as shininess and transparency. While textures must be created externally to JME3, we explored many of their properties.

We examined how materials are defined and created using both j3m and j3md files. JME3 has an editor that allows us to create and modify these types of files. By defining our own materials we can simplify the code we write and avoid errors that can occur when we reuse materials we created using code.

The `AssetManager` class is used extensively when working with materials. Its use and JME3's project file structure were examined to clarify the use of JME3 and how materials-related techniques work.

In the next chapter we will jump into lighting effects! We will explore some new types of light, adding shadows to the game, and techniques on capturing video and screenshots.

6

Lights, Camera, Action!

Introduction

Lighting is an important aspect of 3D graphics and can make all the difference when it comes to the quality of a game's objects. The *interaction* between lights and materials was addressed in Chapter 5, and in this chapter we are concerned with the various light options, sources, and techniques associated with lights.

We will start with a quick review of lights as we have used them in previous chapters. We will then examine how spot lights and point lights work in JME3. As their names suggest, they support specific sources of light and can represent light sources such as street lights, flashlights, and head lights.

Shadows can be an important feature of many games where a villain or a good guy might be lying in wait. Interestingly enough, shadows are not rendered automatically. Instead we need to use one of a couple of approaches to make shadows visible.

The camera provides a perspective into the game. We will address several camera aspects including the `FlyByCamera` class which is provided by default in the classes derived from `SimpleApplication`. As we saw in Chapter 3, the `FlyCamAppState` is added to applications and manages the fly camera. We will dig a little deeper into how this is set up.

Another interesting game technique is the use of multiple cameras. This provides the user with more than one perspective that can aid navigation or provide better feedback on a game's state. One variation is to use a picture in a picture. You may have seen this feature on television where more than one channel is displayed, albeit one channel is a lot smaller than the main channel.

Related to cameras is the capability to capture a screenshot of a game at any given moment or even a video of the game as it runs. JME3 supports both of these features. The video capture capability is supported using an application state.

The last section of this chapter incorporates many of these camera capabilities into the Shades of Infinity game.

Using Lighting Effects

Understanding how cameras work is important. But what they see, and what is ultimately rendered, is dependent on the game's objects, the characteristics of their materials, and the lighting conditions used within the game.

Lights and shadows are usually thought of as part of the same entity. If you have never worked with a 3D engine you may not realize that shadows and lights are completely different entities. When you add light to the scene, an object will be brighter on the side closest to the light source, and darker on the side facing away. This pretty much happens by default in JME3. However, adding a light to the scene does not inherently create shadows from the objects in the scene. This is because shadows and lights are handled separately. In this section we will examine how lights work and then illustrate how shadows can be added to an application.

The Basics of Lights

As we briefly discussed in Chapter 5, light sources are added to the scene by attaching them to the `rootNode` via the `addLight` method. There are four different types of light sources available in JME3 which are found in the `com.jme3.light` package:

- `AmbientLight` – This type of light provides an ever-present light
- `DirectionalLight` - Light appears to originate from a distant source and shines in one direction
- `PointLight` - This light source originates from a specific point
- `SpotLight` - This light also originates from a single point but is focused like a flashlight beam

We discussed ambient and directional light in Chapter 5. Here, we will focus on the other two types of light.

Regardless of the type of light, the color and intensity of light sources can be controlled using the `setColor` method. Typically the color used for light sources is white. It might be a good idea to try out other values and vary the intensities if you want to set a different type of mood for the scene. For example, a shade of red could be used to make part of a game feel more dangerous and exciting. A shade of yellow could be used to make a scene feel warmer and more inviting.

There are two methods that will return a list of lights added to a spatial. The first method is `getWorldLightList` which will return all lights including inherited lights. The second method, `getLocalLightList`, only returns lights that are directly added to a spatial.

In the following example, we demonstrate the use of the `getLocalLightList` method. First we create instances of the four basic light types as shown:

```
DirectionalLight directionalLight =
    new DirectionalLight();
SpotLight spotLight = new SpotLight();
PointLight pointLight = new PointLight();
```

```
AmbientLight ambientLight = new AmbientLight();
```

Two nodes are then created and the lights are added to the nodes and the rootNode:

```
Node carrier1 = new Node();
Node carrier2 = new Node();

carrier1.attachChild(carrier2);
rootNode.attachChild(carrier1);

carrier1.addLight(directionalLight);
carrier1.addLight(spotLight);
carrier2.addLight(pointLight);
carrier2.addLight(ambientLight);
```

The getLocalLightList method is called against the carrier1 node and then displayed:

```
LightList localList = carrier1.getLocalLightList();

for(Light light : localList) {
    System.out.println("Local: " + light);
}
```

The output follows:

Local: com.jme3.light.DirectionalLight@62503aec

Local: com.jme3.light.SpotLight@14c8e61

If we had used carrier2, we would have found the point and ambient lights were attached to it.

Creating a Spot Light

Spot lights are the most complex of the available light sources in JME3. A spot light emits a beam of light which can be thought of as a cone. These lights are typically used to represent a flashlight, a searchlight, or to accentuate a specific element in a scene.

Using a spot light is more complex due to the many options and methods needed to use it effectively. Spot lights are created using the SpotLight class. To implement a spot light:

1. Create a new SpotLight object

2. Set the range of the light (optional)

3. Set the inner and outer angle of the cone (optional)

4. Set the position and location

5. Add the light to the rootNode

The default range is 100. If the angles are not set, they default to 5.26 and 7.5 degrees respectively.

Creating a Spot Light

To demonstrate this process, create a new `SpotLight` instance variable called `spotlight`, as shown next. Set the range of the light to `75` using the `setSpotRange` method in the `SimpleInitApp` method. The distance is measured in pixels. Objects beyond this distance will not be illuminated by the spot light. Objects within range will be illuminated with a magnitude set to the distance/range.

```
SpotLight spotLight;
...
spotLight = new SpotLight();
spotLight.setSpotRange(75);
```

To get a good idea of how this light source works, we will use small angles for the cone of light. Since the methods used to set the angles require arguments in radians, we will use the `FastMath.DEG_TO_RAD` constant to convert degrees to radians. Use the `setSpotInnerAngle` with a parameter of `5` degrees, and the `setSpotOuterAngle` with a parameter of `10` degrees as shown here:

```
spotLight.setSpotInnerAngle(5 * FastMath.DEG_TO_RAD);
spotLight.setSpotOuterAngle(10 * FastMath.DEG_TO_RAD);
```

We will set the color to white using the `setColor` method and then attach it to the `rootNode` using the `addLight` method as shown follows:

```
spotLight.setColor(ColorRGBA.White);
rootNode.addLight(spotLight);
```

Setting the Spot Light's Position

To further illustrate the use of the spot light, we will setup the spot light to emanate from the player's view point, appearing as a headlight or flashlight .This will be accomplished by using the `cam` variables `getLocation` and `getDirection` methods to set the spot light's location and direction in the `simpleUpdate` method.

First we will call the `setPosition` method with `cam.getLocation` as its parameter as shown next. Then we will call the `setDirection` method with `cam.getDirection` as its parameter. In order for these methods to work in `simpleUpdate`, make `spotLight` an instance variable.

```
public void simpleUpdate(float tpf) {
    spotLight.setPosition(cam.getLocation());
    spotLight.setDirection(cam.getDirection());
}
```

To demonstrate this light source we will need an object to test it on. To keep things simple let's just make a red cube with lighted material. This material will use a DiffuseMap. The code to create the cubes and the spot light is shown next:

```
Box b = new Box(3,3,3);
Geometry geom = new Geometry("Box", b);

Material mat = new Material(assetManager,
    "Common/MatDefs/Light/Lighting.j3md");
mat.setColor("Diffuse", ColorRGBA.Red);
mat.setBoolean("UseMaterialColors", true);
geom.setMaterial(mat);

rootNode.attachChild(geom);

spotLight = new SpotLight();
spotLight.setSpotRange(75);
spotLight.setSpotInnerAngle(5 * FastMath.DEG_TO_RAD);
spotLight.setSpotOuterAngle(10 * FastMath.DEG_TO_RAD);
spotLight.setColor(ColorRGBA.White);
rootNode.addLight(spotLight);
}
```

When you get it working you should be able to approach the cube and see a circle of light on the surface of the cube. You can see an example of this in *Figure 1 - SpotLight Example*.

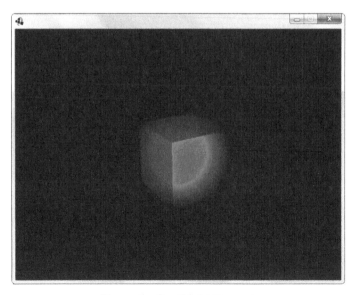

Figure 1 - SpotLight Example

Creating a Point of Light

Point lights are one of the most common single lights in a scene. Point lights have a color and a location. They emit light equally in all directions and start to fade the further you get from them. Some good examples of point lights are lanterns, camp fires, candles, or light bulbs.

This type of light is implemented in JME3 with the `PointLight` class. Point lights have `setColor`, `setRadius`, and `setPosition` methods. The radius of the point light represents the distance that the light covers. To create a point of light:

1. Create an instance of `PointLight`

2. Set its color, position, and radius

3. Add it to the scene

To illustrate this type of light, we will use the same box as developed in the previous section. Create a new `PointLight` object called `pointLight` as shown here:

```
PointLight pointLight = new PointLight();
```

Set the color to white using the `setColor` method as shown in the following code sequence. Next, set the position to `(0,6,6)`. This places the light slightly above, and in front of, the cube. Also, set the radius to `20` using the `setRadius` method.

```
pointLight.setColor(ColorRGBA.White);
pointLight.setPosition(new Vector3f(0, 6, 6));
pointLight.setRadius(20);
```

Finally we need to attach the light to the `rootNode` with the `addLight` method.

```
rootNode.addLight(pointLight);
```

When executed, the end result should appear similar to *Figure 2 - PointLight Example* after the camera has been repositioned. Notice that due to the point light's position, only the top and the side facing the player are illuminated.

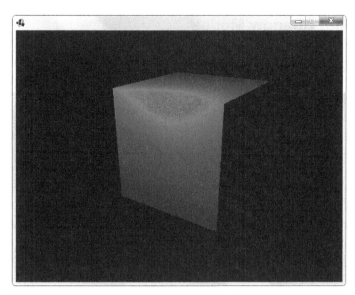

Figure 2 - PointLight Example

Adding Shadows to a Game

Shadows are another important lighting effect. Using shadows in the game requires a lot more computing power than just using lights. For every type of light in JME3, except for ambient light, there are two ways to implement shadow casting. The first is a **shadow renderer** and the second is a **shadow filter**.

Shadow renderers and shadow filters both use shadow modes to set which objects cast and receive shadows. One of the differences between filters and renderers is that filters do not check the shadow mode to determine if an object receives shadows. Renderers, on the other hand, check the shadow mode of an object to see if they are set to receive shadows. Renderers are attached directly to the `viewPort`, where filters are attached through a `FilterPostProcessor`.

You only need one shadow simulation per light source, either shadow rendering or shadow filtering. Each shadow calculation has a significant impact on game play performance, so try not to overuse them if you can avoid it.

The constructors for shadow renderers and shadow filters have three parameters. The `assetManager` is the first parameter. The second parameter is the size of the shadow map. The shadow map represents the size of the area that the shadow effects. The size is represented by an area with 512, 1024, 2048, or 4096 pixels per side. The third parameter is the number of shadow maps used. More shadow maps increases the quality, but decreases performance and reduces the fps.

Each shadow renderer and filter must have a light source attached to them. Shadow renderers and filters must also be attached to the `viewPort` via the `addProcessor` method before they can be used. Viewports will be discussed in more depth in the *Using Viewports* section of this chapter.

Understanding Shadow Modes

Both renderers and filters use various shadow modes to control how the game environment responds to shadow casting. These modes are applied to geometries and nodes using the `setShadowMode` method. A list of shadow modes is found in *Table 1 - Shadow Modes*.

Table 1 - Shadow Modes

Shadow Modes	Meaning
ShadowMode.Inherit	Default setting for new spatials. Inherits ShadowMode from the parent node
ShadowMode.Off	Disables shadows
ShadowMode.Receive	Enables shadows to be shown on the spatial
ShadowMode.Cast	Enables casting shadows but not receiving
ShadowMode.CastAndReceive	Enable shadows to be cast as well as shown

These modes can be applied directly to a spatial, or to the entire scene via the `rootNode`. For example, you may want a flat surface like a floor to only receive shadows and not cast them. Or, you may want to only cast shadows from a spatial like a bird in the sky that would have no other objects between it and the light source.

To test gameplay performance, you may want to disable shadows for the entire scene. The following statement shows how to disable shadows from the entire scene by using the `ShadowMode.Off` option on the `rootNode`:

```
rootNode.setShadowMode(ShadowMode.Off);
```

> Shadow renderers check the shadow mode to see if an object receives shadows. Shadow filters ignore this aspect of the shadow mode.

Using the Shadow Renderer

A shadow renderer is applied to a viewport. There is a separate shadow renderer class for each type of light source except for ambient light as listed in *Table 2 - Shadow Renderer Types*.

Table 2 - Shadow Renderer Types

Light Source	Shadow Renderer
DirectionalLight	DirectionalLightShadowRenderer
PointLight	PointLightShadowRenderer
SpotLight	SpotLightShadowRenderer

The following steps are used to apply a shadow renderer:

1. Determine a shadow map size

2. Create a new shadow renderer

3. Assign a light to the renderer

4. Add the renderer to the viewport

In the following example we will first set up the scene with a few cubes and then follow the previous steps for creating using a shadow render using a `DirectionalLightShadowRenderer`. This class is found in the `com.jme3.shadow` package. The end result is shown in *Figure 3 - Shadow Renderer Example*.

First, we will need a simple floor to catch a shadow. We will create this floor with a simple flat cube as illustrated in the next code sequence. The floor will use a basic unshaded material and a box with a width of `512` in the X and Z directions and a height of `0.3f` in the Y direction. We will then call the `setShadowMode` method against the floor and set it to `ShadowMode.Receive`.

```
Box floorBox = new Box(512, 0.3f, 512);
Geometry floor = new Geometry("Box", floorBox);
floor.setMaterial(mat2);
floor.setLocalTranslation(0, -1, 0);
floor.setShadowMode(ShadowMode.Receive);
```

Next we will create a few red cubes with lighted materials. Since we have done this several times before there is no need to go through all the details. However, the one additional thing we need to do is to call the `setShadowMode` method against each geometry, with `ShadowMode.CastAndReceive` as the parameter as shown next. This will allow each cube to show and cast shadows.

```
Box box = new Box(2,2,2);
Geometry cube1 = new Geometry("Box", box);
cube1.setMaterial(mat);
cube1.setLocalTranslation(0, 5, 0);
cube1.setShadowMode(ShadowMode.CastAndReceive);
```

Next we will create a `DirectionalLight` and use `cam.getDirection` to set the direction of the light. We will need to set the direction in `simpleUpdate` to keep the light source position up to date. This way we can observe how the shadows are cast as we move throughout the scene.

```
light = new DirectionalLight();
...
public void simpleUpdate(float tpf) {
    light.setDirection(cam.getDirection());
}
```

Applying the Shadow Renderer

At this point we have all the pieces to start generating shadows except for the shadow renderer. As listed in the previous steps, the first thing we want to do, when creating a shadow renderer, is determine the size of the shadow map. The size of the shadow map should reflect the size of the scene that will be incorporating shadows. Considering the floor we created is 512x512, an effective shadow map size for this example should be 512.

With our shadow map size determined, the second step is to create a new `DirectionalLightShadowRenderer` object called `shadow` using the `assetManger`, 512 (size of the shadow map), and 2 (number of shadow maps) as parameters as shown here.

```
DirectionalLightShadowRenderer shadow = new
    DirectionalLightShadowRenderer(assetManager, 512, 2);
```

The third step requires us to add a directional light to `shadow` with the `setLight` method. This informs the renderer which light to use to cast shadows. The last step is implemented by applying the `addProcessor` method against the default `viewPort` with `shadow` as the parameter. These actions are shown here:

```
shadow.setLight(light);
viewPort.addProcessor(shadow);
```

The complete source code for this example is found with this book's code download package. When executed you should be able to navigate the scene observing the shadows cast by the red cubes. This is illustrated in *Figure 3 - Shadow Renderer Example*. Notice that the back cube both casts and receives shadows.

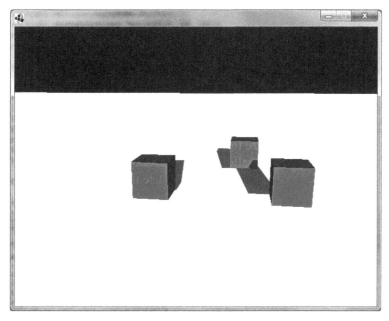

Figure 3 - Shadow Renderer Example

Using the Shadow Filter

Shadow filters work, basically, in the same way as shadow renderers. However, they are applied to the `viewPort` indirectly through a `FilterPostProcessor,` located in the `com.jme3.post package`. A `FilterPostProcessor` is a processor that can apply several filters to a scene. As with shadow renderers, shadow filters have a unique class for each type of light source other than ambient light. These are listed in *Table 3 - Shadow Filter Types*.

Table 3 - Shadow Filter Types

Light Source	Shadow Filter
DirectionalLight	DirectionalLightShadowFilter
PointLight	PointLightShadowFilter
SpotLight	SpotLightShadowFilter

The steps to implement a shadow filter are similar to shadow renderers:

1. Determine a shadow map size

2. Create a new filter

3. Assign a light to the filter

4. Create a new `FilterPostProcessor`

5. Assign the filter to the `FilterPostProcessor`

6. Add the `FilterPostProcessor` to the `viewPort`

For this example let's re-use the scene from the previous example. We will leave the floor, the cubes, and the light source the same, but we will implement a filter instead of a renderer. Considering we are using the same scene as we did with the shadow renderer, we will use a shadow map of 512 to reflect our scene size.

Once we know our shadow map size the next thing we will need to do is create a new `DirectionalLightShadowFilter` called `filter`, as shown next. This type of filter is located in the `com.jme3.shadow` package. We will use the same parameters we used for the renderer.

```
DirectionalLightShadowFilter filter = new
    DirectionalLightShadowFilter(assetManager, 512, 2);
```

To implement the third step, we call the `setLight` method with the directional light as the parameter. Then we call `setEnabled` with `true` as the parameter. This simply activates the filter.

```
filter.setLight(light);
filter.setEnabled(true);
```

In order to complete the remaining three steps, we will create a `FilterPostProcessor` called `fpp` with `assetManager` as the parameter. Then we will need to add `filter` to `fpp` with the `addFilter` method. Finally we will add `fpp` to the `viewPort` via the `addProcessor` method as shown here:

```
FilterPostProcessor fpp = new
    FilterPostProcessor(assetManager);
fpp.addFilter(filter);
viewPort.addProcessor(fpp);
```

The resulting game should appear similar to *Figure 4 – Shadow Filter Example*. In this simple scene there isn't really a recognizable difference between the renderer and filter. However, when using the filter you can remove the `ShadowMode` from the floor and the shadows will still be received.

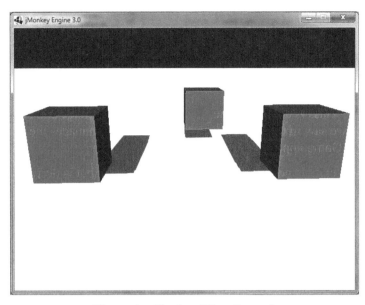

Figure 4 – Shadow Filter Example

Understanding the Projection Matrix

When an object, such as a teapot is created, its mesh is defined using vectors based on a model space coordinate system called the **Model Space**. The center of this coordinate system is (0, 0, 0). Every model uses the same system and coordinates.

When we use an object in an application, we need to transform the object to a position within the application's coordinate system. This system is called the **World Space**. For example, we might have two teapots based on the same model space but they may be mapped to two different world space coordinates.

When an object is added to a world space it may also be scaled or rotated. This transformation is achieved using a **Transformation Matrix** whose details JME3 hides from us. Regardless, it is located relative to the world space's origin (0, 0, 0).

However, the screen represents a 2D view as seen by a camera that looks into a 3D world. We need to map this 3D world into a 2D view. JME3 does this for us using a **Projection Matrix**. Fortunately, most users do not need to worry about how this is done. However, JME3, through the `Camera` class, provides information about projection matrices if needed.

The `Camera` and `FlyByCamera` Classes

There are two camera-related variables that applications can use: `cam` and `flyCam`. They are inherited from the `SimpleApplication` class. These both refer directly or indirectly to the camera used by a game. The relationship and use of these variables can be confusing at times.

The `cam` variable is declared in the `Application` class and is an instance of a `Camera` class. The `Camera` class is found in the `com.jme3.renderer` package. Its job is to render 3D objects to the 2D view a user sees on a screen. The class contains numerous methods to control the camera's frustum and ultimately what the user sees. It can be used to perform basic operations.

The `FlyByCamera` class is defined in the `com.jme3.input` package and controls a first-person view. As we saw in Chapter 3, the `FlyCamAppState` manages the `FlyByCamera` used by the BasicGame application.

The `FlyByCamera` class is not derived from the `Camera` class but is derived from the `Object` class. The `FlyByCamera` class controls the behavior of a `Camera` object as referenced by the `cam` variable. This instance of the `Camera` class is used as the argument to the `FlyByCamera` class' constructor. The `FlyByCamera` class will use the `cam` variable to affect its methods. For example, in the `FlyByCamera` class' `raiseCamera` method, a new position is calculated based on the `cam` instance's `getLocation` method.

The `flyCam` variable is defined and initialized in the `SimpleApplication` class. It references a `FlyByCam` object. Its location and orientation is bound to the input events such as the *W* key and mouse movement. This provides access to the camera which can be used to further control its use. The `FlyByCamera` provides an alternative way of controlling the camera used by applications.

When working with cameras, there are several terms that are helpful to keep in mind. The **Frustum** was defined in Chapter 1. As you may remember it defines a six plane region which represents what the camera is able to view in the game space. **Frustum Culling** is the process used to render only those objects that are in the frustum.

Based on the frustum, a camera has an orientation which is generally conceived of as an up and a down. Usually, this is a directional change on the Y axis.

An application's **Viewport** is a rectangular area of the screen used to render the game. The screen can be split into multiple viewports to provide different views of the game. For example, we may have a main view which occupies most of the screen and a second view which shows a map of the game.

> The default camera used by `SimpleApplication` is not suitable for all applications. Often, it is desirable to create your own fly camera to affect the behavior your application needs.

Using the `flyCam` Variable

The `flyCam` is active by default. This camera can be turned on and off with the `setEnabled` method with `true` or `false` as the parameter. The `flycam`'s movement and rotation speeds can be altered with the `setMoveSpeed` and `setRotationSpeed` methods respectively. These methods are illustrated here:

```
flyCam.setEnabled(true);
flyCam.setMoveSpeed(10);
flyCam.setRotationSpeed(10);
```

> Play with the move and rotation speeds to achieve the feel you want your game
> to have.

Using Positional Sounds

`AudioNode`s can be used for positional sounds. This type of sound is tied to a specific set of coordinates in the game space. As the player approaches the origin of the sound it will get louder and as the player departs the sound will fade. Positional sounds can be either ambient or situational.

To make a sound positional we will need to call the `setPositional` method with a parameter of `true`. We will also need to call the `setLocalTranslation` method and provide the coordinates for the positional sound. These two methods are the key to making a sound positional.

To use positional sound 3D, sound needs to be supported by your system. To test whether your system supports this feature and to enable it, use the following sequence for application settings:

```
settings = new AppSettings(true);
if(settings.useStereo3D()) {
    System.out.println("3D Sound Supported");
    settings.setStereo3D(true);
} else {
    System.out.println("3D Sound is not Supported");
}
app.setSettings(settings);
```

If 3D sound is supported then you can continue and setup a sound. In the following sequence, a new audio node is created using a beep sound from the jme3-test-data library. Its volume is set to `0.3f` so that it is not too annoying and is positioned at the application's origin.

```
AudioNode background = new AudioNode(assetManager,
    "Sounds/Beep.ogg");
background.setVolume(0.3f);
background.setLooping(true);
background.setPositional(true);
background.setLocalTranslation(0, 0, 0);
rootNode.attachChild(background);
background.play();
```

To make use of positional sounds, our player will need a set of ears that move with them! To do this we will make use of the `listener` object which is provided automatically by `SimpleApplication`. The best way to think of the `listener` object is to picture it as the player's ears in the game. To keep those ears tied to the player we will use the `simpleUpdate` method to get the position of the player's camera and move the listener to that position. Basically we are keeping the player's ears with the player's eyes.

In the following `simpleUpdate` method, we use two methods to keep the `listener` updated: the `setLocation` and `setRotation` methods. The arguments to these methods will be `cam.getLocation` and `cam.getRotation`, respectively. This will set the `listener` object's movements to the default camera's movements.

```
public void simpleUpdate(float tpf) {
    listener.setLocation(cam.getLocation());
    listener.setRotation(cam.getRotation());
}
```

When the application executes, moving the camera away from the origin should result in the volume of the sound decreasing.

Positional sounds must always be mono audio files. If they are not, then an exception will be thrown when played

If you attach a positional sound to the root node it will not move. However, attaching it to a node that moves, will result in the sound moving as the node moves. This is a way to associate a sound with a character or element of the game.

Handling Multiple Cameras

Multiple cameras can make a game more interesting by providing multiple perspectives. For example, we might want to have two views for a race car. The first view is looking out the front of the car and a second view looking backwards to see who is chasing us, or behind us.

Using Viewports

We can support multiple cameras through multiple root nodes with different scene graphs or by using one scene graph with different **Viewports**. A viewport defines what the user is able to see from a camera's perspective. It can be envisioned as a rectangle window in front of the camera that restricts the visible parts of a scene. With a single camera, the entire screen is available. With multiple cameras, then the screen needs to be divided into sections, one for each camera.

The `cam` object's default viewport occupies the entire window. The `setViewPort` method specifies the area of the application's window to use. It has four arguments: `left`, `right`, `bottom`, `top`. The values for these argument range from 0.0f to 1.0f representing the percentage of the screen to use. The values start in the lower left-hand corner of the screen.

A viewport that uses the entire window, the default setting for `cam`, uses the values (0.0, 1.0, 0.0. 1.0). A viewport that uses the lower right hand corner of the window uses the values (0.5, 1.0, 0.0, 0.5) as depicted in *Figure 5 - Viewport Examples*.

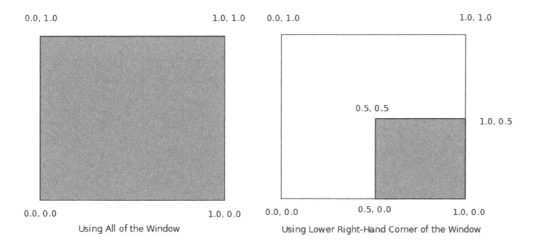

Figure 5 - Viewport Examples

To use the entire widow, which is the default camera setting, use the following statement:

```
cam.setViewPort(0f, 1f, 0f, 1f);
```

The next statement sets results in the camera view only using the lower right corner of the screen:

```
cam.setViewPort(0.5f, 1.0f, 0f, 0.5f);
```

This statement will use the lower left corner:

```
cam.setViewPort(0f, 0.5f, 0f, 0.5f);
```

Setting up Multiple Viewports

Multiple viewports require multiple cameras. To demonstrate how to use multiple cameras we will use the default camera but set it to use the lower right-hand corner of the screen. A second camera is created that will use the lower left-hand corner of the screen. This will leave the upper half of the screen unused.

In the following code sequence the `cam` object's viewport is set. To make the viewports clearly visible, we will set the background color of the viewport using its `setBackgroundColor` method. The viewport is not directly accessible through the `cam` variable so we will use the `Application` class' `getViewPort` method to get a reference to it. The background color is then set to light gray.

```
cam.setViewPort(.5f, 1f, 0f, 0.5f);
this.getViewPort().setBackgroundColor(
    ColorRGBA. LightGray);
```

A cube is then added to the scene using lighted material and diffuse and ambient colors added as shown next. In addition, the cube is rotated by 45 degrees to make it more visible.

```
Box box = new Box(1, 1, 1);
geom = new Geometry("Box", box);
Material mat = new Material(assetManager,
    "Common/MatDefs/Light/Lighting.j3md");
mat.setBoolean("UseMaterialColors", true);
mat.setColor("Diffuse", ColorRGBA.Red);
mat.setColor("Ambient", ColorRGBA.Gray);
geom.setMaterial(mat);
geom.rotate(0, 45 * FastMath.DEG_TO_RAD, 0);
rootNode.attachChild(geom);
```

We setup a second camera, `cam2`, by cloning the first one as shown next. Its viewport is then set for the lower left-hand corner. We want this camera to be positioned in a different location to the first one. Here, it is set to look directly down on the scene by placing it 10 units above the origin. We also need to change the direction it is pointing, so we use the `lookAtDirection` method to have it look down the Y axis. Its `Vector3f` object is set to point relative to the origin. A negative value of the Y axis means it will look downward. The last argument specifies that the up and down direction of the camera is along the X axis.

```
Camera cam2 = cam.clone();
cam2.setViewPort(0f, 0.5f, 0f, 0.5f);
cam2.setLocation(new Vector3f(0, 10, 0));
cam2.lookAtDirection(
    new Vector3f(0, -1, 0), Vector3f.UNIT_X);
```

The `RenderManager` class is responsible for rendering a scene. To associate the second camera with the application and to obtain its viewport, the `createMainView` method is used as shown next. Its first argument is the name of the view and its second argument is the camera we want to use.

```
ViewPort viewPort =
    renderManager.createMainView("Camera 2", cam2);
```

To make the viewport useable, we need to enable it and clear its frame buffer. The easiest way of doing this is to use setClearFlags method and set each argument to true as shown next. These arguments correspond to the color, depth, and stencil buffers. These buffers are used to assist in rendering the scene. The rootNode is then attached to the viewport and its background is set to red to make it easily seen.

```
viewPort.setEnabled(true);
viewPort.setClearFlags(true, true, true);
viewPort.attachScene(rootNode);
viewPort.setBackgroundColor(ColorRGBA.Red);
```

To take advantage of the lighted materials, directional and ambient lights were added as shown:

```
DirectionalLight sun = new DirectionalLight();
sun.setDirection(new Vector3f(-1, 0, 0));
sun.setColor(ColorRGBA.White);
rootNode.addLight(sun);

AmbientLight ambient = new AmbientLight();
ambient.setColor(ColorRGBA.White.mult(0.25f));
rootNode.addLight(ambient);
```

To demonstrate how these views work, we will bind the *K* and *L* keys to an action listener that will move the cube left and right.

```
// Instance variable declarations
private final static Trigger TRIGGER_K =
    new KeyTrigger(KeyInput.KEY_K);
private final static Trigger TRIGGER_L =
    new KeyTrigger(KeyInput.KEY_L);
private final static String MAP_MOVE_CUBE_LEFT =
    "Move cube left";
private final static String MAP_MOVE_CUBE_RIGHT =
    "Move cube right";

// Added to simpleInitApp method
inputManager.addMapping(MAP_MOVE_CUBE_LEFT, TRIGGER_K);
inputManager.addMapping(MAP_MOVE_CUBE_RIGHT, TRIGGER_L);
inputManager.addListener(
    actionListener, MAP_MOVE_CUBE_LEFT);
inputManager.addListener(
    actionListener, MAP_MOVE_CUBE_RIGHT);
```

The action listener follows:

```
        private ActionListener actionListener =
              new ActionListener() {
          @Override
          public void onAction(String name,
                  boolean isPressed, float tpf) {
              if (MAP_MOVE_CUBE_LEFT.equals(name) &&
                      isPressed) {
                  x -= 0.1f;
                  geom.setLocalTranslation(x, 0, 0);
              } else if (MAP_MOVE_CUBE_RIGHT.equals(name) &&
                      isPressed) {
                  x += 0.1f;
                  geom.setLocalTranslation(x, 0, 0);
              }
          }
        };
```

When this example is executed, the application will appear as shown in *Figure 6 - Multiple Views Example*. The *K* key was used to move the cube to the left along the X axis in the right view. This resulted in the cube moving downward in the left window. This is because the left view was created with the X axis running up and down.

Figure 6 - Multiple Views Example

Setting Up a Picture in a Picture

Another viewing option is to display a picture in a picture. Usually one camera uses the entire screen while a second camera view is displayed in a smaller window located somewhere in the larger window. The process of creating this type of display is very similar to using multiple views. The main difference is the order the views are created in, and where they overlap.

To demonstrate how this done we will reuse the code from the previous section. There are only two changes that need to be made. First, set the `cam` object's viewport to use the entire window as shown:

```
cam.setViewPort(0f, 1f, 0f, 1f);
```

Second, change the `cam2` object's viewport to overlap the first camera and place it in the upper right-hand part of the screen as illustrated next:

```
cam2.setViewPort(0.75f, 0.95f, 0.7f, 0.9f);
```

The result is shown in *Figure 7 - Picture in a Picture Example* where the cube has been moved to the left.

Figure 7 - Picture in a Picture Example

The order in which the viewports are created is important. The larger one must be created first.

Capturing Screenshots

There are times when a user, or the game itself, may wish to capture a screen shot. This is a useful feature that allows the user to capture "the moment" such as when the game ends. Win or lose, the last scene can be saved and displayed.

While most operating systems provide a way of doing this, such as using *Alt-PrtScrn* on a Windows platform, this involves the subsequent saving of the screenshot using an editor. JME3 provides a way of capturing a screenshot and automatically saving it for you.

The `ScreenshotAppState` class, found in the `com.jme3.app.state` package, can be added to your application using the `StateManager` class' `attach` method as shown next. Valid arguments to the constructor are listed in *Table 4 - ScreenshotAppState Constructor Parameters*. In this case, we specified that the project's application folder be used to save the images.

```
ScreenshotAppState screenShotState =
    new ScreenshotAppState("");
this.stateManager.attach(screenShotState);
```

To programmatically take a screenshot, use the `takeScreenshot` method as shown here:

```
screenShotState.takeScreenshot();
```

The user can also use the `KeyInput.KEY_SYSRQ` key. On windows, this is the *Print Screen* or *Alt-Print Screen* key. It doesn't make any difference which key combination is used. On Mac OS you need to use either *Command+Shift+3* to capture the full screen or *Command+Shift+4* to select a window.

The images are saved as `.png` files and are named after the application's class name. For example, if the class is `Main`, the files are named `Main1.png`, `Main2.png`, and so forth.

The folder location can be changed using the `setFilePath` method as shown next. Its argument follows the same conventions as that for the class' constructor listed in *Table 4 - ScreenshotAppState Constructor Parameters*.

```
screenShotState.setFilePath("C:\\Applications\\");
```

Table 4 - ScreenshotAppState Constructor Parameters

Argument	Meaning
No argument	System's default folder. For Windows this is located at `C:\Users\UserName\.jme3` where UserName is the name of the logged in user.
Empty string	The project's application folder
A string containing a path	The location to store the images. The string needs to end with the file separator for the system.

Capturing Video

Capturing the game as it is played in a video can be useful. Such videos can be used to capture some great, or not so great, moments in a game. It can be used to provide a promotional video for your game.

Video capture is easy in JME3 if you want to save it as an `.avi` file with M-JPEG content. If you want some other file type it will be necessary to convert the `.avi` to that format.

To capture video of a game, add the `VideoRecorderAppState` to your application. This class is found in the `com.jme3.app.state` package. Video recording will begin when the application state is added to an application and will terminate when the application quits or the application state is detached from the application.

In the following example, an instance of the `VideoRecorderAppState` is created and attached to the application using the `StateManager` class' `attach` method:

```
VideoRecorderAppState  videoRecorderAppState =
    new VideoRecorderAppState();
stateManager.attach(videoRecorderAppState);
```

The file is saved in the user's home directory with a file name of `jMonkey-timestamp.avi`, where `timestamp` is the time of the video. The location of the file can be specified in one of several constructors or by using the `setFile` method. An example using a constructor follows:

```
videoRecorderAppState =
    new VideoRecorderAppState(new File("video.avi"));
```

The quality of a video can be specified in a constructor or using the `setQuality` method. A float value is used which ranges from `0.0f`, the worst, to `1.0f`, the best. The default value is `0.8f`. In addition, the frame rate can be set using a constructor.

Shades of Infinity Enhancements

Our new version of the game incorporates many of the topics discussed in this chapter. These include:

- The use of shadows for the ships

- The addition of a picture in a picture

- The ability to capture screenshots and video of the game

Adding Shadows

We added shadow rendering to the planets as well as the AI ships using a
`DirectionalLightShadowRenderer`. Either we need to individually set the shadow
mode of each object we want to be affected, or we need to set the shadow mode for the
entire `rootNode`, affecting all children. In the `PlanetsAppState` class we set the
shadows individually as shown:

```
planetGeometry.setShadowMode(ShadowMode.CastAndReceive);
...
moon.setShadowMode(ShadowMode.CastAndReceive);
...
enemy.setShadowMode(
    RenderQueue.ShadowMode.CastAndReceive);
```

Once we have the ships and planets set to `ShadowMode.CastAndReceive`, we are ready to
add a renderer. For this we will use the same parameters as the example in Using the
Shadow Renderer. Since our light source, the `sun`, is in the `PlanetsAppState` we can
add the renderer to the application state. As you may recall from the earlier example, a
shadow renderer must have a light source set to it before it will know what to cast
shadows from.

In the `addLights` method we call the `addShadow` helper method:

```
addShadow(sun);
...
private void addShadow(DirectionalLight light){
    DirectionalLightShadowRenderer shadow =
        new DirectionalLightShadowRenderer(
            assetManager, 512, 2);
    shadow.setLight(light);
    viewPort.addProcessor(shadow);
}
```

With these simple additions you can now observe shadows when you run the game.
Notice that if you destroy the AI ship casting the shadow, the shadow on the other AI
ship will disappear immediately. The shadow cast by the space ship is shown in *Figure 8
- Spaceship Shadow*.

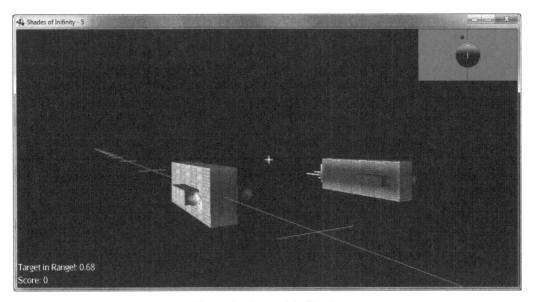

Figure 8 - Spaceship Shadow

You can also observe the shadow of the smaller planet moving across the surface of the larger one. This is seen in *Figure 9 - Planet Shadow*.

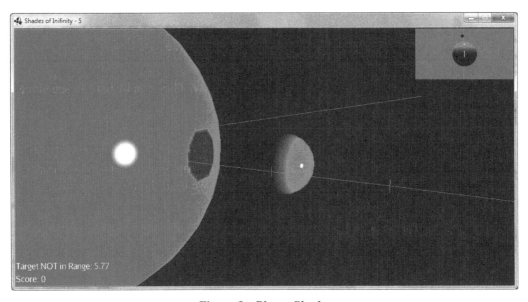

Figure 9 - Planet Shadow

Creating a Picture in a Picture

You may have noticed the picture in a picture shown in the previous section's figures. The process we used is very similar to that described in Setting Up a Picture in a Picture. We started by moving the ships about a bit:

```
enemy.setLocalTranslation(0, 0, 4);       // Enemy 1
...
enemy.setLocalTranslation(-0.5f, 0, 4);  // Enemy 2
```

The default camera is set explicitly to use the entire window as shown next:

```
cam.setViewPort(0f, 1f, 0f, 1f);
```

The second camera was then created and set to use part of the upper right-hand corner of the window as shown next. The background is set to blue to make it more visible.

```
Camera cam2 = cam.clone();
cam2.setViewPort(0.8f, 1.0f, 0.8f, 1.0f);
cam2.setLocation(new Vector3f(0, 10, 0));
cam2.lookAtDirection(
    new Vector3f(0, -1, 0), Vector3f.UNIT_X);

ViewPort viewPort =
    renderManager.createMainView("Camera 2", cam2);
viewPort.setEnabled(true);
viewPort.setClearFlags(true, true, true);
viewPort.attachScene(rootNode);
viewPort.setBackgroundColor(ColorRGBA.Blue);
```

The two AI ships should be visible in the smaller window. They can be hard to see since they are small relative to the planets.

Capturing Screenshots and Videos

The approach used is the same as illustrated in the Capturing Screenshots and Capturing Video sections. To enable the capturing of screenshots we used the following code sequence:

```
ScreenshotAppState screenShotState =
    new ScreenshotAppState("");
stateManager.attach(screenShotState);
```

The video recorder is enabled and we specified the file name for the video as shown next:

```
VideoRecorderAppState videoRecorderAppState =
    new VideoRecorderAppState(new File("SOI.avi"));
stateManager.attach(videoRecorderAppState);
```

Conclusion

In this chapter we examined two new light sources and demonstrated how shadows are added to a scene. The spot light is similar to a flashlight and has a cone shape and a range. The point light also has a range but radiates in all directions. The brightness of these lights decrease over distance.

Shadows are not automatically added to scenes. Special renderers are needed along with a light source. We demonstrated how to use both a shadow renderer and a shadow filter which produce similar results. Shadows can be computationally intense, so they should be used carefully.

The default camera and its relationship with the `FlyByCamera` were examined. Games based on `SimpleApplication` automatically have a default camera and fly-by-camera. However, it is common to change how a camera behaves for a game. The use of multiple camera views can add a different perspective to a game. This was discussed along with the use of positional sounds.

Capturing an image of the current game state or even a video can be a positive application feature. These are supported in JME3 and are easy to implement. Many of these chapter's topics were incorporated into the Shades of Infinity game.

In the next chapter we will jump into animation! We will explore techniques used to animate models, configure waypoints, and use cinematics.

7

Animation

Introduction

Animation is an important aspect in most games. Using animation injects dynamic behavior into a game and can make it a more pleasing and interesting affair. Animation can be used to make a character walk, a ship move across a sea, or a door open and close.

JME3 supports animation using simple techniques based on the `simpleUpdate` method; model animation supplied by a model; movement of a character or object through a series of predefined points in a game; and with **Cinematics**. The last technique uses a series of steps which can combine movement, sound, animation, and HUD updates.

We start the chapter off with examples of using the `simpleUpdate` method and `tpf` variable to control simple animations. While this is not as powerful as the other animation techniques discussed in this chapter, it is a simple and quick technique for handling some basic animations.

Many animations are based on complex 3D models developed with other applications. JME3 allows us to load many of the models and control the animations embedded within these models. These types of animations are often easier to handle. However, we are reliant upon other tools such as Blender to create the models.

The topic of cinematics is then covered starting with a discussion of way points. These points are simple `Vector3f` objects representing points in the scene. An object can be made to move through a path defined by these points. Cinematics is also illustrated where we combine movement with sound.

The last section describes how many of this chapter's techniques are incorporated into the Shades of Infinity game. These include the use of motion paths and cinematics to move the AI ships separately.

Animation Basics

At the most basic level, animation simply involves moving an object that would otherwise be static. The easiest way to animate an object is to apply a transformation to the object repeatedly.

In this section we will examine the use of the `tpf` variable more closely and how the `Application` class' `speed` variable can be used. Bear in mind that the `tpf` variable is used in many places and the techniques discussed here are equally applicable wherever the variable is found.

Animating with the `simpleUpdate` Method

Creating a simple animation in the update loop involves applying a transformation to an object in `simpleUpdate`. An object is transformed, by the specified amount, every frame. You may recall that we did this with our planetary system in Chapter 4 where we moved the AI ships along a straight path as shown here:

```
public void simpleUpdate(float tpf) {
    shootables.move(0.1f * tpf, 0, 0);
}
```

The use of a movement transformation is a simple one. We could have used more complex transformations such as a scale or rotate or even a combination of transformations. We used the `tpf` (time per frame) variable to support a smooth transformation (as explained in the next section).

Using `tpf` to Control the Speed of an Animation

The `tpf` parameter is used in a number of update methods including the `simpleUpdate` method. It represents the amount of time, in seconds, since the last time the update was called. It is larger for slower computers or more computationally intensive applications. It is smaller for faster machines or where the computations are simpler.

To illustrate its use, we will move a simple cube across the scene. In the following sequence, which should be placed in the `simpleInitApp` method, lights and axes and a simple box are added to the scene using the helper method `getBox`. The `drawAxes` method was used in Chapter 1 and the `addLights` method was introduced in Chapter 6. The variable `cubeNode` is declared as an instance variable of type `Box` to allow access from multiple methods.

```
drawAxes();
addLights();

cubeNode = getBox("Simple Cube", 0.5f, 0.5f,
    0.5f, ColorRGBA.Blue);
cubeNode.setLocalTranslation(0, 0, 0);
cubeNode.rotate(0, FastMath.DEG_TO_RAD * 45, 0);
rootNode.attachChild(cubeNode);
...
private Node getBox(String name, float width,
        float height, float depth, ColorRGBA color) {
    Node boxNode = new Node(name);
    Box box = new Box(width, height, depth);
    Geometry boxGeometry = new Geometry(name, box);
    Material mat = new Material(assetManager,
        "Common/MatDefs/Light/Lighting.j3md");
    mat.setBoolean("UseMaterialColors", true);
```

```
            mat.setColor("Diffuse", ColorRGBA.White);
            mat.setColor("Ambient", color);
            mat.setColor("Specular", ColorRGBA.White);
            mat.setFloat("Shininess", 128f);

            boxGeometry.setMaterial(mat);
            boxNode.attachChild(boxGeometry);
            return boxNode;
        }
```

The `simpleUpdate` method is modified as shown next. The `move` method will move the cube along the X axis at a rate determined by the expression: `0.5f * tpf`.

```
        public void simpleUpdate(float tpf) {
            cubeNode.move(0.5f * tpf, 0, 0);
        }
```

The `0.5f` value controls the rate at which the cube will move. The larger the value, the faster the cube will move. This, combined with the `tpf` variable, results in the smoother movement of objects. If the `tpf` is small, the object does not move as far. If the `tpf` is large, the object will move farther. If we had used a variable for the `0.05f` value instead, we could control the rate that multiple objects move at (all expressed as a factor of this variable).

The `tpf` variable can also be used as a simple clock. In the next example, a `currentTime` variable keeps track of elapsed time. When it reaches `1.0f`, one second has elapsed. The variable `currentTime` is declared as an instance variable of type `float` to allow access from multiple methods.

```
        public void simpleUpdate(float tpf) {
            currentTime += tpf;
            if (currentTime > 1.0f) {
                // Do something
                currentTime = 0.0f;
            }
        }
```

Using the speed Variable

The `speed` variable is defined in the `Application` class. It represents the relative speed of your game and is initialized to `1.0f`. You can use it to speed up the game by setting it to a different value. As shown here the speed of the game is increased by a factor of 5:

```
        speed = 5*speed;
```

Depending on the machine in use, faster values can affect how well 3D graphics are rendered. Some effects, such as how fast a sound is played, are not affected.

Understanding Model Animation

A model animation uses a series of files developed by an external editor such as Blender. These models usually have one or more animations built into them. For example, the character represented by a model can be made to walk, jump, or squat. Each of these actions is represented by an animation.

Before a model can be used it must be loaded into JME3. It can then be controlled using a combination of controls, channels, and animation cycle methods. The class `AnimControl` controls how the model's skeleton is animated. Various animation transitions, skin usage, and event listeners can be handled by the controller.

For each animation you will need an animation channel. This is supported by the `AnimChannel` class. Switching between animations is fairly common. For example, a player may walk along a path and then fight an evil troll. To control switching between animations the `onAnimCycleDone` and `onAnimChange` methods of the `AnimEventListener` interface are used.

These classes and techniques will be discussed in this section. But first, we will discuss a number of terms used in model animation. Understanding these terms allows you to converse with other developers and helps you understand how JME3 handles model animation.

Animation Terms

Model animations are much more complex than update loop animations. There are three primary components to model animations: **Rigging**, **Skinning**, and **Keyframes**. All these components are created outside of JME3 but are loaded in JME3. To animate a model the skeletal structure must be rigged, the structure must be linked to the mesh in a process called skinning, and the animation sequence must be defined using keyframes.

Rigging is basically the creation of the bones, or skeletal structure, of the model. The bones are the part of the model that moves. They are invisible in the game. The bones are created in a hierarchy so the proper parts move during animation. For example, the thigh bone might have the leg bone as a child, and the leg bone might have the foot bone as a child, etc. It would be uncommon for one part of the leg to move without the others.

> The more bones a model has, the greater the potential impact on performance.

Skinning relates to how bones correspond to sections of skin. Skin also includes the model's clothing or other items. Animating the unseen bone also moves the skin, and may add realistic distortion. In the skinning process, the modeler decides how much each polygon of skin is affected by each bone. The degree that the skin segment is affected is referred to as the **weight**. One skin segment can be affected by more than one bone.

Keyframes are the building blocks of an animation. A keyframe is an instance of a specific pose in the animation. Model animations are created from a combination of keyframes. You can think of this as a series of snapshots that add up to become a moving scene.

Understanding Model Files

Every model animation has a file that stores the skeletal structure along with the keyframes used in the animation process. To demonstrate models in this chapter, we will use the Sinbad model found in the `jme3-test-data` library under `Model Sinbad`. This model is made of several files including the `Sinbad.skeleton.xml` file.

This file specifies the organization of the bones, hierarchy, keyframes, and animations for the Sinbad model. You don't have to worry about this file unless you want to see exactly how the structure of a model is saved. A partial listing of the file is shown next, to give you an idea of how it is organized. This is a large file and would be difficult to create in JME3 and therefore editors such as Blender are used instead.

```
<skeleton>
    <bones>
        <bone id="52" name="Root">
            <position x="0.000000" y="0.000000" z="0.000000"/>
            <rotation angle="0.000000">
                <axis x="-1.000000" y="0.000000" …/>
            </rotation>
        </bone>
...
    </bones>
    <bonehierarchy>
        <boneparent bone="Thigh.R" parent="Root" />
        <boneparent bone="Thigh.L" parent="Root" />
        <boneparent bone="Waist" parent="Root" />
        <boneparent bone="Calf.R" parent="Thigh.R" />
...
    </bonehierarchy>
    <animations>
        <animation name="RunBase" length="0.666667">
            <tracks>
                <track bone="Root">
                    <keyframes>
                        <keyframe time="0.000000">
                            <translate x="0.200000" …/>
                            <rotate angle="0.171706">
                                <axis x="1.000000" …/>
                            </rotate>
                            <scale x="1.000000" …/>
                        </keyframe>
...
                    </keyframes>
                </track>
...
            </tracks>
        </animation>
```

```
        </animations>
    </skeleton>
```

Loading Animations

The loading process is simple. Use the `loadModel` method of the `assetManager` to load the model. The method is passed the location of the model and returns a `Spatial` representing the model.

To demonstrate this process, create a new `Spatial` called `sinbad` as shown next and then use the `loadModel` method to load it. The specific location we will use is `Models/Sinbad/Sinbad.mesh.xml`. Then we will attach it to the `rootNode`.

```
    Spatial sinbad = assetManager.loadModel(
        "Models/Sinbad/Sinbad.mesh.xml");
    rootNode.attachChild(sinbad);
```

Once the model has been loaded, we can set up the animations using an animation control and an animation channel.

Using Animation Controls

The animation control, or `AnimControl`, is found in the `com.jme3.animation` package. This class is a control that gives us access to the skeletal animation of a model. This control can support multiple channels and animation listeners. After we implement a control, we will create an animation channel to use with an animation, as illustrated in the next section.

In this example, we add code to the `simpleInitApp` method to move the camera back a bit so we can see Sinbad in his entirety. Then we add ambient light. The model is then loaded and Sinbad is added to the scene.

```
    cam.setLocation(new Vector3f(0,0,14));
    AmbientLight light = new AmbientLight();
    rootNode.addLight(light);
    Spatial sinbad = assetManager.loadModel(
        "Models/Sinbad/Sinbad.mesh.xml");
    rootNode.attachChild(sinbad);
```

Next, create an instance variable of type `AnimControl` called `control`. Continuing with the `simpleInitApp` method, instantiate the control using the `getControl` method with `AnimControl.class` as the parameter. This method will return the control for Sinbad's animations. Finally, we will add a listener to the control with `this` as the parameter.

```
    control = sinbad.getControl(AnimControl.class);
    control.addListener(this);
```

Your class will need to implement the `AnimEventListener` interface. This will require you to implement two methods as we will detail in *Switching Between Animations*. At this time you can use the empty implementations.

There are several other useful methods available for animation controls as described in *Table 1 - AnimControl Methods*.

Table 1 - AnimControl Methods

AnimControl Methods	Uses
createChannel	Returns a new channel that controls all bones
getNumChannels	Return the number of channels on the control
getChannel	Returns a channel by index
clearChannels	Clears all channels on the control
addListener	Adds listeners to receive animation events
getAnimationNames	Returns a collection of the names of all the animations available for the model
getAnimationLength	Returns the length of the animation in seconds
getSkeleton	Returns the model's skeleton object
getTargets	Returns the model's skin object

One of these methods that you may find useful is the `getAnimationNames` method. It will return the names of all of the available animations for the given model. This is useful with models that may not be well documented.

In the following code sequence, a list of animation names is displayed for the Sinbad model.

```
Collection<String> list = control.getAnimationNames();
    for(String name : list) {
        System.out.println(name);
    }
```

The output follows. We will use the Dance animation in the next example.

Dance

SliceHorizontal

StandUpFront

StandUpBack

JumpLoop

JumpStart

Chapter 7

DrawSwords

RunTop

SliceVertical

HandsClosed

JumpEnd

RunBase

IdleBase

HandsRelaxed

IdleTop

Using Animation Channels

The animation channel, or `AnimChannel`, is found in the `com.jme3.animation` package. Each animation controller can have multiple animation channels. Each channel will run one animation sequence at a time. Multiple channels are needed to support multiple animation sequences.

Sometimes you will want to run two animation sequences at the same time. For example, you may want to have a model jump while attacking. This would require two channels running at the same time, each assigned to a separate animation sequence: one for jumping and the other for attacking.

Let's build on the previous example by adding an instance variable of type `AnimChannel` called `danceChannel`. This channel will be used to control Sinbad's dance animation. Instantiate the channel by calling the `createChannel` method against `control` as shown next. Then call the `setAnim` method with the string `"Dance"` as the parameter. This will set the current animation on this channel to dance.

```
danceChannel = control.createChannel();
danceChannel.setAnim("Dance");
```

Take a look at *Table 2 - AnimChannel Methods* to see the various methods available for channels.

Table 2 - AnimChannel Methods

`AnimChannel` **Methods**	**Uses**
`setLoopMode`	Controls how the animation plays (See *Table 3 - LoopMode Enumeration*)
`setSpeed`	Controls the speed of the animation with 1 being the default. Values bigger than 1 are faster and values smaller than 1 are slower.
`setTime`	Sets the time of the animation
`getAnimationName`	Returns the name of the animation on the current channel

`AnimChannel` **Methods**	**Uses**
`getControl`	Returns the control that controls the current channel

Table 3 - LoopMode Enumeration

`LoopMode` **Enumeration Values**	**Meaning**
`LoopMode.Loop`	Animation repeats
`LoopMode.DontLoop`	Animation plays only once
`LoopMode.Cycle`	Animation plays forward then backward

Playing Animations

At this point we have an animation control, animation channel, and a model all set up and ready to go. Now let's play the animation. We will use two examples to show how this can be accomplished. First, we will map the left mouse button click event to start an animation. Then, we will demonstrate how to switch between animations.

Triggering Animations

We will map the left mouse click to start the animation. We won't go into much detail here since we covered this in Chapter 3. Then we will create an action listener to respond to the input. When the mouse button is clicked Sinbad will perform the dance animation as pictured in *Figure 1 - Sinbad Dance*. The code to perform the mapping is shown here and goes in the `simpleInitApp` method:

```
inputManager.addMapping("Dance",
    new MouseButtonTrigger(MouseInput.BUTTON_LEFT));
inputManager.addListener(actionListener, "Dance");
```

Next, we will set up the action listener to activate the dance animation when the player clicks the left mouse button as shown next. The second argument to the `setAnim` method specifies what is called the **Blend Time**. This is the time that the animation will be mixed with the currently executing animation. When used, it can result in a smoother transition between animations.

```
private ActionListener actionListener =
            new ActionListener() {
    public void onAction(String name,
            boolean keyPressed, float tpf) {
        if (name.equals("Dance") && !keyPressed) {
            danceChannel.setAnim("Dance", 0.50f);
        }
    }
};
```

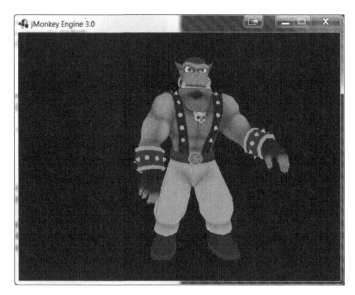

Figure 1 - Sinbad Dance

Switching Between Animations

Some situations require that animations play sequentially. They often form a cycle where the first animation is followed by a second animation and so on until the last animation is executed. Then, the first animation plays again repeating the cycle. If a model only uses one animation it won't be necessary to implement the animation cycle.

The `AnimEventListener` interface supports cycles of this type and is found in the `com.jme3.animation` package. The interface has two methods: `onAnimCycleDone`, and `onAnimChange`.

The first method, `onAnimCycleDone`, is used for handling animations' ending(s). If the animation is not set to loop, this method will be invoked when an animation has finished playing. If the animation is set to loop, this method will be invoked each time the loop restarts. The `onAnimCycleDone` method has three parameters: an `AnimControl`, an `AnimChannel`, and the name of the animation. You do not need to explicitly call this method because it responds to the animation cycle automatically.

In this method we usually just check to see if an animation has finished and then set the channel to some other animation. In the example shown next, we will check to see if the dance animation just ended, since we are starting with the `Dance` animation. If it did, then we will set the animation to idle using `IdleBase`. `IdleBase` is just an idle position where Sinbad will stand still. Instead of `IdleBase`, we could use other Sinbad animations such as `RunBase` or `JumpLoop`.

```
public void onAnimCycleDone(AnimControl control,
    AnimChannel channel, String animName) {
  if (animName.equals("Dance")) {
    channel.setAnim("IdleBase");
  }
}
```

The `onAnimChange` method is invoked when it is set to play. This method uses the same parameters as the previous method. For the implementation of this method, we will do the opposite of what we did in the `onAnimCycleDone` method. This method checks for the idle animation and sets it back to the dance animation.

```
public void onAnimChange(AnimControl control,
    AnimChannel channel, String animName) {
  if (animName.equals("IdleBase")) {
    channel.setAnim("Dance");
  }
}
```

At this point we have setup an animation cycle that transitions from `IdleBase` to `Dance` and then back to `IdleBase`. Sinbad in `IdleBase` is pictured in *Figure 2 - Sinbad Idle*. When we run this example, a left click causes the Sinbad model to perform the dance animation. Once the animation completes Sinbad will return to idle.

> If you want to have a model perform the same animation continuously you can call the `setLoopMode` method against a channel with `LoopMode.Loop` as the parameter.

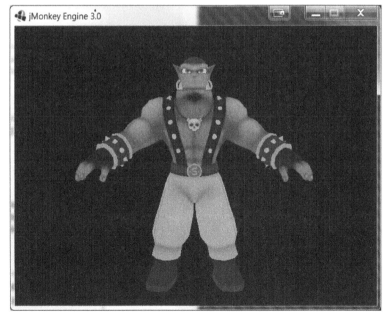

Figure 2 - Sinbad Idle

197

Motion Paths and Way Points

When an object moves through a scene it can be envisioned as moving through a series of points along a path. These points are called **Way Points**. The path the object follows is referred to as a **Motion Path**.

In JME3, the `MotionPath` object defines the waypoints for the path as a series of `Vertex3f` objects. We can create a motion path and then use it with an object so that the object will move along the path. When the motion begins and when it ends is controlled by an instance of the `MotionEvent` class.

To use this technique:

1. Create an instance of `MotionPath`

2. Use the `addWayPoint` method to add points to the path

3. Set any additional behaviors desired

4. Create a `MotionEvent` class to control the motion

5. Use the `play` method to start the motion

Additional behaviors may include whether the path cycles or how "smooth" the movement will be. To illustrate this technique we will move a simple cube in a circle around the origin along the X and Y axes.

First the `MotionPath` object is created:

```
MotionPath path = new MotionPath();
```

Next, four points are added corresponding to four points around the origin:

```
path.addWayPoint(new Vector3f(3, 0, 0));
path.addWayPoint(new Vector3f(0, 3, 0));
path.addWayPoint(new Vector3f(-3, 0, 0));
path.addWayPoint(new Vector3f(0, -3, 0));
```

These points are illustrated in *Figure 3 - Motion Path Coordinates* where the X and Y axes are displayed only. The direction of movement is defined by the order of the way points. In this case it defines a counter-clockwise rotation as viewed from the Z axis.

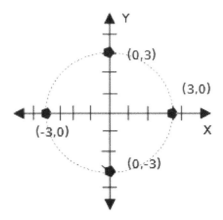

Figure 3 - Motion Path Coordinates

To modify its behavior, we will use the `setCycle` method to specify that the points form a cycle and the `setCurveTension` method to make the cycle round. The argument of this latter method can vary from `0.0f` to `1.0f` where the lower values will result in more of a straight path between the waypoints and larger values result in a more circular transition between the waypoints.

```
path.setCycle(true);
path.setCurveTension(1.0f);
```

We need an object to move so we will use a simple cube. The `cubeNode` is created using a helper method: `getBox` as defined earlier in *Using `tpf` to Control the Speed of an* Animation. Lights and axes are rendered but this code is not shown here. The cube is located 3 units to the right of the origin as viewed from the camera's initial position. It is rotated 45 degree to make it more visible. The `cubeNode` is declared as an instance variable of type `Node`.

```
cubeNode = getBox(
    "Simple Cube", 0.5f, 0.5f, 0.5f, ColorRGBA.Blue);
cubeNode.setLocalTranslation(3, 0, 0);
cubeNode.rotate(0, FastMath.DEG_TO_RAD * 45, 0);
rootNode.attachChild(cubeNode);
```

To execute the motion, create a `MotionEvent` object using the `cubeNode` and `path` instances. Then, use the `play` method as shown next. We will examine the `MotionEvent` class in more detail in the next section

```
MotionEvent motionEvent = new MotionEvent(cubeNode,path);
motionEvent.play();
```

When executed, it will appear as shown in *Figure 4 - Motion Path Example* (a red circle has been superimposed to show the cube's path). The full source code can be downloaded from `www.p8tech.com`. It differs from what we illustrated here. In the fill version it has been setup to start, pause, and stop using the F1, F2, and F3 keys respectively.

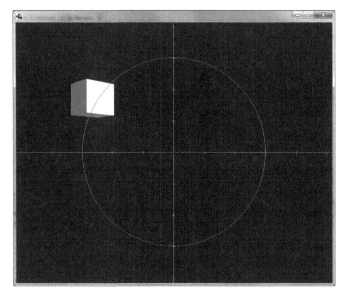

Figure 4 - Motion Path Example

There are several useful `MotionPath` methods as summarized in *Table 4 - MotionPath Methods* We will use a few of these in later sections.

Table 4 - `MotionPath` Methods

`MotionPath` **Methods**	**Parameter**	**Meaning**
`getLength`	None	Returns the length of the path in world units
`getNbWayPoints`	None	Returns the number of way points for the path
`getWayPoint`	`int`	Returns a `Vector3f` object for the way point at the specified index
`setCycle`	`boolean`	Specifies whether the way points represent a cycle

Configuring the Motion Event

The `MotionEvent` class is found in the `com.jme.cinematic.events` package and is derived from `AbstractCinematicEvent`. Between these two classes there are a number of useful methods to configure the motion as summarized in *Table 5 - Motion Event*

Configuration Methods. In the following example, the spatial will rotate in the direction of the path.

```
motionEvent.setDirectionType(MotionEvent.Direction.Path);
```

These methods provide more flexibility in how an object behaves when controlled by a `MotionEvent` object.

Table 5 - Motion Event Configuration Methods

Method	Argument	Usage
play	None	Start the motion
pause	None	Pauses the motion
stop	None	Stops the motion
setTime	float	Results in the motion being fast-forwarded to the specified time
setLoopMode	LoopMode	Controls how the motion loops
setDirectionType	MotionEvent.Direction	Controls the direction the spatial uses (See *Table 6 - MotionEvent.Direction Constants*)
setLookAt	**Two** Vector3f objects	Specifies the direction the spatial looks if the direction type specifies look at
setRotation	Quaternion	Sets the rotation based on the direction type

Table 6 - MotionEvent.Direction Constants

MotionEvent.Direction **Constant**	Meaning
LookAt	Looks at a specific point as specified by the setLookAt method
None	The spatial does not rotate
Path	The spatial rotates with the path
PathAndRotation	Rotates in the direction of the path plus a value
Rotation	Spatial rotates as specified by the setRotation method

Other potentially useful methods are summarized in *Table 7 - MotionEvent State Methods*.

Table 7 - MotionEvent State Methods

`MotionEvent` **Method**	**Meaning**
`getTraveledDistance`	Returns the distance traveled
`getDuration`	Returns the actual duration of the motion as calculated by initialDuration/speed

`getPlayState`	Returns a play state of either:
	`PlayState.Paused`
	`PlayState.Playing`
	`Playstate.Stopped`

`getTime`	Returns the current time of the motion

Capturing Motion Path Events

During the motion, it is possible to get information about the motion when a way point is encountered. The `com.jme3.cinematic` package's `MotionPathListener` interface supports this need. The interface has a single method: `onWayPointReach`.

In the following sequence, an anonymous inner class using this interface is created and added to the path defined in *Motion Paths and Way Points*. When a way point is reached, its index is displayed along with the current time and distance traveled.

```
path.addListener(new MotionPathListener() {
    public void onWayPointReach(
            MotionEvent control, int wayPointIndex) {
        System.out.print("Way point: " + wayPointIndex +
            path.getWayPoint(wayPointIndex));
        System.out.print(" Time: " + control.getTime() +
            "/" + control.getDuration());
        System.out.println(" Distance: " +
            control.getTraveledDistance() + "/" +
            path.getLength());
    }
});
```

When executed, you will get an output similar to the following. Notice that the first way point listed is *actually* the second way point added to the path. This is because the motion starts before the first way point can be processed. The last way point listed is the first way point added because the `setCycle` method was passed a value of `true`. If it had been set to `false`, then the motion would stop at the last waypoint added: way point 3.

Way point: 1(0.0, 3.0, 0.0) Time: 7.7078557/15.0 Distance: 4.774579/19.4729

Way point: 2(-3.0, 0.0, 0.0) Time: 15.009551/15.0 Distance: 9.724064/19.4729

Way point: 3(0.0, -3.0, 0.0) Time: 22.515575/15.0 Distance: 14.594003/19.4729

Way point: 4(3.0, 0.0, 0.0) Time: 30.024704/15.0 Distance: 19.46932/19.4729

Understanding Cinematics

Cinematics in JME3 is a technique to control the behavior of nodes or cameras "remotely". By remotely, we mean the ability to orchestrate a sequence of actions in a game. For example, you might want a character in your game to move from one place to another while playing a sound. This type of sequence is sometimes called a **Cut Scene** or **Event Scene**.

Another use of cinematics is to prerecord an event, such as a bridge falling down, and play it back at a later time. This can often be more efficient than using your graphics card to compute the movement in real time. We can also play it back faster or slower than the original sequence.

A cinematic is represented by an instance of the `Cinematic` class and derives from the `AppState` class. Since it is an application state, it must be added to the application before it can be used. The class manages the cinematics based on cinematic events attached to it. These events may result in a node being moved, sounds being played, or various GUI updates.

The steps to use cinematics include:

1. Create an instance of the `Cinematic` class
2. Add one or more cinematic events to it
3. Attach it to the application using `stateManager`
4. Start it using the `play` method

There are several types of cinematic events as summarized in *Table 8 - Cinematic Event Types*. We will demonstrate all of these events with the exception of the `GuiEvent` since we have not covered **Nifty**.

One of the advantages of using these objects in a cinematic is that the motion can also be combined with sound and other events. We will see how this is done in the next section.

Table 8 - Cinematic Event Types

Cinematic Event	Purpose
MotionEvent	A spatial will be moved through a series of points
SoundEvent	A sound will be played for a specified duration
GuiEvent	This uses Nifty to display information
AnimationEvent	Supports a model animation

When browsing through the JME3 API documentation you may encounter the following classes: `AnimationTrack`, `MotionTrack`, `GuiTrack`, and `SoundTrack`. These are all deprecated and should not be used. The corresponding event classes should be used instead.

Using a Motion Event

The creation and use of `MotionEvent` and `MotionPath` objects was explained in *Motion Paths and Way Points*. We will use the same code to demonstrate how they can be used with a cinematics.

To use a motion event with a cinematic, use the following steps:

1. Create an instance of `MotionPath`

2. Use the `addWayPoint` method to add points to the path

3. Set any additional behaviors desired

4. Create an instance of a `MotionEvent` using a spatial and the motion path

5. Set any desired behavior for the event

6. Use the `Cinematic` object to play the motion

Use the same `MotionPath` and `MotionEvent` objects as before. Create a `Cinematic` object, as shown next. The `Cinematic` constructor uses the same cube and a second argument specifying how long the cinematic is to run in seconds. In this instance, it is set to run for 30 seconds. The `Cinematic` object is attached to the application and the motion event is added to the cinematic. The first argument of the `addCinematicEvent` method determines when the cinematic will start. In this case, it will be 3 seconds after the start of the cinematic. The `play` method starts the cinematic.

```
Cinematic cinematic = new Cinematic(cubeNode, 30);
stateManager.attach(cinematic);
cinematic.addCinematicEvent(3, motionEvent);
cinematic.play();
```

When this sequence is executed you will see the cube rotating around the origin as shown in *Figure 5 – Cinematic Motion Example* (again, a red circle has been superimposed to show the cube's path). The full source code can be downloaded from `www.p8tech.com`. It differs from what we illustrated here. Once again, in the full version it has been setup to start, pause, and stop using the F1, F2, and F3 keys respectively.

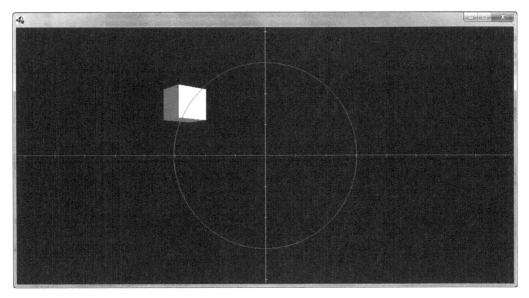

Figure 5 – Cinematic Motion Example

Using a Sound Event

A sound event can be used as part of a cinematic. It is supported by the com.jme3.cinematic.events package's SoundEvent class. The class possesses several constructors that allow the user to specify the sound resource, whether the audio is streamed, the initial duration of the sound, and the loop mode. In the following example, footsteps are played in a continuous loop:

```
SoundEvent soundEvent = new SoundEvent(
    "Sounds/Foot steps.ogg",LoopMode.Loop);
```

The event is then added to the cinematic as shown next. In this case, we are using the cinematic object created in the previous section.

```
cinematic.addCinematicEvent(0, soundEvent);
```

When executed, the footsteps sound is played and then, 3 seconds later, the cube will rotate.

Using a Listener with a Cinematic

When a cinematic is active, a listener can be attached to it and will be invoked on three conditions:

- `onPlay` – When the cinematic starts

- `onPause` – When the cinematic is paused

- `onStop` – When the cinematic stops

The `CinematicEventListener` interface is found in the `com.jme3.cinematic.events` package. It consists of the previous three methods. In the following sequence, an anonymous inner class is created with these methods implemented. Depending on the needs of the cinematic, various actions can be taken on these events. Here the fly-by-camera is disabled while the cinematic is active.

```
CinematicEventListener cel =
        new CinematicEventListener() {
    public void onPlay(CinematicEvent cinematic) {
        flyCam.setEnabled(false);
    }

    public void onPause(CinematicEvent cinematic) {
        flyCam.setEnabled(true);
    }

    public void onStop(CinematicEvent cinematic) {
        flyCam.setEnabled(true);
    }
};
```

To associate this inner class with a cinematic, the `addListener` method is used as shown here:

```
cinematic.addListener(cel);
```

Using an Animation Event

To demonstrate how to use an animation event, we will use the Sinbad model explained in *Understanding Model Animation* and combine it with music. The code used is similar to what we have used in previous sections.

The camera is moved and light is added to make Sinbad visible, as shown next. The model is loaded and then attached to the root node.

```
cam.setLocation(new Vector3f(0, 0, 14));
AmbientLight light = new AmbientLight();
rootNode.addLight(light);
```

```
Spatial sinbad = assetManager.loadModel(
    "Models/Sinbad/Sinbad.mesh.xml");
rootNode.attachChild(sinbad);
```

A controller is created for the animation and an anonymous inner class is used to create a listener for the control. We did not use the previous listener because in its onAnimCycleDone method, it sets the animation channel to IdleBase. In this example we want to let it run until the cinematics have completed so we left the methods empty. The control is then added to the model.

```
control = sinbad.getControl(AnimControl.class);

control.addListener(new AnimEventListener() {
    public void onAnimCycleDone(AnimControl control,
        AnimChannel channel, String animName) {
    }
    public void onAnimChange(AnimControl control,
        AnimChannel channel, String animName) {
    }
});
sinbad.addControl(control);
```

While the listener is not necessary for this example to work, it does illustrate how we can add one if needed.

Next, the channel is created. This is followed by the creation of an AnimationEvent object. This object is used by a Cinematic object to support the use of model animations within a cinematic. As shown next, it uses three arguments specifying the model, the name of the animation that is to be performed, and its loop mode. Sinbad is the model to be animated, the animation will be the dance animation, and it will loop for the duration of the cinematic.

```
danceChannel = control.createChannel();
AnimationEvent animationEvent = new AnimationEvent(
    sinbad, "Dance", LoopMode.Loop);
```

A sound event is also created as shown next. The Cinematic object is created with a 10 second cinematic. The model animation and the sound both start 5 seconds after the cinematic begins using the addCinematicEvent method. The cinematic is then started.

```
SoundEvent soundEvent = new SoundEvent(
    "Sounds/The_old_grey_goose.ogg", LoopMode.Loop);

cinematic = new Cinematic(rootNode, 10);
stateManager.attach(cinematic);
cinematic.addCinematicEvent(5, animationEvent);
cinematic.addCinematicEvent(5, soundEvent);
cinematic.play();
```

When executed, Sinbad will dance for 5 seconds.

Shades of Infinity - 7

This version of the game has been enhanced in several ways:

- The AI ships have been modified to allow separate motions

- One of the AI ships will follow a path

- We will then use a cinematic to achieve a similar effect

The use of a path provides one way of implementing behavior for the ships. Multiple paths can be defined and then applied, perhaps randomly, to one or more ships to provide a more challenging game. Levels of game difficulty can be supported where the more difficult levels use more difficult paths.

Ship Modifications

Normally you would not expect the enemy ships to travel together. To allow separate movement of the ships it is necessary to modify certain aspects of their nodes. To split them apart, the shootables reference variable was changed to an ArrayList of Nodes in the Main class as defined here:

```
static ArrayList<Node> shootables;
shootables = new ArrayList<Node>();
...
shootables.add(enemy1Node);
shootables.add(enemy2Node);
```

This resulted in the modification of the simpleUpdate method where we use a for-each loop:

```
public void simpleUpdate(float tpf) {
    ...
    for (Spatial spatial : shootables) {
        float d = cam.getLocation().distance(
            spatial.getWorldTranslation());
        if (d < distance) {
            distance = d;
        }
    }
    ...
}
```

In the CombatAppState the declaration of shootables and the onAction method were also modified:

```
public void onAction(String name, boolean keyPressed,
            float tpf) {
```

```
        if (name.equals(MAP_FIRE) && !keyPressed) {
            for (Spatial spatial : shootables) {
                addCollision(spatial);
            }
            laser.playInstance();
        }
    }
```

These changes allow for the independent movement of the ships. These can now be used with motion events and cinematics.

Adding the MotionEvent

We will use `MotionEvent` and `MotionPath` objects to control the behavior of one of the AI ships. The code used to create a path followed by the ship is similar to that used in Motion Paths and Way Points. Declare two instance variables for these objects so that we can access them in multiple methods as shown here:

```
private MotionPath path;
private MotionEvent motionEvent;
```

The path is defined using five way points as shown in the following code sequence:

```
path = new MotionPath();
path.addWayPoint(new Vector3f(0, 0, 4));
path.addWayPoint(new Vector3f(2, 2, 2));
path.addWayPoint(new Vector3f(3, 1, 0));
path.addWayPoint(new Vector3f(2, -2, 2));
path.addWayPoint(new Vector3f(3, -1, 3));
path.setCycle(true);
path.setCurveTension(1.0f);
```

We will use the first enemy from our previous version of the game with the path. In the following sequence, a `MotionEvent` object is created using the enemy and the previously defined path. A duration of 90 seconds is specified. The direction type is set so that the ship will always point in the direction of the path. The motion is then started.

```
motionEvent = new MotionEvent(enemy1Node, path);
motionEvent.setInitialDuration(90);
motionEvent.setDirectionType(
    MotionEvent.Direction.Path);
motionEvent.play();
```

The ship will follow the path as illustrated in *Figure 6 – Shades of Infinity MotionEvent Example*. In this figure, the ship is near the surface of the planet. Notice the ship's shadow. Axes have been added to make it easier to determine the position and orientation of the ships.

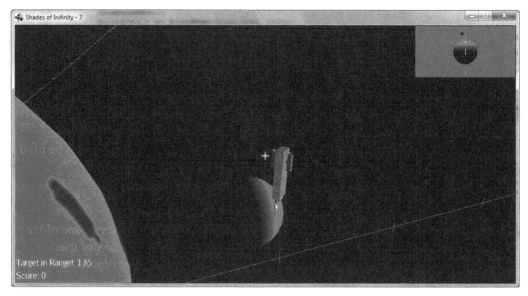

Figure 6 – Shades of Infinity MotionEvent Example

Adding Cinematics

We added a cinematic to the application to duplicate the behavior of the previous section. However, it differs in that it will loop for the duration of the cinematic and also uses a sound.

The code is similar to that used in *Understanding Cinematics* and is shown next. The code for the path is the same as used in the previous section. Again we used the first enemy and the duration of the cinematic is set for 60 seconds. We added the MotionEvent and SoundEvent instances to the cinematic.

```
motionEvent = new MotionEvent(enemy1Node, path);
motionEvent.setLoopMode(LoopMode.Loop);
motionEvent.setDirectionType(
    MotionEvent.Direction.Path);

SoundEvent soundEvent = new SoundEvent(
    "Sounds/Acid_techno.ogg", LoopMode.Loop);

cinematic = new Cinematic(enemy1Node, 60);
stateManager.attach(cinematic);
cinematic.addCinematicEvent(0, motionEvent);
cinematic.addCinematicEvent(0, soundEvent);
cinematic.play();
```

When executed, it will behave in the same way as for the earlier example but with sound added. In addition, it will loop until the ship is destroyed or the game ends. Cinematic is preferred over the use of a motion path alone because it can combine events and offers a more flexible way of controlling an animation.

Conclusion

We have covered how JME3 supports animation in this chapter. This includes the use of the `simpleUpdate` method to implement simple animations. More sophisticated model animations were discussed and illustrated using the Sinbad model. Models provide interesting and flexible ways of animating an object. However, they must be developed outside of JME3.

The use of way points provides a very useful technique for supporting cutscenes. Their use and potential was illustrated and then incorporated into a cinematic demonstration. These types of approaches can simplify "canned" animations in often efficient ways.

We also saw how many of this chapter's techniques can be added to a game using our Shades of Infinity game. This allowed us to provide more realistic movement to the AI ships.

In the next chapter we will learn how to create landscapes, skies, and how to show reflections off water.

8

Creating Landscapes

Introduction

Landscapes and their associated elements are an important aspect in many games. In this chapter we examine how we create terrains, sky, and water using JME3. These techniques are often fairly simple to use and can produce high quality images.

Terrains are created using a material whose appearance is controlled by a height map. We will see how we can create terrains in code and how they can be created using the JME3 Scene Composer.

Skies are also easy to add to a game. The process involves creating a spatial and attaching a sky texture to it. There is a `SkyFactory` class that assists in this process.

Water can be used in a number of ways in a game. It can be used to simulate an ocean, river, and smaller bodies such as ponds. JME3 supports two techniques for rendering water: the `SimpleWaterProcess` class and the `WaterFilter` class. The `SimpleWaterProcess` class offers a technique that is less CPU intensive but is limited in some features. The `WaterFilter` class is more capable, including the ability to render underwater scenes, but requires more computational power.

Due to the nature of the Shades of Infinity game, we won't apply this chapter's techniques to the game.

Understanding and Creating Terrains

Terrain is the fundamental element of a landscape. The terrain usually refers to the ground level of the game world. This includes grass, water, trees, mountains, roads, and any other objects you would find on the surface of your game world. Terrain in JME3 can be created using only code, or using the scene creation tool called the **Scene Composer**. When working with code there are three important concepts we need to cover:

- **Heightmaps** – A heightmap can be either a special type of image or an array of float values that represent varying heights to be applied to a terrain.

- **Alpha Textures** – An Alpha texture, or **Alpha Map**, is an image using various colors or transparencies as placeholders for appropriate textures such as dirt or grass.

- **TerrainQuad** – The `TerrainQuad` class supports a height-based terrain system. The base of the system has four children and each child has four children of its own. This pattern continues down to the actual patches of terrain.

We will see how each of these are used to create terrains in this section.

Creating Code-Based Terrain

In this section we will use code to create a terrain. In Creating a Terrain with the Scene Composer, we will use JME3's Scene Composer to create a terrain. The code-based process uses the following steps:

1. Create a Material
2. Create the Heightmap
3. Create an Alpha Texture
4. Create and apply the various terrain textures
5. Create a `TerrainQuad` object

Throughout this section we will create a terrain that has a valley surrounded by mountains. We will be able to create much of this terrain using components that are available in JME3.

The first step is fairly obvious. Like most elements we have created thus far, we will need a material to make the object visible. The next step involves developing a heightmap that will represent the hills and valleys of the terrain. As we will see later, there are several ways to create a heightmap.

Once we have a heightmap in place we can use an Alpha map to prepare the terrain for various textures. Each different color on the Alpha map can have a different texture applied to it, representing different types of terrains.

The final step is creating the `TerrainQuad` object. This object ties all the pieces together to create a complete terrain. When we finish these steps we should have a terrain similar to the one pictured in *Figure 1 - Final Terrain*. This is a zoomed out view of the completed terrain example.

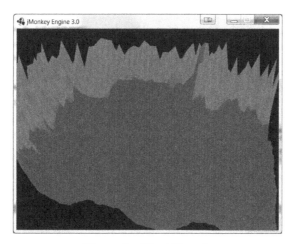

Figure 1 - Final Terrain

Defining the Material

The first step is defining the material. In the following example we use the
`Terrain.j3md`, which has been configured to act as terrain.

```
Material terrainMaterial = new Material(assetManager,
    "Common/MatDefs/Terrain/Terrain.j3md");
```

JME3 has several preloaded images in the `test-data` library. Several of the images we
will use are found in the `Textures/Terrain/splat` folder.

Defining the Heightmap

Heightmaps are one of the most efficient ways to represent the hills and curves of a
landscape. Heightmaps can be created using two different methods. The first method
uses an image to represent height values. The second method uses an array of float
values between 0 and 255 to represent low and high values.

Creating a Heightmap from Image

Heightmap images are grayscale, where lighter shades represent high points and darker
shades represent low points. In the next example we will use `fortress512.png` for our
heightmap as shown in *Figure 2 - Fortress512 Image*. This image defines our heightmap.
The light area represents a ridge surrounding a valley.

Figure 2 - Fortress512 Image

To create a heightmap based on a texture:

    1. Create a `Texture` object with a heightmap image

    2. Create an `AbstractHeightMap` object from an `ImageBasedHeightMap`

    3. Load the heightmap

The `AbstractHeightMap` object will represent the heightmap in the game.

The `Texture` class is located in the `com.jme3.texture` package. The next statement creates a heightmap using a `Texture` object. The texture is called `heightMapImage` and uses the `assetManager` to load the fortress512 image.

```
Texture heightMapImage = assetManager.loadTexture(
    "Textures/Terrain/splat/fortress512.png");
```

The `AbstractHeightMap` class is located in the `com.jme3.terrain.heightmap` package. This class provides the base implementation for height map terrain rendering. To create an `AbstractHeightMap` object we will create a new `ImageBasedHeightMap`. The parameter will be the `heightMapImage` object. This may seem a little convoluted at first, but it will make more sense when you examine the code segment here:

```
AbstractHeightMap heightmap =
    new ImageBasedHeightMap(heightMapImage.getImage());
```

The final step is loading the heightmap. This is accomplished by calling the `load` method against an `AbstractHeightMap` object. This method simply populates the heightmap data that was extracted from the image.

```
heightmap.load();
```

Now we have a functional heightmap called `heightmap` that can be used with the terrain.

Creating a Heightmap from Array

You can also create a heightmap by specifying an array of float values to represent heights. Rather than storing each pixel individually, heightmaps use a grid of samples to outline the terrain. The points between the samples are interpolated. Interpolation is a mathematical concept that basically creates new points based on a range of known points.

A heightmap is defined as a float array with values between 0 and 255. The following are guidelines for values used to represent various heights:

- 0-100 represents valleys or low areas

- 100-200 represents average areas

- 200-255 represents the hills

In order to create a heightmap, we need an array of `float` values. Rather than creating various heightmap objects like we did in the previous example, we can populate an array with values between 0 and 255. The array can then be added to the `TerrainQuad` in place of a heightmap.

We need to determine the number of values you need for a functional heightmap. In the previous heightmap example, we created an image that has 262,143 float values (512^2-1) to represent the heights. So, if you decide to manually populate a heightmap using the array method, you will probably want to stick to a much smaller terrain.

Defining an Alpha Texture

An **Alpha Texture** uses colors to represent textures. Alpha textures like this allow us to place specific textures on to the differently colored areas. We will apply a dirt texture to the green mountains and a grass texture to the surrounding red areas.

To apply an alpha texture, use the following steps:

1. Color a heightmap image with red, green, and blue colors

2. Add the image to JME3

3. Load the image with the `setTexture` method

Alpha textures are created from grayscale heightmaps as we discussed in the previous section. We will be using the `Fortress512.png` image as the basis for our alpha map. To create our alpha texture we will take the fortress512 image and add color to it using an outside editor such as Microsoft Paint. The colors used to make alpha textures are red, green, and blue. For this example we will color the mountains green and the surrounding area red. The resulting image is shown in *Figure 3 - Alpha Map*.

Figure 3 - Alpha Map

After coloring the image we will save it as `fortressAlpha.png`. Then we can simply drag and drop the image into the appropriate assets folder.

Finally, to set the alpha texture we call the `setTexture` method against our material, as shown next. The first parameter defines the texture as an Alpha texture by using the `Alpha` string. The second parameter defines the location of the texture through the `assetManager.loadTexture` method. This sets the alpha texture to the material we created earlier.

```
terrainMaterial.setTexture("Alpha",
    assetManager.loadTexture(
        "Textures/fortressAlpha.png"));
```

Defining the Terrain Textures

To create the grass for the terrain we will create a new texture using the `assetManager` to load the grass texture as shown next. Then we set a wrap mode, `WrapMode`, to repeat the texture using the `setWrap` method. This allows the texture to repeat across the designated area on the terrain.

```
Texture grass = assetManager.loadTexture(
        "Textures/Terrain/splat/grass.jpg");
grass.setWrap(WrapMode.Repeat);
```

The grass texture is smaller than the material. We need to duplicate it to fill a scene. Unfortunately, at a distance the tiles may be noticeable. Next we will set the texture to the terrain material using `Tex1` and the grass texture as parameters.

```
terrainMaterial.setTexture("Tex1", grass);
```

Optionally you can set the scale of the texture by calling the `setFloat` method against the terrain material as shown in the next statement. The larger the value used, the more repeating textures are used on the terrain.

```
terrainMaterial.setFloat("Tex1Scale", 64f);
```

The appearance of different texture values is shown in *Figure 4 - Grass Texture Scales*. Both of these images are taken from the same distance.

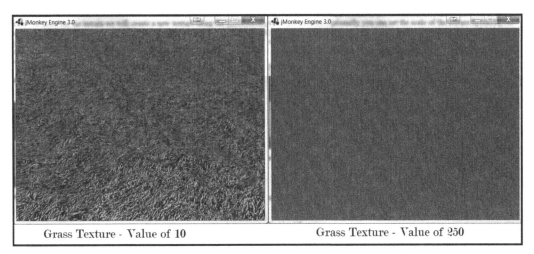

| Grass Texture - Value of 10 | Grass Texture - Value of 250 |

Figure 4 - Grass Texture Scales

Next, we will apply a dirt texture in a similar fashion as shown. The only difference here is that we will use a different name: `Tex2` instead of `Tex1`.

```
Texture dirt = assetManager.loadTexture(
        "Textures/Terrain/splat/dirt.jpg");
dirt.setWrap(WrapMode.Repeat);
terrainMaterial.setTexture("Tex2", dirt);
terrainMaterial.setFloat("Tex2Scale", 32f);
```

Now that we have the textures applied to the Alpha map we are ready to bring it all together using `TerrainQuad`.

Defining the `TerrainQuad`

The `TerrainQuad` class is located in the `com.jme3.terrain.geomipmap` package. We will use this class to create the final terrain. This is the object that takes all the elements we have created so far and brings them together.

Use the following steps to create/apply a `TerrainQuad`:

1. Create a `TerrainQuad` object

2. Set the material

3. Translate the `TerrainQuad` object if necessary

4. Attach it to the `rootNode`

We will create a `TerrainQuad` called `terrain`. The first parameter to the `TerrainQuad` constructor is a string that identifies the terrain. This can be any name you like. The next two parameters are the tile size and the block size. These values represent the size and detail of the terrain. We will describe these in more detail in the next section. The final parameter is the heightmap.

For the following example, we will use the heightmap that we created earlier. We need to call the `getHeightMap` method against our `heightmap`. This will return the height values we extracted from our image. If you created a heightmap from an array, you can place the array here. If this value is `null`, a flat heightmap will be generated.

```
TerrainQuad terrain = new TerrainQuad(
    "my terrain", 65, 513, heightmap.getHeightMap());
```

The second step is applying our material to the `TerrainQuad`. This is accomplished using the `setMaterial` method as shown here:

```
terrain.setMaterial(terrainMaterial);
```

The third step involves applying transformations if they are needed. `TerrainQuad`s can be transformed just like any other spatial if you would like to alter their position, rotation, or scale. For this example we will move the terrain 100 units lower. Otherwise the terrain will load above our starting position.

```
terrain.setLocalTranslation(0, -100, 0);
```

The final step is attaching the terrain to the `rootNode`:

```
rootNode.attachChild(terrain);
```

Understanding the Tile and Block Size

The tile size, or patch size, is an integer value that represents the number of individual tiles in the terrain. A tile, or patch, is a visible piece of the terrain that can be individually culled. The number of tiles must be smaller than the total size of the terrain. The total size of the terrain we have been creating will be 512, because this is the size of our heightmap. Our tiles must also be smaller than this. Tiles must be a power of 2 plus 1. For our example we will use 65. In most cases 65 is a good starting value for terrain tiles.

The block size represents the actual size of the terrain in World Units. For our example we will use 513. We used a heightmap of size 512, and like the tiles we must add 1 to get 513. You will usually want to create a terrain of the same size as the heightmap you used. If we defined a block size of 2x the heightmap, the terrain would be stretched out and flat. If we defined a block size of ½ the heightmap, the terrain would be smaller and more detailed.

When you run the code you should see something similar to *Figure 5 - Terrain Example*.

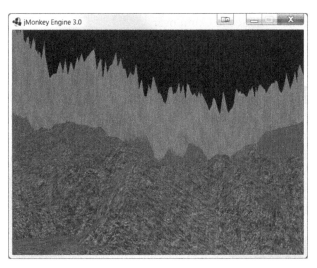

Figure 5 - Terrain Example

Optimizing the Level of Detail

JME3 provides a `TerrainLodControl` class that is used to optimize terrain rendering. This class is found in the `com.jme3.terrain.geomipmap` package. This class is technically a control that uses the camera distance to determine how much of the terrain to render. The level of detail will increase as the camera approaches sections of the terrain. As the camera moves away from the terrain, details will be reduced. This allows us to load larger terrains without burning up all of our processing resources. When we add this control to the terrain it will optimize the rendering process automatically behind the scenes. The `TerrainLodControl` class' constructor will also accept a list of cameras rather than a single camera, if you are using multiple cameras in your game.

To create a new `TerrainLodControl` object we will need our `TerrainQuad` and the camera we are using. As shown next, we will use `terrain` that we created earlier, and `getCamera` to return our camera. Once we have the new `TerrainLodControl` created we can attach it to our terrain via the `addControl` method.

```
TerrainLodControl lodControl =
    new TerrainLodControl(terrain, getCamera());
terrain.addControl(lodControl)
```

Creating a Terrain with the Scene Composer

We can create a terrain using the Scene Composer and the Terrain Editor, also known as **TerraMonkey**. This will allow us to develop a terrain and a heightmap using visual tools. When we create terrain using this method, the default material will be a lighted terrain material. As you may recall, this means that we will need a light source to make the terrain visible. To create a terrain using the Scene Composer:

1.   Create an Empty Scene

2.   Edit the scene with Scene Composer

3.   Add a terrain spatial

4.   Fill in details with the Terrain Wizard

5.   Optionally use the Terrain Editor to further configure the terrain

Creating an Empty Scene

To create an empty JME3 Scene, right click on the Texture folder where you want to store the terrain and select Other. In the Categories list box, select Scene and then Empty JME3 Scene. The resulting dialog box is shown in *Figure 6 - Create Empty Scene*.

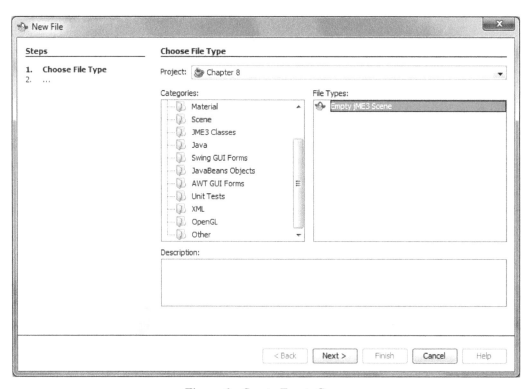

Figure 6 - Create Empty Scene

Use any name you like to the empty scene and click Finish. This will create an empty scene using the name you provided with a .j3o file type as shown in *Figure 7 - Scene Composer.*

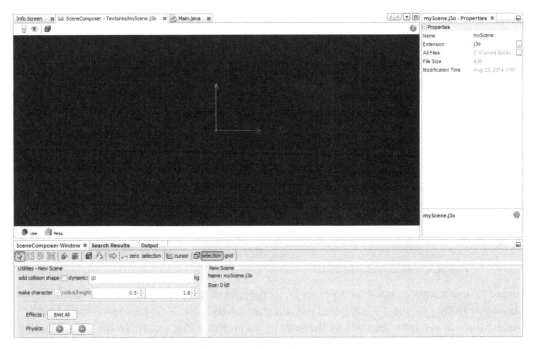

Figure 7 - Scene Composer

Using the Scene Composer

We need to edit the scene using the Scene Composer. Right click the .j3o file and click Edit in Scene Composer. This will open up the Scene Composer in JME3 as shown in in the bottom left- hand corner of *Figure 7 - Scene Composer*. Right click on New Scene in the SceneExplorer tab and select Add Spatial -> Terrain as demonstrated in *Figure 8 - Create Terrain*.

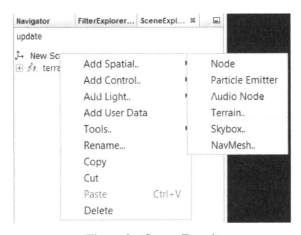

Figure 8 - Create Terrain

This will bring up the Terrain Wizard as shown in *Figure 9 - Terrain Size*. This wizard uses three steps:

1. Configure the total and patch sizes

2. Configure the heightmap

3. Configure the Alpha-blend texture size

The wizard provides the ability to customize the terrain.

Configuring the Total and Patch sizes

The first step in the process is defining the total terrain and patch sizes. This works pretty much the same way as with the `TerrainQuad` we created in the previous section. You will provide values for:

*   The total size, similar to block size

*   The patch size, similar to tile size

Both of these numbers must be a power of 2. A good default total size to use when playing with this tool is 512. A good default patch size is 64. You can play around with these values to see how they affect the terrain. Remember, the patch size must be smaller than the total size.

Figure 9 - Terrain Size

Configuring the Heightmap

Select Next, which brings up the Heightmap window in the Terrain Wizard. This window will give us three options as seen in *Figure 10 - Heightmap Options*.

Figure 10 - Heightmap Options

These three options include: Flat, Image Based, and Hill:

- The Flat option is used for a field, the floor of a building, or any other surface that would be level without any hills

- The Image Based option creates a heightmap based on a grayscale image. This works in the same way as discussed in the Using Heightmaps section.

- The Hill option has four integer values that must be specified: Iterations, Flattening, Min radius, and Max radius.

If the Hill option is selected, then the Terrain Wizard dialog will appear as shown in *Figure 11 - Heightmap Hill Options*.

Figure 11 - Heightmap Hill Options

These hill values will create random hills across the terrain. Iterations define the number of hills that will be generated. The Min radius value defines the minimum radius of the generated hills. The Max radius value determines the maximum radius of the generated hills. Increasing the Flattening value makes the terrain less hilly. A comparison between a low flattening value and a high flattening value is shown in *Figure 12 - Flattening*.

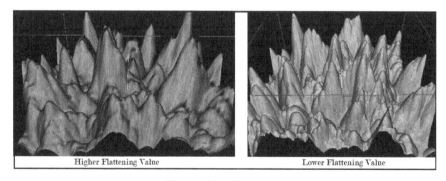

Figure 12 - Flattening

Select the Flat heightmap option. We will use this in the next section because a flat terrain will allow us to make changes using the Terrain Editor. The default terrain will look like *Figure 13 - Flat Terrain*

Figure 13 - Flat Terrain

Configuring the Alpha-blend Texture Size

The last step in the terrain creation process defines the Alpha-blend texture size. This screen looks like *Figure 14 - AlphaBlend Texture*. This value is used to blend several textures together into one texture for the terrain. The default value is the same as the terrain size.

Figure 14 - AlphaBlend Texture

Select Finish and the terrain defined in the .j3o file has been configured.

Using the Terrain Editor

JME3 provides a terrain editor that is referred to in the JMonkey community as **TerraMonkey**. This editor gives precise control over where hills, mountains, and textures are placed. To begin the texture painting process, right click on the .j3o scene and select Edit Terrain. This will open up the Terrain Editor in JME3. The editor works similar to the scene composer and will appear as shown in *Figure 15 - Terrain Editor*.

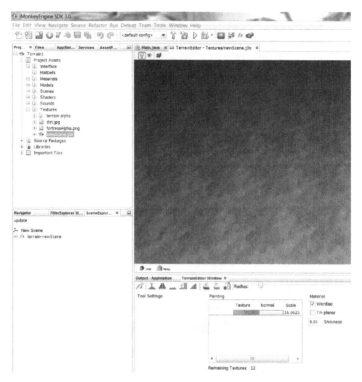

Figure 15 - Terrain Editor

There are three sets of buttons on the toolbar found below the image. The first set adds a terrain, the second adds heightmap features to the terrain, and the third set is used for painting a texture. The first button is fairly self-explanatory. It simply brings up the Terrain Wizard from the Scene Composer section.

Using the Terrain Editor Heightmap Tools

The second set of tools is used for editing the height of the terrain. An image of the available heightmap tools is found in *Figure 16 - Heightmap Tools*.

1. Raise Terrain
2. Smooth Terrain
3. Rough Terrain
4. Level Terrain
5. Slop Terrain

Figure 16 - Heightmap Tools

The first button is used to raise the terrain, or create hills. Clicking the button brings up a polygon sphere on the terrain. You can move an editing sphere around the terrain by moving the mouse. Holding down the left click button raises the terrain. The longer you hold down the left mouse button on one spot, the bigger the hill becomes.

You can move the mouse while holding down the button to upraise the terrain in a more natural way. There is also a slider to determine the radius of the sphere as well as the height. You can see a hill being created in *Figure 17 - Height Tool*.

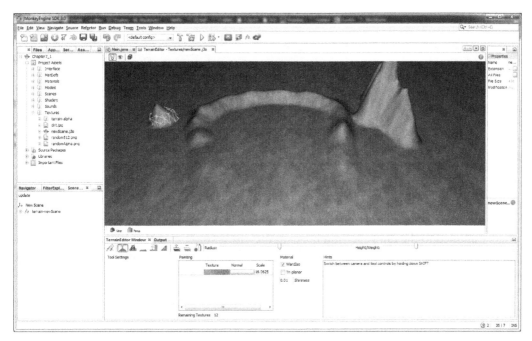

Figure 17 - Height Tool

The second button does the exact opposite of the height tool. This is the smooth terrain tool. It reduces hills rather than creating them. Simply hold down the left button in the same way as before.

The third button creates rough terrain. This basically makes the terrain more textured and natural looking. Take a look at *Figure 18 - Rough Terrain Tool* to see the effects of the rough terrain tool. The yellow sphere determines which areas are roughened.

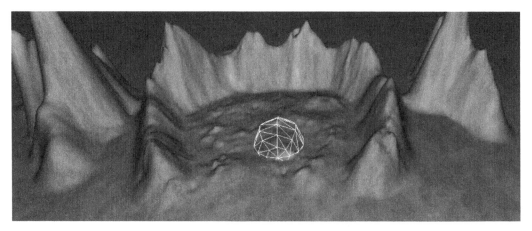

Figure 18 - Rough Terrain Tool

The fourth button is used to level the terrain back to its original flat state. The last button adds slope to the terrain. The effect of the slope tool is frequently not very noticeable.

Painting Textures

Textures are applied in layers in TerraMonkey. The terrain is originally created with one texture layer. As we have seen so far, the original texture layer is dirt. The phrase "painting textures" is a little bit misleading. When you want to add a new texture it is actually applied to the entire terrain beneath the dirt texture, completely out of sight. Rather than painting a new texture on top of the original texture, we erase parts of the top layer revealing the new texture underneath. This is essentially the same as painting on a texture in reverse. The end result is the same.

The terrain editor gives you several tools to paint textures onto the terrain as shown in *Figure 19 - Texture Painting Tools*. You can add up to 12 layers of textures. We will examine each of the features depicted in the figure.

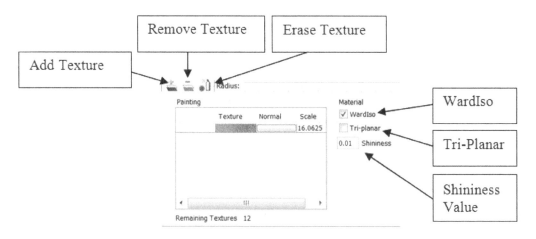

Figure 19 - Texture Painting Tools

The first button on the top left allows you to add a new texture. When selected, it will bring up a dialog box as shown in *Figure 20 - Texture Browser Dialog Box*.

To demonstrate this process we will paint a grass texture onto the terrain. Click on the add texture button, this is the first button of the three texture painting buttons. This will bring up a window to choose a texture. You can find this texture, `Grass_256.png`, in the `Blender/2.4x/textures` folder as shown in *Figure 20 - Texture Browser Dialog Box*. The second button is used to remove a texture layer.

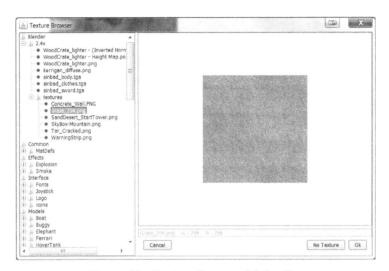

Figure 20 - Texture Browser Dialog Box

Next, click on the Erase Texture button, which technically erases a texture from the terrain. Every time we add a texture it is added beneath the previous texture. Therefore we can erase the top texture wherever we want, revealing the grass texture underneath. We simply left click wherever we want the grass to appear. Painting the grass, or erasing the texture above the grass, should look similar to *Figure 21 - Grass Texture*.

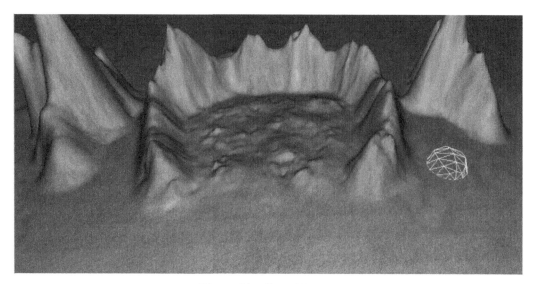

Figure 21 - Grass Texture

There is also a shininess box used to control the shininess of the texture. You can see this box on the right side of *Figure 19 - Texture Painting Tools*. It is set to 0.01 by default. If you decide to increase the shininess using the box provided it will look similar to *Figure 22 - Shiny Terrain*.

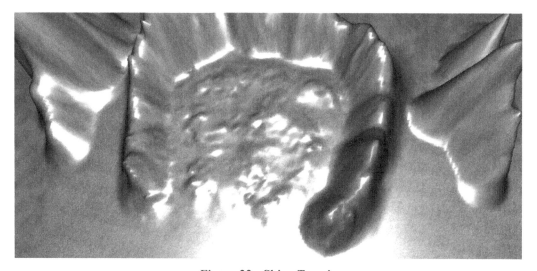

Figure 22 - Shiny Terrain

There is a checkbox on the texture painting panel that enables a WardIso option, which stands for Ward Isotropic Gaussian Specular Shader. You can see why they chose to shorten it to WardIso. This is a type of shader. You may recall that shaders are used in the GPU to accelerate rendering. Re-examine Chapter 5 for a refresher on shaders.

You may have noticed that this option is enabled by default. This particular type of shader is typically used for a metal or plastic appearance. It will have different effects with varying levels of shininess. A comparison between enabling and disabling WardIso is shown in *Figure 23 - Effects of WardIso*.

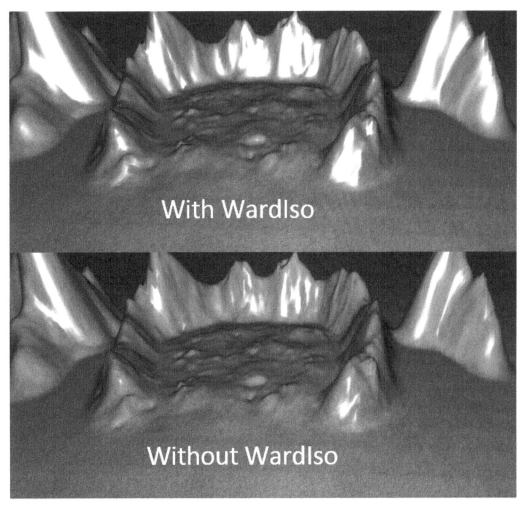

Figure 23 - Effects of WardIso

On the same panel there is a check box to enable Tri-planar Mapping. For completely flat terrain you will not need to enable this option. Tri-planar Mapping enables rendering in the Y plane. Without it, rendering only takes place on the X and Z planes, which can make mountain and hill textures appear stretched out. If you have a lot of hills and mountains you may want to enable Tri-planar mapping. You should keep in mind that while this will make your terrain more aesthetically pleasing, it will also have an impact on performance.

The texture painting tools have an option to add a normal map to a texture as well. You may recall from Chapter 5 that a normal map is used to create a more realistic appearance by adding bumps or cracks to the surface. By default no normal map is added. To add a normal map, click on the button pointed to in *Figure 24 - Texture Painting Table* and select a normal map. You may also notice that you can change the scale of the texture as specified by the last column of the table.

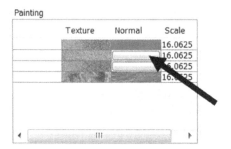

Figure 24 - Texture Painting Table

Adding a Light Source

When using TerraMonkey and the Scene Composer you have the option to add a light source directly to the terrain. Because the terrain breaks down into tiles, or patches, we can add lights to individual tiles or the entire terrain. You may find this much easier than adding light sources in code later on.

To add a light source, right click on the scene in the bottom left corner of JME3, which will bring up a list of items you can add to the terrain. Selecting Add Light will bring up a list of lights you can add including: Ambient, Directional, Spot, and Point lights. Take a look at *Figure 25 - Add Lights* to see how this looks.

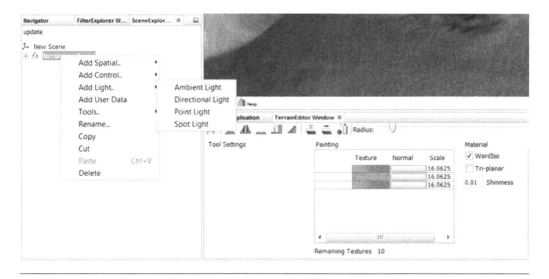

Figure 25 - Add Lights

If you add multiple lights you will notice the scene gets brighter. You also have the option to add lights to specific sections or even individual tiles of the terrain. To do this, expand the terrain by clicking the plus box to the left of the terrain as depicted in *Figure 26 - Expand Terrain*.

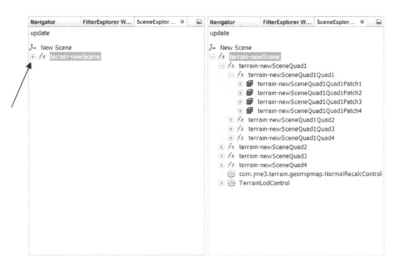

Figure 26 - Expand Terrain

You will notice the terrain splits into quads, or groups of four, all the way down to the individual patches. Hopefully this will give you a better understanding of how `TerrainQuads` work. You can add a light source to any of these components by right clicking and choosing the Add Light option for that item.

Loading New Terrain

At this point we have successfully created a terrain using the Scene Composer and TerraMonkey. Now we need to load it into the game. We will treat the new scene as a model and load it using the `assetManager`'s `loadModel` method. First, create a new spatial called `terrain` and load our scene into it. Then we will simply attach it to the `rootNode` as shown here:

```
Spatial terrain =
    assetManager.loadModel("Textures/newScene.j3o");
rootNode.attachChild(terrain);
```

Remember, when you create a terrain in TerraMonkey it uses a lighted terrain material by default. This means you will need a light source for this terrain to be visible unless we add light as we did in the previous section.

Understanding and Creating a Sky

A sky is important because it provides a more visually pleasing backdrop than the default black background that we have been using thus far. To add a sky we need to:

1. Create a new `Spatial`

2. Load the sky texture using the `SkyFactory`

3. Attach the spatial to the `rootNode`

Creating a sky texture is a process that must be carried out using a graphic editor like Blender. JME3 provides a few different textures we can use for sky. Once we have a sky texture to use, we will need to create a new spatial and load the texture into it using the `SkyFactory` class. The final step is attaching the spatial to the `rootNode` to make it visible.

Loading a Sky

A sky is created in JME3 using the `SkyFactory` class found in the `com.jme3.util` package. For this example we will use `BrightSky.dds` from the test-data library. The exact location of this sky is `Textures/Sky/Bright/BrightSky.dds`.

The `SkyFactory` class' `createSky` method will load the sky texture as specified by its second parameter. Its first parameter is the `assetManager`. The last parameter is a boolean value that is set to `false` when using a box texture, and set to `true` when using a sphere. The default sky texture uses a box texture, which is why we used the `false` parameter. It returns a `Spatial` object representing the sky. The last step is to add the sky to the scene graph as shown here:

```
Spatial sky = SkyFactory.createSky(assetManager,
    "Textures/Sky/Bright/BrightSky.dds", false);
rootNode.attachChild(sky);
```

The result should appear similar to *Figure 27 - SkyFactory Image*.

Figure 27 - SkyFactory Image

You will notice that the sky texture we chose to use in the example has mountains. You may not want mountains in your landscape. Luckily, JME3 provides a few alternative choices we can use. You may want to try out `FullskiesBlueClear03.dds`. This is located in the same folder as the previous example. The new sky texture can be seen in *Figure 28 - Alternate Sky*.

Figure 28 - Alternate Sky

There is also a sky texture located in `Scenes/Beach/FullskiesSunset0068.dds`. This sky texture is pictured in *Figure 29 - Sunset Sky*.

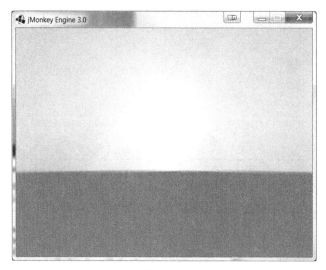

Figure 29 - Sunset Sky

Behind the scenes, `SkyFactory` calls a couple of additional methods that aid in sky texture rendering. The first of these methods is the `sky.setQueueBucket(Bucket.Sky)` method. This method ensures that the sky is rendered behind all the other landscape elements. The `setCullHint` method is also called and set to `CullHint.Never`. This ensures that the sky texture is never invisible.

Building a Sky Box with Individual Images

It is also possible to load a sky using separate images as sections of the texture. In the next example we will load a sky texture using an image for West, East, North, South, Up and Down. This allows us to create a sky texture using a variation of the `createSky` method. This version takes the `assetManager` and 6 textures as parameters. The default sky is a box with the order of the images being West, East, North, South, Up and Down, as defined in the API. Optionally, we could add an integer to represent a sphere radius as a final parameter to build a dome sky. It is a good idea to take a look at the `SkyFactory` API to get a better feel for the different `createSky` methods available.

We will use the images located at `Textures/Sky/Lagoon` where there are six images named for their position in the sky texture layout. These images are: `lagoon_down`, `lagoon_up`, `lagoon_east`, `lagoon_west`, `lagoon_south`, and `lagoon_north`. These images are shown in *Figure 30 - Lagoon Sky Images*.

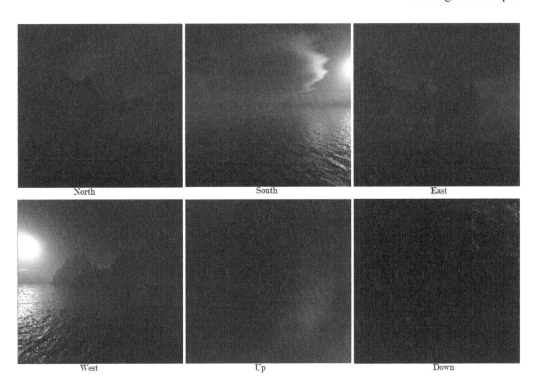

| North | South | East |
| West | Up | Down |

Figure 30 - Lagoon Sky Images

As you can see there is a separate image for each section. First, we need to create a texture from each image. Create an array of textures and assign the images to the textures in the correct order as shown below. Next, insert the textures as parameters to the createSky method.

```
Texture[] skyTex = new Texture[6];
skyTex[0] = assetManager.loadTexture(
    "Textures/Sky/Lagoon/lagoon_west.jpg");
skyTex[1] = assetManager.loadTexture(
    "Textures/Sky/Lagoon/lagoon_east.jpg");
skyTex[2] = assetManager.loadTexture(
    "Textures/Sky/Lagoon/lagoon_north.jpg");
skyTex[3] = assetManager.loadTexture(
    "Textures/Sky/Lagoon/lagoon_south.jpg");
skyTex[4] = assetManager.loadTexture(
    "Textures/Sky/Lagoon/lagoon_up.jpg");
skyTex[5] = assetManager.loadTexture(
    "Textures/Sky/Lagoon/lagoon_down.jpg");
Spatial sky = SkyFactory.createSky(assetManager,
    skyTex[0], skyTex[1], skyTex[2], skyTex[3],
    skyTex[4], skyTex[5]);
rootNode.attachChild(sky);
```

The result is the sky texture pictured in *Figure 31 - Lagoon Sky*.

Figure 31 - Lagoon Sky

Loading a Dome Sky

Up until this point we have been using sky textures based on a cube. It is also possible to load a sky using a spherical approach. To do this we can provide any image to the createSky method using the true parameter instead of false. However, there is a side effect to using this approach. Applying an ordinary image to a sphere will cause a blemish on the scene where the corners come together.

In the following example we will use the image located at Textures/Sky/St Peters/StPeters.jpg. We will load this the same way as before, however we will use true as the final parameter instead of false.

```
Spatial sky = SkyFactory.createSky(assetManager,
    "Textures/Sky/St Peters/StPeters.jpg", true);
rootNode.attachChild(sky);
```

The result should be similar to *Figure 32 - St. Peter's Sky*.

Figure 32 - St. Peter's Sky

There are two negative side effects to using the dome method in this way. The first is that the images appear upside down in the scene. This particular problem is easily fixed by rotating an image before adding it to JME3. The second problem is the blemish caused by the edges coming together. The blemish appears on the side of the sky dome. Half of the dome appears correctly and the other half has the blemish where the sides of the original image are pulled together as highlighted in *Figure 33 - Sky Dome Blemish.*

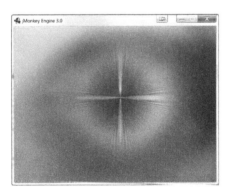

Figure 33 - Sky Dome Blemish

Creating a Sky Texture

JME3 does not have a built in way to create sky textures. However, there are tools like Blender that have the ability to create these textures. There are also a variety of free textures available online. These textures are typically created in box or sphere formats, but JME3 will also accept a more complex node that contains geometries for moving clouds and other objects.

Using Water and Reflection

There are several techniques for generating scenes using water and reflections. We will examine the use of the `SimpleWaterProcess` class and the SeaMonkey `WaterFilter` class to render water.

Using the `SimpleWaterProcess` Class

The `SimpleWaterProcess` class is used for simple water surfaces that are typically shallow and need limited wave motion. It does not support underwater effects but requires fewer resources than the SeaMonkey `WaterFilter` class.

To achieve a water effect, this technique uses shaders and the `SimpleWater.j3md` material found in `Common/MatDefs/Water/`. A quad is created to represent the water's surface and a normal is used to create the wave effect. A quad is a rectangular plane defined by four vertices.

Water does not normally exist by itself. It is frequently used in conjunction with a terrain and a sky. To use water, the terrain and sky are added to the scene first. After this is done, there are three tasks to perform:

1. Create and configure an instance of the `SimpleWaterProcess` class

2. Create and configure a `Quad` object

3. Create a geometry to represent the water from the `Quad` object

The `SimpleWaterProcess` instance sets up the processor so that it can properly render the water. The `Quad` object represents the water and is also used to specify how high any waves may be. The geometry determines where the water will appear and is the target of the processor.

We will reuse the terrain and sky developed in the previous sections. If simulating an ocean, the following method may be useful to add an ocean sound to the application:

```
private void createWaterSound() {
    AudioNode background = new AudioNode(assetManager,
        "Sound/Environment/Ocean Waves.ogg");
    background.setVolume(0.3f);
    background.setLooping(true);
    rootNode.attachChild(background);
    background.play();
}
```

Creating and Configuring the `SimpleWaterProcess` class

An instance of the `SimpleWaterProcessor` class needs to be created and configured. The configuration includes:

- Specifying the scene to be reflected

- Determining where the water surface will be

- Adding the processor to the current viewport

- Specifying the water's depth

- Specifying the amount of water distortion

- Specifying the wave speed

At a minimum, we need to accomplish the first three tasks. In the following code sequence, an instance of the `SimpleWaterProcessor` class is created and the `setReflectionScene` method uses the `rootNode` as its argument. This informs the water processor that the scene formed by the `rootNode` is to be reflected.

```
SimpleWaterProcessor waterProcessor =
    new SimpleWaterProcessor(assetManager);
waterProcessor.setReflectionScene(rootNode);
```

If a directional light source was not created for a scene, then the `setLightPosition` method needs to be used to specify a source as shown here:

```
waterProcessor.setLightPosition(
    new Vector3f(0.55f, -0.82f, 0.15f));
```

A plane is used to represent the water's surface. The `setPlane` method specifies the origin of the water quad and the direction of reflections. The origin and reflection normal of the plane is specified using two `Vector3f` objects. In the following code sequence, a `Vector3f` object is created with a value of `-6` for the Y axis. This corresponds to the position of the quad as we will see shortly. A second `Vector3f` object representing `(0,1,0)` is used to specify the direction of reflection which is along the Y axis.

```
Vector3f waterLocation = new Vector3f(0, -6, 0);
waterProcessor.setPlane(
    new Plane(Vector3f.UNIT_Y,
        waterLocation.dot(Vector3f.UNIT_Y)));
```

It is necessary to add the water processor to the view port as shown here:

```
viewPort.addProcessor(waterProcessor);
```

We can also control the transparency of the water, how rough it appears, and how fast the waves move using the `setWaterDepth`, `setDistortionScale`, and `setWaveSpeed` methods respectively. These are all optional with default values used if they are not specified explicitly.

In the following sequence, the depth is set to be fairly shallow with a moderate level of distortion and slow wave movement. When you execute the completed example, play with these values to see how the appearance of the water changes.

```
waterProcessor.setWaterDepth(10);
waterProcessor.setDistortionScale(0.15f);
waterProcessor.setWaveSpeed(0.05f);
```

Creating and Configuring the Quad class

The Quad class is found in the com.jme3.scene.shape package. This class represents a 2D rectangle plane defined by four vertices. It is used here to represent the area used by the water. As shown in the following code, the constructor used takes a width and a height as its parameters. The scaleTextureCoordinates method uses a Vector3f object to scale the texture coordinates. The values used here will result in the texture being tiled.

```
Quad quad = new Quad(400, 400);
quad.scaleTextureCoordinates(new Vector2f(6f, 6f));
```

Creating the Water's Geometry

A Geometry object needs to be added to the scene. In the following example a Geometry object is created based on the previously created Quad object:

```
Geometry water = new Geometry("water", quad);
```

It is then rotated and translated as follows. The Y value should be the same as the one used for the quad.

```
water.setLocalRotation(new Quaternion().
    fromAngleAxis(-FastMath.HALF_PI, Vector3f.UNIT_X));
water.setLocalTranslation(-200, -6, 250);
```

In order for the water to receive shadows we need to use the setShadowMode method as shown next. Shadows were discussed in Chapter 6. The material used by the water is provided by the WaterProcessor class.

```
water.setShadowMode(RenderQueue.ShadowMode.Receive);
water.setMaterial(waterProcessor.getMaterial());
```

The last step is to attach the water geometry to the scene as shown here:

```
rootNode.attachChild(water);
```

When this example is executed, it will appear as shown in *Figure 34 - SimpleWaterProcess Example*.

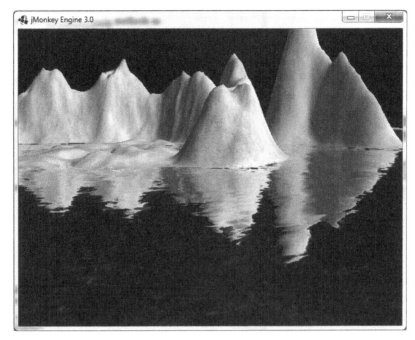

Figure 34 - SimpleWaterProcess Example

Using the SeaMonkey WaterFilter

The SeaMonkey `WaterFilter` class is based on Wojciech Toman's technique as explained in gamedev.net's article *Rendering Water as a Post-process Effect* (http://www.gamedev.net/page/reference/index.html/_/technical/graphics-programming-and-theory/rendering-water-as-a-post-process-effect-r2642).

While this is a fairly simple technique to use, it can be configured in a number of ways. It supports not only the rendering of water, but also underwater effects. The approach uses a height map to generate waves and ripples are created using a normal map. In addition, foam is also supported.

Here, we are interested in how we can use the filter. However, this approach is more computationally intensive than the `SimpleWaterProcessor` class as discussed in Using the `SimpleWaterProcess` Class.

To use water, we need:

- Terrain and, optionally, a sky
- A directional light source for reflection
- A `FilterPostProcessor` and `WaterFilter` objects

The `FilterPostProcessor` class performs the rendering computations and the `WaterFilter` class configures the water. In the following statement a `FilterPostProcessor` is created using the `assetManager` as an argument:

```
FilterPostProcessor fpp = new
    FilterPostProcessor(assetManager);
```

A `WaterFilter` object is then created and the wave height is set using the `setWaterHeight` method.

```
WaterFilter water = new WaterFilter(rootNode,
    new Vector3f(-1, 0, 0));
water.setWaterHeight(1.0f);
```

The `WaterFilter` object is then added to the post processor and the processor is attached to the current view port.

```
fpp.addFilter(water);
viewPort.addProcessor(fpp);
```

The use of this approach based on the terrain created earlier using TerraMonkey is shown in *Figure 35 - WaterFilter Example Above Water* and *Figure 36 -* WaterFilter *Example Below Water*.

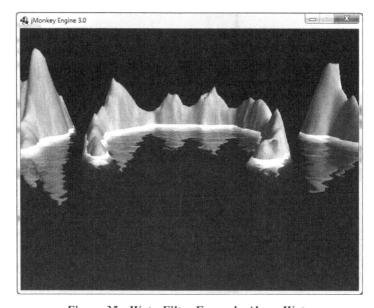

Figure 35 - WaterFilter Example Above Water

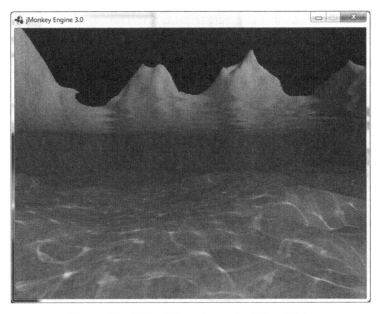

Figure 36 - WaterFilter Example Below Water

The WaterFilter class possesses a number of methods to customize the behavior of the water. Many of these are summarized in *Table 1 - Useful WaterFilter Methods*.

Table 1 - Useful WaterFilter Methods

Method	Purpose
setLightDIrection	Sets the direction of the light
setSunScale	Determines the size of the sun's reflection
setWindDirection	Specifies the direction of the wind
setWaveScale	Specifies how far apart the waves will be
setMaxAmplitude	Specifies how high the waves will be
setWaveTransparency	Determines how clear the water will be
setWaterColor setDeepWaterColor	Together, they specify how the color of the water changes with depth

Conclusion

We have examined how landscapes and their associated elements can be created and managed in JME3. Some of these techniques were fairly easy to use and often produced high quality images.

We used height maps and a quad to create terrain. A terrain can be implemented in code or using the Scene Composer. In both cases, the heightmap controls the height of the landscape. Also, skies can be created easily in JME3.

Two approaches for generating water scenes were examined. The first one used the `SimpleWaterProcess` class, which produced good images but did not support underwater scenes. We found that the `WaterFilter` class was more capable and included the ability to render underwater scenes. However, this latter technique required more computational power.

In the next chapter we will see how physics is added to a game. This capability adds a new level of realism to a game.

9
Physics

Introduction

Games can be made more realistic by adding collision detection, solid objects, and gravity in accordance with the principles of physics. Up to this point in our game design journey, we have been able pass right through objects with no gravitational or collision effects. Some common physics effects you may want to implement include: sliding, jumping, bouncing, friction, falling, ragdoll effects, and pendulum effects.

The primary way to implement physics in JME3 is through an `AppState` called the `BulletAppState`, and a `Control` called `RigidBodyControl`. There are additional components to control the physics of the game, but the two mentioned above will do the bulk of the work in most cases.

Gravity is actually rather easy to implement in JME3; we will see its use in several sections. In turn, when a collision occurs, we will want to be able to deal with it. While there are several techniques available for handling collisions, we will examine the `GhostControl` and Physics Listeners specifically.

Many of the physics elements supported by JME3 are implemented by classes in the `com.jme3.bullet` packages. These are ports of the Bullet Physics Engine (`http://bulletphysics.org/wordpress/`). Bullet has been used with many video games and movies. Some titles you may recognize include the Grand Theft Auto series, Sonic the Hedgehog, The A-Team, and Sherlock Holmes. More details about JBullet can be found at `http://jbullet.advel.cz/`.

Handling Collisions

The first aspect of physics we will implement is collisions. This means that instead of the player passing through objects, a collision will occur – thus making the player and the object appear solid. We will use the `BulletAppState` class to implement the physics space and the `RigidBodyControl` class to apply physics to objects, respectively. Additionally, to apply physics to the player, we will need to implement a `CapsuleCollisionShape` and character control. With these pieces in place, a player's character will be able to walk on solid ground and run into solid walls using collision detection.

Adding a Physics Space

The `BulletAppState` class, found in the `com.jme3.bullet` package, will provide the foundation for our physics components. This class simulates the collision detection and rigid body dynamics that we will use in this chapter. The JME3 implementation of JBullet gives the game access to a `PhysicsSpace`, which allows you to use `PhysicsControls` to apply physics to nodes. Thanks to the `BulletAppState` most of the actual work is done behind the scenes.

To get started we will add bullet physics to the game by instantiating `BulletAppState` and attaching it the `stateManager` via the `attach` method as shown next. If you need a refresher on `AppState`s - they were covered in Chapter 4.

```
BulletAppState bulletAppState = new BulletAppState();
stateManager.attach(bulletAppState);
```

We can access the physics space via the `getPhysicsSpace` method. The physics space is used by those elements of the game that need to interact. You can add elements such as walls and NPCs to the physics space.

Adding Physics to Objects

The `RigidBodyControl` class, located in the `com.jme3.bullet.control` package, is used to apply gravity and to make objects appear solid. A new `RigidBodyControl` must be created for each object that needs to be solid. There are three different constructors you can use to instantiate this type of control:

- The first takes a single float value parameter that represents the mass of the object

- The second constructor takes a `CollisionShape` as a parameter providing a shape to interact with

- The third constructor takes a `CollisionShape` and a float value for mass as parameters

The `CollisionShape` class will be discussed in the next section. The mass determines how objects will be affected by collisions. For static objects, or objects that do not move, like the terrain and walls, use a mass of 0. With a mass of 0, objects will not be affected by physical forces like gravity. For dynamic objects we can apply varying masses depending on the size of the object and how much we want the object to be affected by physical forces.

To use a `RigidBodyControl`:

1. Create a new `RigidBodyControl` object
2. Add the control object to a spatial object using the `addControl` method
3. Add the control object to the physics space

Once we create a `RigidBodyControl` we need to add it to the object we want to make solid. If a `CollisionShape` is not explicitly used in the constructor, JME3 will automatically choose one that fits best. Then we need to add that object to the physics space before it will take effect. Be sure to remember to attach the original object to the `rootNode`.

To avoid starting from scratch, let's pick up where we left off with the terrain we created in Chapter 8. Recall that we created a `TerrainQuad` called `terrain` using the `fortess512` heightmap and corresponding alpha map. You can use any terrain you like with this technique and it will have similar affects.

Create a new `RigidBodyControl` called `terrainPhysics` with a mass of `0` as shown next. Remember, we set the mass to 0 when an object is static. Next, add `terrainPhysics` to `terrain` via the `addControl` method. Add `terrainPhysics` to the physics space by calling the `getPhysicsSpace` method against `bulletAppState` that we created earlier.

```
RigidBodyControl terrainPhysics =
    new RigidBodyControl(0f);
terrain.addControl(terrainPhysics);
bulletAppState.getPhysicsSpace().add(terrainPhysics);
```

At this point, if you run the game you will notice that you can still pass right through the terrain even though it is supposedly solid. You may also notice that the player is not affected by any sort of gravity. The reason for this is that our player character is not solid. Therefore the physics of the terrain has no effect on the player.

Keep in mind that once a `RigidBodyControl` is added to the physics space, it will remain in the physics space even if the object is removed. For example, if you have a door with physics that opens, the `RigidBodyControl` object will remain in its original position barring passage to the next area. To solve this problem, remove the `RigidBodyControl` object from the physics space when the original object is removed.

```
bulletAppState.getPhysicsSpace().remove(terrainPhysics);
```

Adding Physics to the Player

Adding physics to the player allows us to interact with objects in the game space. Up until this point our player still passes through solid objects. There are a couple of ways we can solve this problem. The first way uses the `CharacterControl` and `CapsuleCollisionShape` classes.

The second way uses an instance of the `BetterCharacterControl` class. `BetterCharacterControl` is intended to replace the original `CharacterControl`. However, at this time the consensus among the JME3 community is that the `BetterCharacterControl` is still a bit too buggy. Because of this we will address both methods of adding physics to the player. Keep in mind that the original `CharacterControl` may become deprecated in the future.

Using the `CharacterControl` and `CapsuleCollisionShape` Classes

The `CharacterControl` provides the physics controls for the player. This is similar to the `RigidBodyControl` but is designed specifically for the player. The `CapsuleCollisionShape` class provides a collision boundary around the player. This is what actually collides with other physics-enabled objects. You can imagine this capsule as a cylinder that surrounds a standing character.

To use this technique and add physics to the player, we must create the `CapsuleCollisionShape` first and then use it as a parameter to the `CharacterControl`'s constructor. The `CapsuleCollisionShape` can be found in the `com.jme3.bullet.collision.shapes` package. `CharacterControl` is found in the `com.jme3.bullet.control` package. We will also need to implement mapping controls and a custom `onAction` method. For this to work correctly we need our class declaration to implement `ActionListener`.

To implement the player with physics using this technique:

1. Create a `CapsuleCollisionShape`

2. Create a `CharacterControl` using the capsule

3. Add the `CharacterControl` to the physics space

4. Set the location of the player using `setPhysicsLocation`

5. Update the camera in `simpleUpdate`

6. Implement controls for walking

When completed, a player can move about the terrain and not pass through solid objects. There are two primary parameters to the `CapsuleCollisionShape` constructor. The first is a float representing the radius of the capsule. The second parameter is a float representing the height of the capsule. There is also a third optional integer parameter that represents an axis. The default axis, if one is not specified, is the y axis.

- 0 creates a capsule around the x axis

- 1 creates a capsule around the y axis

- 2 creates a capsule around the z axis

We will create a `CapsuleCollisionShape` called `capsule`, with a radius of `1.5f` WU, and a height of `6` WU. These values can vary depending on the size of your character in relation to the game. We chose the aforementioned values to represent the average shape of a character. It may help to picture these units as feet in the current scope.

```
CapsuleCollisionShape capsule =
    new CapsuleCollisionShape(1.5f, 6);
```

With `capsule` in place we can now set up our `CharacterControl`, which will roughly represent our player's shape. Define a `CharacterControl` called `player` as an instance variable. Call the `CharacterControl` constructor using `capsule` and a float value that represents the step height. For a player of height 6 WU an appropriate step height might be around .05f. The step height represents the height of the player character's footsteps. This will have an effect on how the player maneuvers over stairs and hills. Once we have our player set up, we need to add it to the physics space using bulletAppState.

```
private CharacterControl player;
player = new CharacterControl(capsule, 0.05f);
bulletAppState.getPhysicsSpace().add(player);
```

Next, we set the location of the player using setPhysicsLocation. The parameter for this method is a Vector3f representing coordinates in the game. We set the Y axis value to 70 due to the hills of the terrain. Alternatively we could lower the terrain. If the player is loaded beneath the terrain it will fall endlessly.

```
player.setPhysicsLocation(new Vector3f(0, 70, 0));
```

In order to position the camera correctly, we need to add some code to simpleUpdate. We need to keep the camera with the player as the player moves. To position the camera, call the setLocation method against the default cam object with the physics location of the player as an argument.

```
public void simpleUpdate(float tpf) {
        cam.setLocation(player.getPhysicsLocation());
    }
```

At this point if we load the game our player will fall onto the terrain. Try it - it can be fun! We can look around using the camera, but we will be unable to move. To solve this problem we need to implement some movement controls. Let's start out by adding some additional instance variable declarations. We will use these variables as we progress.

```
private Vector3f walkDirection = new Vector3f();
private boolean left = false;
private boolean right = false;
private boolean up = false;
private boolean down = false;
```

Next, have your class implement the ActionListener interface. Then, add the following onAction method to handle the new inputs:

```
public void onAction(String binding, boolean isPressed,
        float tpf) {
    if (binding.equals("Left")) {
      if (isPressed) { left = true; } else { left = false; }
    } else if (binding.equals("Right")) {
      if (isPressed) { right = true; } else { right = false; }
    } else if (binding.equals("Up")) {
      if (isPressed) { up = true; } else { up = false; }
    } else if (binding.equals("Down")) {
      if (isPressed) { down = true; } else { down = false; }
```

```
    } else if (binding.equals("Jump")) {
      player.jump();
    }
  }
```

You will get an error here if you have not implemented `ActionListener` in the class declaration!

Next we will set up the controls for player movement and jumping using triggers as described in Chapter 3. Use the code next to set up the key bindings. Add a call to this method in the `simpleInitApp` method.

```
private void setUpKeys() {
    inputManager.addMapping("Left",
        new KeyTrigger(KeyInput.KEY_A));
    inputManager.addMapping("Right",
        new KeyTrigger(KeyInput.KEY_D));
    inputManager.addMapping("Up",
        new KeyTrigger(KeyInput.KEY_W));
    inputManager.addMapping("Down",
        new KeyTrigger(KeyInput.KEY_S));
    inputManager.addMapping("Jump",
        new KeyTrigger(KeyInput.KEY_SPACE));
    inputManager.addListener(this, "Left");
    inputManager.addListener(this, "Right");
    inputManager.addListener(this, "Up");
    inputManager.addListener(this, "Down");
    inputManager.addListener(this, "Jump");
}
```

Finally we need to add some code to `simpleUpdate` in order to update the player's movement. Next, in the `simpleUpdate` method, we will add a variable for camera direction and a variable for camera left. We will reset the `walkDirection` variable to (0,0,0). We will respond to the variables left, right, up, and down. Also, we will call the `setWalkDirection` method against the player with the `walkDirection` variable as the parameter.

```
public void simpleUpdate(float tpf) {
    Vector3f camDir = cam.getDirection();
    Vector3f camLeft = cam.getLeft();
    walkDirection.set(0, 0, 0);
    if (left)  { walkDirection.addLocal(camLeft); }
    if (right) { walkDirection.addLocal(camLeft.negate()); }
    if (up)    { walkDirection.addLocal(camDir); }
    if (down)  { walkDirection.addLocal(camDir.negate()); }
    player.setWalkDirection(walkDirection);
    cam.setLocation(player.getPhysicsLocation());
}
```

Notice the `left` responds to `camLeft` and `right` responds to `camLeft.negate`. In case you are unfamiliar with the `negate` method, it will create a `Vector3f` object that points in the exact opposite of the direction of the vector it is running against. Therefore `camLeft.negate` is equivalent to camera right. This allows the camera to move with the player.

When you run the game, at this point, you should be able to walk across the terrain. You can use the keys to navigate the terrain. If you walk to the edge of the terrain map, then you will discover that, at least for this application, the world is flat.

Using `BetterCharacterControl`

The `BetterCharacterControl` class is similar to `CharacterControl`, as the name suggests. However, you do not need to provide a capsule. This class is found in the `com.jme3.bullet.control` package. The parameters to its constructor are a float representing a radius, a float representing a height, and an integer representing a mass.

To use this control:

1. Create a `Node` object to represent the player
2. Create a new `BetterCharacterControl` object and add it to the player node
3. Add the control object to the physics space
4. Implement controls for walking
5. Update movement in the `simpleUpdate` method

Create a new node to represent the player as we did earlier. Call the node `playerNode`. We need to attach the `playerNode` object to the `rootNode` object as shown here:

```
Node playerNode = new Node();
rootNode.attachChild(playerNode);
```

Declare a `BetterCharacterControl` instance variable called `playerControl`. We use an instance variable so that we can use it throughout the class.

```
private BetterCharacterControl playerControl;
```

As we mentioned earlier, the `BetterCharacterControl` constructor expects two floats to represent the width and height of the player, and an integer to represent the player's mass. We will use a width of `1.5f`, a height of `6f`, and a mass of `80`. We use a value of `80` to give the player a realistic mass for the size we have defined. Feel free to vary these values depending on the world scope of your game, and how you want the player to be affected by gravity and other objects.

```
playerControl = new BetterCharacterControl(1.5f, 6, 80);
```

We now want to add the `playerControl` we created to our `playerNode`, as well as the physics space as shown here:

```
playerNode.addControl(playerControl);
bulletAppState.getPhysicsSpace().add(playerControl);
```

We have the option to set the force of the player's jump using the `setJumpForce` method. We can also set the gravity of the player using the `setGravity` method. Both of these methods take a `Vector3f` as the parameter.

Next we set the location of the player using the `warp` method. The `warp` method works in the same way as the `setPhysicsLocation` method in the old character control by placing the player at a location in the physics space. The parameter for this method is a `Vector3f` representing coordinates in the game. We set the Y value to 70, just like the previous example, due to the hills of the terrain. Alternatively we could lower the terrain. If the player is loaded beneath the terrain it will (once more) fall endlessly.

```
playerControl.warp(new Vector3f(0, 70, 0));
```

Next we will need to set up the same movement system boolean variables that we used in the previous example. Declare these as instance variables. These variables correspond to movement in each direction. For now we will set them all to `false`. We will also use the `walkDirection` variable.

```
private boolean left = false;
private boolean right = false;
private boolean up = false;
private boolean down = false;
private Vector3f = walkDirection = new Vector3f(0,0,0);
```

Add a new instance variable, `location`, as shown here:

```
private Vector3f location = new Vector3f(0,0,0);
```

Also, add the following declarations. These will be used in `simpleUpdate` to update the movement of the player.

```
private Vector3f camDir = new Vector3f(0, 0, 0);
private Vector3f camLeft = new Vector3f(0, 0, 0);
private Vector3f location = new Vector3f(0, 0, 0);
```

At this point we need to implement a system for movement. We will use the same implementation of the movement keys that we did in the `CharacterControl` section. Since we are using the same key mapping you can refer back to the previous example to see how this is implemented.

This set up uses the same keys for movement as for the previous player, but with a slightly different update method. To make this work correctly we will need to add some code to `simpleUpdate`. This section of code uses a combination of various techniques we have seen before to make the camera move with the player. The `walkDirection` vector is used to determine the direction the player is walking. Each time the player moves, the vector is reset to (0, 0, 0). The input provided from the user determines the new value for `walkDirection` and it is applied to the player.

```
public void playerUpdate() {
    float walkSpeed = 15;
    camDir.set(cam.getDirection());
    camLeft.set(cam.getLeft());
    walkDirection.set(0, 0, 0);
    if (left) {
        walkDirection.addLocal(camLeft);
    }
    if (right) {
        walkDirection.addLocal(camLeft.negate());
    }
    if (up) {
        walkDirection.addLocal(camDir);
    }
    if (down) {
        walkDirection.addLocal(camDir.negate());
    }

    playerControl.setWalkDirection(
        walkDirection.mult(walkSpeed));
    ...
```

The only real difference between this implementation and the previous example is that we need to acquire the location of the `playerNode` object and store its `location`. We do this to set the location of the camera. Then we will move the camera up using the `add` method as shown next. This may seem strange, but it is necessary to keep the camera above the terrain due to a quirk of `BetterCharacterControl`.

```
    ...
    location.set(playerNode.getLocalTranslation());
    cam.setLocation(location.add(0,3.5f,0));
    }
```

Add the following statement to the `simpleUpdate` method:

```
    playerUpdate();
```

At this point your player should be ready to go. To see the player in action, simply add a terrain to the game and run the project. Play with various values for the jump force, `walkSpeed`, and mass to see how it affects the player.

Collisions in Action

Your terrain, your character, and your objects are affected by physics. We now have the tools to apply the principles of physics to our objects. We will start by creating a pyramid of boxes and knocking them down with a high velocity ball. For this example we will use a flat terrain to support a pyramid of box geometries.

Create a new method called createBox. In this method we will create a new box-shaped geometry and apply an unshaded material with a metal texture. We will then add a RigidBodyControl object to apply physics principles to the box. Finally, we will add the box to the physics space as well as attach the box to the rootNode object. We will pass a Vector3f parameter to the createBox method so that we can place the bricks at various locations. We will also pass an integer parameter so we can create boxes of various colors. We will switch between colors using a switch statement.

```java
public void createBox(Vector3f location, int color){
    Box box = new Box(2,2,2);
    Geometry brick = new Geometry("Box", box);
    Material brickMat = new Material(assetManager,
        "Common/MatDefs/Misc/Unshaded.j3md");
    Texture brickTex = assetManager.loadTexture(
        "Textures/metalTex.png");
    brickMat.setTexture("ColorMap", brickTex);
    switch(color){
        case 0:
        case 6: brickMat.setColor("Color", ColorRGBA.Red);
            break;
        case 1:
        case 7: brickMat.setColor("Color", ColorRGBA.Green);
            break;
        case 2:
        case 8: brickMat.setColor("Color", ColorRGBA.Yellow);
            break;
        case 3:
        case 9: brickMat.setColor("Color", ColorRGBA.Blue);
            break;
        case 4:
        case 10: brickMat.setColor("Color", ColorRGBA.Orange);
            break;
        case 5: brickMat.setColor("Color", ColorRGBA.Pink);
            break;
    }

    brick.setMaterial(brickMat);
    brick.setLocalTranslation(location);

    RigidBodyControl boxPhysics = new RigidBodyControl(10);
    brick.addControl(boxPhysics);
    bulletAppState.getPhysicsSpace().add(boxPhysics);
    rootNode.attachChild(brick);
}
```

Next, we need to define a method to build a destructible wall out of our physics-enabled boxes. This is done in the `buildPyramid` method here:

```
public void buildPyramid(){
    createBox(new Vector3f(0,2,0), 0);
    createBox(new Vector3f(6,2,0), 1);
    createBox(new Vector3f(12,2,0), 2);
    createBox(new Vector3f(18,2,0), 3);
    createBox(new Vector3f(3,6,0), 4);
    createBox(new Vector3f(9,6,0), 5);
    createBox(new Vector3f(15,6,0), 6);
    createBox(new Vector3f(6,10,0), 7);
    createBox(new Vector3f(12,10,0), 8);
    createBox(new Vector3f(9,14,0), 9);
}
```

We need to create a floor for the pyramid to sit on. Use the following method to create this floor. This approach should be familiar to you as we are using the earlier techniques to make the floor solid.

```
private void createFloor() {
    Box box = new Box(100, 0.1f, 100);
    Geometry floorGeometry = new Geometry("Box", box);
    Material floorMat = new Material(assetManager,
        "Common/MatDefs/Misc/Unshaded.j3md");
    Texture floorTex = assetManager.loadTexture(
        "Textures/BrickWall.jpg");
    floorMat.setTexture("ColorMap", floorTex);
    floorGeometry.setMaterial(floorMat);
    floorGeometry.setLocalTranslation(location);

    RigidBodyControl boxPhysics = new RigidBodyControl(0);
    floorGeometry.addControl(boxPhysics);
    bulletAppState.getPhysicsSpace().add(boxPhysics);
    rootNode.attachChild(floorGeometry);
}
```

Call the `createFloor` and `buildPyramid` methods from the `simpleInitApp` method. When the program executes, you should see a pyramid as shown in *Figure 1 - Pyramid*.

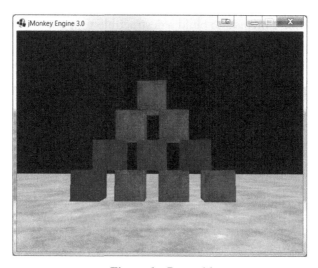

Figure 1 - Pyramid

Now we have a pyramid of blocks with physics enabled. Although we could destroy the pyramid by running into it with our player, we will instead shoot a spherical object at the blocks. To do this we will need to add a `createSphere` method similar to the `createBox` method.

The code that follows illustrates how this is done. For the parameter of the `setLocalTranslation` method we had to call the `scaleAdd` method against the camera direction. This method is required because of the capsule around the player. Without this, the ball will ricochet off the invisible capsule. We color the sphere white so we can easily see it against the background and colored boxes.

```
public void createSphere(){
    Sphere sphere = new Sphere(32, 32, 0.5f);
    Geometry ball = new Geometry("ball", sphere);
    Material ballMat = new Material(assetManager,
        "Common/MatDefs/Misc/Unshaded.j3md");
    ballMat.setColor("Color", ColorRGBA.White);
    ball.setMaterial(ballMat);
    rootNode.attachChild(ball);
    ball.setLocalTranslation(cam.getDirection().
        scaleAdd(5, cam.getLocation()));

    RigidBodyControl ballPhysics = new RigidBodyControl(15);
    ball.addControl(ballPhysics);
    bulletAppState.getPhysicsSpace().add(ballPhysics);
    ballPhysics.setLinearVelocity(
        cam.getDirection().mult(50));
    }
```

Notice that we introduced a new method here, `setLinearVelocity`. As the name implies, this will add a velocity to the sphere we are creating, allowing us to shoot it at the wall. Increasing the `mult` value from 50 will allow you to propel the sphere at a higher velocity causing greater destruction to the pyramid.

Next we will want to add some mapping to our existing player controls. We will simply add a left mouse click to shoot our newly created sphere. This is similar to what we have seen before.

```
inputManager.addMapping("shoot",
    new MouseButtonTrigger(MouseInput.BUTTON_LEFT));
inputManager.addListener(this, "shoot");
```

We will also need to update the `onAction` method to include the new control.

```
if (binding.equals("shoot") && !isPressed) {
    createSphere();
  }
```

This will allow us to fire a sphere at the pyramid when the left mouse button is clicked. You can see this in *Figure 2 - Shooting Ball*.

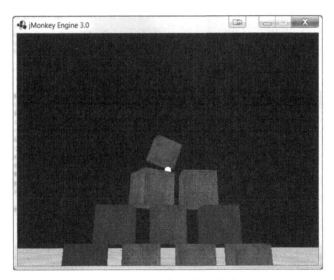

Figure 2 - Shooting Ball

Gravity

In most cases gravity is represented as a vector that is directed down the negative Y axis. This vector simulates gravity toward the terrain. For the most part this is handled behind the scenes via the physics space, specifically the `bulletAppState` class. We can set the intensity of the gravity by calling the `setGravity` method against the `bulletAppState` object. For a standard Earth-like gravity, set the gravity to `-9.81f` in the Y axis.

```
        bulletAppState.getPhysicsSpace().setGravity(
            new Vector3f(0, -9.81f, 0));
```

Other than setting the gravity vector, there is not much you have to do to enable gravity. In fact, in our previous examples, gravity is enforced by default when using RigidBodyControls, CharacterControls, and BetterCharacterControls. Once we have added them to the physics space gravity is automatically enabled.

Observing Gravity

In this section we will create a simple demonstration of JME3 gravity by adding some objects above the scene and allowing them to fall and collide with the terrain. This will give some insight into the effects of gravity on our game components.

We will apply what we learned in Handling Collisions to create some physics-enabled falling objects. We will also use previous code, so if you run into a problem go back and make sure you are not missing a key element from the previous examples. You will only need to implement one of the two available character controls to interact with the environment. For this example we will use the CharacterControl class for our player.

We will create blocks using the createBlock method defined earlier. For this example, let's create a new version of this method adding some capabilities. We will add an integer parameter called randSize to create blocks of random size and a corresponding mass that is 10 times the size. This will allow us to observe falling blocks of varying mass. The following is the second version of the createBlock method.

```
public void createBox(Vector3f location, int i, int randSize){
    Box box = new Box(randSize,randSize,randSize);
    Geometry brick = new Geometry("Box", box);
    Material brickMat = new Material(
    assetManager, "Common/MatDefs/Misc/Unshaded.j3md");
    Texture brickTex = assetManager.loadTexture(
        "Textures/BrickWall.jpg");
    brickMat.setTexture("ColorMap", brickTex);
    switch(i){
        case 0:
        case 6: brickMat.setColor("Color", ColorRGBA.Red);
            break;
        case 1:
        case 7: brickMat.setColor("Color", ColorRGBA.Green);
            break;
        case 2:
        case 8: brickMat.setColor("Color", ColorRGBA.Yellow);
            break;
        case 3:
        case 9: brickMat.setColor("Color", ColorRGBA.Blue);
            break;
        case 4:
        case 10: brickMat.setColor("Color", ColorRGBA.Orange);
            break;
```

```
        case 5: brickMat.setColor("Color", ColorRGBA.Pink);
            break;
    }

    brick.setMaterial(brickMat);
    brick.setLocalTranslation(location);

    RigidBodyControl boxPhysics =
        new RigidBodyControl(randSize*10);
    brick.addControl(boxPhysics);
    bulletAppState.getPhysicsSpace().add(boxPhysics);
    rootNode.attachChild(brick);
}
```

Now let's create another method called `fallingBlocks` to create falling blocks of random size and corresponding mass. In this method we will use a `randomGenerator` to generate a random X and Z location, a random color, and a random size as shown next. If you are unfamiliar with the random number generator, the `nextInt` method takes an integer parameter, X, and will generate a number from 0 to X-1.

```
public void fallingBlocks(){
    float y = 100;
    Random randomGenerator = new Random();
    int randomX = randomGenerator.nextInt(10);
    int randomZ = randomGenerator.nextInt(10);
    int randomColor = randomGenerator.nextInt(10);
    int randomSize = randomGenerator.nextInt(8);
    createBox(new Vector3f(randomX, y, randomZ),
        randomColor, randomSize);
}
```

Call this method from the `simpleUpdate` method as shown next. We will surround the `fallingBlocks` method with a conditional statement that will run the method every time the `time` variable gets bigger than 5. Declare the `time` variable as an instance variable.

```
private float time = 0;
...
@Override
public void simpleUpdate(float tpf) {
    time+=tpf;
    if(time>5){
        fallingBlocks();
        time=0;
    }
}
```

This will cause randomly colored and sized blocks to fall periodically. As the blocks pile up you will be able to observe the collisions and gravitational effects more easily. The bigger the block, the greater the corresponding mass will be. This is illustrated in *Figure 3 - Falling Blocks*.

Notice that each time a block falls, the game will run slightly slower. This is because the more physics-enabled objects you have in the scene, the bigger the impact on game performance. It is a good idea to limit the amount of physics implemented as your project grows in size.

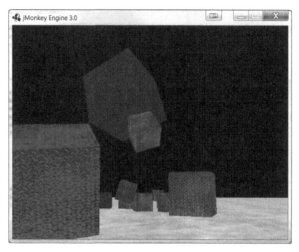

Figure 3 - Falling Blocks

Physics Listeners

Physics listeners are useful for responding to collisions and applying forces to objects. When a component of the game is hit, we may want to decrease its health level. An obstacle in a game may need to be moved. We can allow the user to move the object using a physics listener.

One approach is to use the `GhostControl` class found in the `com.jme3.bullet.control` package. An instance of this class is attached to a spatial object and will automatically follow the spatial object as it moves. This "ghost" object is not visible and will handle collisions in a passive manner.

Typically a ghost control is added to a rigid body. The body normally has a visible geometry attached to it. When a ghost is created, a `CollisionShape` object is associated with it. This shape may be the same as the body it is attached to but it doesn't have to be. If it is larger than the body, then a buffer is created around the original object. We will see an example of this control shortly.

Using the Tick Listener

The implementation of the JBullet Physics engine performs calculations at 60 physics ticks per second of the frame rate. Any updates to the environment are performed at the end of the physics update cycle. When you need to interact with the physics of the game you need to be careful as physics calls can be dropped if not used at the appropriate time.

To address this issue, a tick listener based on the `com.jme3.bullet` package's `PhysicsTickListener` interface should be implemented. The use of this interface will ensure that physics updates will not be dropped or lost. Use methods such as the `GhostControl` class' `getOverLappingObjects` method in one of the methods of the interface to determine the state of the application.

> This interface is not always needed. If you just need to gather information about the current state of an object you don't need to use the tick listener.

To use the tick listener:

1. Create a class that implements the `PhysicsTickListener` interface
2. Override its methods
3. Add the desired functionality to the overridden methods

The `PhysicsTickListener` interface has two methods:

- `prePhysicsTick` - This is called before each physics step and is used to change the state of an object

- `physicsTick` - This method is called after each step and is used to get the state of an object

Both of these methods are passed a `PhysicsSpace` object and `tps`, which is the number of seconds that has elapsed since the last frame. The `tps` value can be used to time actions.

Using the `PhysicsCollisionListener` Interface

The collision listener is based on the `com.jme3.bullet.collision` package's `PhysicsCollisionListener` interface. When two solid objects collide, any effect from these collisions is applied automatically by the physics engine. However, if the listener is used, you can respond to the collision event. For example, when two objects collide you might want to increase a score, decrease the health of an opponent, apply a special effect, or a combination of similar actions.

To use the `PhysicsCollisionListener` interface:

1. Create an object that implements the `PhysicsCollisionListener` interface

2. Use the `PhysicsSpace` class' `addCollisionListener` methods to add the listener to the objects

3. Override the `collision` method

4. Use the `getNodeA` and `getNodeB` methods to handle the event

The `collision` method is passed a `CollisonEvent` object, which provides access to several aspects of the collision. Many of the `CollisonEvent` class' methods are detailed in *Table 1 - CollisionEvent Methods.*

This class' `getNodeA` and `getNodeB` methods return references to the two objects that collided allowing you to identify and then process the event. It is not known which object is returned by either the `getNodeA` or `getNodeB` method until the collision occurs. You will need to deal with this as shown in the next example.

Table 1 - CollisionEvent Methods

Method	Meaning
`getNodeA` `getNodeB`	Returns a reference to the objects involved in the collision

`getAppliedImpulse`
`getAppliedImpulseLateral1`
`getAppliedImpulseLateral2`
	Returns a float representing different collision impulses

`getCombinedFriction`	Returns the amount of collision friction as a float
`getCombinedRestitution`	Returns the amount of bounciness as a float

The `PhysicsCollisionListener` class' `collision` method is invoked whenever a collision occurs anywhere in the game. Here, we will combine the use of the ghost control with the `collison` method. One advantage of this approach is that it helps partition our code.

Create a class named `ExtendedGhostControl` that extends the `GhostControl` class and implements the `PhysicsCollisionListener` interface as shown here:

```
public class ExtendedGhostControl extends GhostControl
        implements PhysicsCollisionListener {

    ...
}
```

Add an instance variable, shown next, that we will use to update the HUD.

```
private BitmapText hudText;
```

Add a constructor that accepts a `BitmapText` and `BoxCollisionShape` objects. The `BitmapText` object will be used to update the HUD and the `BoxCollisionShape` will be used with the base class constructor so that the ghost control has a specified shape associated with it.

```
public ExtendedGhostControl(BitmapText hudText,
        BoxCollisionShape bcs) {
    super(bcs);
    this.hudText = hudText;
}
```

To make the HUD output more readable, we will use the following helper method. This converts a `Vector3f` object into a formatted string.

```
private String getFormattedVector(Vector3f vector) {
    NumberFormat nf = NumberFormat.getNumberInstance();
    nf.setMaximumFractionDigits(2);
    StringBuilder sb = new StringBuilder();
    return sb.append(" at (").
        append(nf.format(vector.x)).append(",").
        append(nf.format(vector.y)).append(",").
        append(nf.format(vector.y)).
        append(")").toString();
}
```

The `collision` method follows. We use the `getNodeA` and `getNodeB` methods to determine which objects collided. We restricted the objects we observe to those whose names start with either "Collision", "Floor", or "Box". We use a `StringBuilder` class to create a description of the collision and then use the `hudText` parameter to update the HUD.

```
@Override
public void collision(PhysicsCollisionEvent event) {
    StringBuilder sb = new StringBuilder();
    if (event.getNodeA().getName().
            startsWith("Collision")) {
        sb.append("A: ").append("GhostControl").
            append(getFormattedVector(
            this.getPhysicsLocation()));
    }
    if (event.getNodeA().getName().startsWith("Box") ||
            event.getNodeA().getName().startsWith(
            "Floor")) {
        Geometry geometry = (Geometry) event.getNodeA();
        sb.append("A: ).
            append(geometry.getName()).
```

```
                        append(getFormattedVector(
                        this.getPhysicsLocation()));
            }

            if (event.getNodeB().getName().
                        startsWith("Collision")) {
                sb.append(" collided with B: ").
                append("GhostControl").
                append(getFormattedVector(
                    this.getPhysicsLocation()));
            }
            if (event.getNodeB().getName().startsWith("Box") ||
                        event.getNodeB().getName().startsWith(
                        "Floor")) {
                Geometry geometry = (Geometry) event.getNodeB();
                sb.append(" collided with B: ").
                    append(geometry.getName()).
                    append(getFormattedVector(
                    this.getPhysicsLocation()));
            }
            hudText.setText(sb.toString());
        }
    }
}
```

To demonstrate the use of the ghost control, we will create a floor and a box. We will attach a ghost control to the default camera and use the collision method to show the collisions between the floor, the box, and the ghost control as they occur in the HUD.

Declare an instance variable for the ghost control as shown here:

```
    private ExtendedGhostControl ghostControl;
```

In the simpleInitApp class we will add code to create the scene. Enable the physics engine by adding the BulletAppState class to the program as illustrated next. Set the default camera location and create the floor. We will use the createFloor method that we developed in Collisions in Action.

```
    bulletAppState = new BulletAppState();
    stateManager.attach(bulletAppState);
    cam.setLocation(new Vector3f(0, 1, 10));
    createFloor();
```

We want to use the HUD to display collisions as they occur. The following code sequence does this. The management of a HUD was discussed in Chapter 1.

```
    BitmapText hudText = new BitmapText(guiFont, false);
    hudText.setSize(
        guiFont.getCharSet().getRenderedSize());
    hudText.setColor(ColorRGBA.Blue);
    hudText.setText("");
```

```
        hudText.setLocalTranslation(0,
            hudText.getLineHeight(), 0);
        guiNode.attachChild(hudText);
```

The `ExtendedGhostControl` object is created next using a small cube that is `0.25` units on each side as shown next. A `Node` object is then created. This will be used to attach the ghost control. The node will be positioned with the camera using the `setLocalTranslation` method.

```
        Vector3f halfExtents = new Vector3f(0.25f, 0.25f, 0.25f);
        ghostControl = new ExtendedGhostControl(
            bulletAppState,hudText,
            new BoxCollisionShape(halfExtents));
        collisionBox = new Node("Collision Node");
        collisionBox.setLocalTranslation(cam.getLocation());
        collisionBox.addControl(ghostControl);
```

The ghost control needs to be added to the physical space using the `add` method. Also, for the `ExtendedGhostControl` class' collision method to be called, we need to use the `addCollisionListener` method.

```
        PhysicsSpace physicsSpace =
            bulletAppState.getPhysicsSpace();
        physicsSpace.add(ghostControl);
        physicsSpace.addCollisionListener(ghostControl);
```

Next, add the `collisionBox` node to the game and create the brick as shown here:

```
            rootNode.attachChild(collisionBox);
            createBrick(new Vector3f(0, 10, 0));
```

The `createBrick` method follows:

```
public void createBrick(Vector3f location) {
    Box box = new Box(1, 1, 1);
    Geometry brick = new Geometry("Box", box);
    Material brickMat = new Material(assetManager,
        "Common/MatDefs/Misc/Unshaded.j3md");
    Texture brickTex = assetManager.loadTexture(
        "Textures/Terrain/BrickWall/BrickWall.jpg");
    brickMat.setTexture("ColorMap", brickTex);
    brick.setMaterial(brickMat);
    brick.setLocalTranslation(location);

    RigidBodyControl brickPhysics = new RigidBodyControl(5);
    brick.addControl(brickPhysics);
    bulletAppState.getPhysicsSpace().add(brickPhysics);
    rootNode.attachChild(brick);
}
```

Add the following statement to the `simpleUpdate` method. This will ensure that the node and the ghost control both move with the camera.

```
collisionBox.setLocalTranslation(cam.getLocation());
```

When the program is executed you will see a box drop and collide with the floor. The HUD will be empty until this collision occurs. When the collision occurs, you will see the collision reflected in the HUD as shown in *Figure 4 - GhostControl Box-Floor Collision*.

Figure 4 - GhostControl Box-Floor Collision

If you move the camera into the box, and then out, you will record a collision with the ghost control and the box as shown in *Figure 5 - GhostControl Ghost-Box Collision*. Only the last collision is displayed in the HUD.

A: Floor Box at (0,1,1) collided with B: Box at (0,1,1)

Figure 5 - GhostControl Ghost-Box Collision

Move through the floor. You will also observe a collision between the floor and the ghost control.

Using Collision Groups

One of the problems with collisions is the potential performance hit that can occur with a large number of collisions. One way of reducing this overhead is to use **Collision Groups**. This technique groups objects (that are of interest) together, and ignores the remaining objects.

To create and use a collision group:

1. Assign an object to a group using the `setCollisionGroup` method

2. Assign the object to collide with another group using the `setCollideWithGroups` method

There are a fixed number of groups available: `PhysicsCollisionObject` fields `COLLISION_GROUP_01`, `COLLISION_GROUP_02`, ... `COLLISION_GROUP_16`.

Using this technique with the previous example to simplify the collision method is left as an exercise for the reader.

Adding Physics to Shades of Infinity

We will apply several of the techniques illustrated in this chapter to our game in this section. Since our game is set in space, we will do things a bit differently by applying a gravity of 0 to the active objects. Otherwise the elements of the game possessing mass will "fall" like they would on a surface or terrain. However, applying rigid bodies and physics to the ships will allow them to collide and send them spinning off into space.

To demonstrate these effects we will:

- Add an BulletAppState instance to the game
- Add rigid bodies to the ship
- Set the gravity for the ship

We will also modify the player ship to allow it to collide with the enemy ships.

Applying the Physics Space

In the Main class we will apply the BulletAppState to the game in the same way we did earlier in the chapter. We will add a BulletAppState instance variable to the Main class called bulletAppState as shown here:

```
private BulletAppState bulletAppState;
```

To enable this state, add the following statements to the createScene method:

```
bulletAppState = new BulletAppState();
stateManager.attach(bulletAppState);
```

Applying Physics to the Player's Ship

We will add physics to the player's ship using the CharacterControl. This will give our ship the necessary physical attributes to collide with the AI ships. We can set this up in the same way we did for Adding Physics to the Player.

However, we need to turn off any "naturally" occurring gravitational forces. To do this we will simply call the setGravity method against the playerShip with a parameter of 0.

The code to add the physics is shown next. An instance of the CapsuleCollisionShape is created and added to the play ship. Physics is then added along with a location, and gravity for the player is set to 0.

```
CapsuleCollisionShape capsule =
    new CapsuleCollisionShape(0.2f, 0.2f);
```

```
playerShip = new CharacterControl(capsule, 50);
bulletAppState.getPhysicsSpace().add(playerShip);
playerShip.setPhysicsLocation(new Vector3f(-2, 0, 15));
playerShip.setViewDirection(new Vector3f(5,0,0));
playerShip.setGravity(0);
```

Now the playerShip will be unaffected by gravity, which is what we want for this game.

Applying Physics to the AI Ships

In order to add physics to the AI ships we will need to make a few alterations to the AISpaceShip class. First, add a BulletAppState instance reference variable called state:

```
private BulletAppState state;
```

Next, add a BulletAppState parameter to the AISpaceShip class' constructor and assign it to the corresponding BulletAppState instance variable. This will allow the AISpaceShips class to access the same physics space as the Main class.

```
public AISpaceShip(String name, Node rootNode,
        Vector3f location, int health,
        BulletAppState state) {
    super(name, location, 100, 100, 0, health, 0);
    this.name = name;
    this.state = state;
}
```

We will use the shipLinearVelocity method to apply an initial velocity to the AI ships. This requires modification of the getAIShip and createAIShip methods to accept this value. The getAIShip is shown here where the new parameter is passed to the createAIShip method. This will permit the ships to move along the velocity vector until acted upon by other forces.

```
public Node getAIShip(float x, float y, float z,
        Vector3f shipLinearVelocity) {
    AIShipNode = createAIShip(name, x, y, z,
        shipLinearVelocity, ColorRGBA.Blue);
    AIShipNode.scale(0.05f);
    AIShipNode.setUserData("AINodeEnclosingObject", this);
    return AIShipNode;
}
```

Next, we will need to alter the createAIShip method to include some physics. To make this work correctly we will create a CapsuleCollisionShape called cs, with 0.2f as both parameters. As you may recall, the parameters represent the height and width of the collision capsule. For different objects or effects you will need to adjust these values so they match their associated objects.

273

```
    private Node createAIShip(String name,
        float x, float y, float z,
        Vector3f shipLinearVelocity,ColorRGBA color) {
      ...
    CapsuleCollisionShape cs =
        new CapsuleCollisionShape(0.02f,0.02f);
      ...
    }
```

Define a `RigidBodyControl` instance variable called `shipPhysics`. Then create a new `RigidBodyControl` object using `cs` and `40` as the parameters and assign it to `shipPhysics`. The `40` represents the ship's mass and `cs` is our collision capsule.

```
    RigidBodyControl shipPhysics =
        new RigidBodyControl(cs, 40);
```

Associate the ship's physics with the AI ship and the `BulletAppState` as referenced by the `state` variable. The location of the physics needs to be set. We do this using the location coordinates passed to the method. The gravity of the ship is also set to 0. This effort is shown here:

```
    AIShip.addControl(shipPhysics);
    state.getPhysicsSpace().add(shipPhysics);
    shipPhysics.setPhysicsLocation(new Vector3f(x, y, z));
    shipPhysics.setLinearVelocity(shipLinearVelocity);
    shipPhysics.setGravity(Vector3f.ZERO);
```

Demonstrating AI Ships in Collision

To demonstrate these additions to the game, we will force our two AI ships to collide. In the `Main` class' `createShips` method, replace the creation of the ship with the next code sequence. The two ships are positioned along the Z axis with the second enemy slightly above the first one. In the `getAIShip` method, slightly different linear velocities are applied to each ship. They are both given a value of `1`, which will move them along the Z axis. However, the second enemy is given a Y axis value of `-0.2f`, which moves it slowly toward the first ship forcing them to collide.

```
    enemy1 = new AISpaceShip("Enemy 1", rootNode,
        new Vector3f(0, 0, 8), 20, bulletAppState);
    enemy1.setAssetManager(assetManager);
    enemy1Node = enemy1.getAIShip(0, 0, 10,
        new Vector3f(0,0f,1));
    enemy1Node.setShadowMode(
        RenderQueue.ShadowMode.CastAndReceive);
    rootNode.attachChild(enemy1Node);
    shootables.add(enemy1Node);

    enemy2 = new AISpaceShip("Enemy 2", rootNode,
        new Vector3f(0, 0, 8), 15, bulletAppState);
```

```
enemy2.setAssetManager(assetManager);
enemy2Node = enemy2.getAIShip(0, 0.5f, 10,
    new Vector3f(0,-0.2f,1));
enemy2Node.setShadowMode(
    RenderQueue.ShadowMode.CastAndReceive);
rootNode.attachChild(enemy2Node);
shootables.add(enemy2Node);
```

When you execute the game, the AI ships will collide causing them to move away from each other. Since we have also enabled physics for the player, you can collide with the ships and watch them spin and fly off. This is shown in *Figure 6 - AI Ship Spinning*. The effect can be more dramatic than the collision of the two ships.

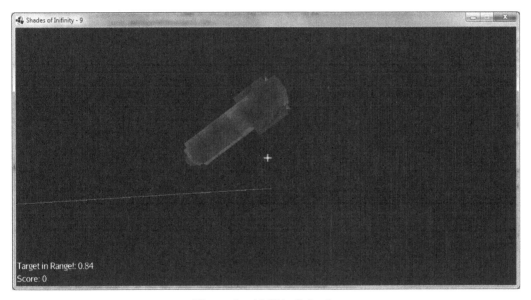

Figure 6 - AI Ship Spinning

Further enhancements are possible but will require more effort. For example, when the ships collide, perhaps damage could be shown using a replacement element for the ship. Another option is to add physics to the projectiles shot at a ship. These are left as exercises for the reader.

Creating an Orbiting Moon

Another example of using gravity in space is shown here where a smaller moon is placed in an elliptical orbit around a larger planet. The example places the planet at (0,0,0) with its gravity set to 0 preventing it from moving. The moon is placed at (40,0,0) and is given an initial linear velocity of (0,0,-2.5f). This will get it moving upon which it settles into its orbit. Axes are drawn to help set how the moon orbits.

The complete code listing can be found at www.p8tech.com. Here we will show the more relevant code sections. The planet is created and set up in the next code segment. Its position is set to (0,0,0) and its gravity is set to 0. Its mass is also set to 0 when the planetRigidBodyControl is instantiated. We do this to keep the planet in place if the moon were to collide with it.

```
planetRigidBodyControl = new RigidBodyControl(0);
Geometry planet = getSphere(32,32,6);
planet.addControl(planetRigidBodyControl);
Material mat = new Material(assetManager,
    "Common/MatDefs/Misc/Unshaded.j3md");
mat.setColor("Color", ColorRGBA.Blue);
mat.getAdditionalRenderState().setWireframe(true);
planet.setMaterial(mat);
state.getPhysicsSpace().add(planetRigidBodyControl);
planetRigidBodyControl.setPhysicsLocation(
    new Vector3f(0, 0, 0));
planetRigidBodyControl.setGravity(Vector3f.ZERO);
rootNode.attachChild(planet);
```

The moon is created in a similar manner as shown next. The primary difference is where the gravity is set to the center of the planet.

```
moonRigidBodyControl = new RigidBodyControl(15);
Geometry moon = getSphere(32,32,1);
moon.addControl(moonRigidBodyControl);
moonRigidBodyControl.setPhysicsLocation(
    new Vector3f(40,0,0));
Material mat2 = new Material(assetManager,
    "Common/MatDefs/Misc/Unshaded.j3md");
mat2.setColor("Color", ColorRGBA.White);
mat2.getAdditionalRenderState().setWireframe(true);
moon.setMaterial(mat2);
state.getPhysicsSpace().add(moonRigidBodyControl);
moonRigidBodyControl.setGravity(
    planetRigidBodyControl.getPhysicsLocation());
```

The linear motion is imparted with the following statement where the force is exerted along the Z axis:

```
moonRigidBodyControl.setLinearVelocity(
    new Vector3f(0,0,-2.5f));
```

The simpleUpdate method, shown next, consists of code that creates a gravitational pull attracting the moon to the planet. You might think that we could simply set the gravity of the moon to the location of the planet. However, this would cause the moon to travel in a straight line following the vector directly, ignoring the planet. To correct this issue we subtract the location of the moon from the location of the planet, creating a vector from the moon toward the planet. We use the normalize function on the vector to produce the proper direction. We use the `mult` function on the end of the vector to reduce the strength of the pull. The `mult` function could also be used to magnify the pull, or be left off completely depending on the situation.

```
public void simpleUpdate(float tpf) {
    moonRigidBodyControl.setGravity(
        planetRigidBodyControl.getPhysicsLocation().
            subtract(moonRigidBodyControl.
            getPhysicsLocation()).
            normalize().mult(0.75f));
}
```

The orbiting moon is shown in *Figure 7 - Orbiting Moon* where the camera is looking down the Y axis.

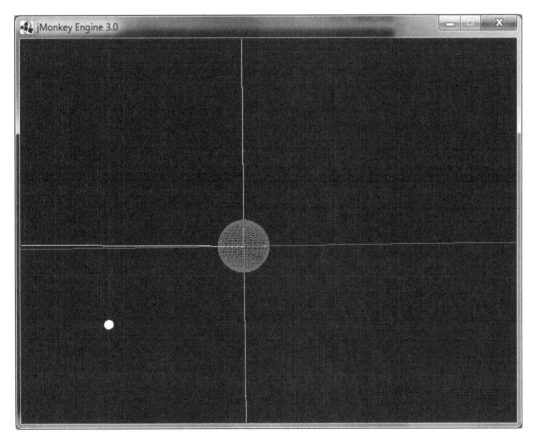

Figure 7 - Orbiting Moon

Conclusion

Adding physics to a game can make it more interesting and realistic. In this chapter we illustrated how the JBullet implementation of Bullet is used to add physics elements to the game. In particular, we showed several approaches for handling collisions between object.

To make an object solid, we need to add a RigidBodyControl object to a node. This combination with the BulletAppState enables the underlying physics engine to determine how objects should interact.

Details of collisions can be obtained using the PhysicsCollisionListener interface. We saw how we can use the collision event object passed to its collision method to determine which objects are colliding. We also illustrated how the GhostControl class can be used to handle collisions.

We augmented the Shades of Infinity game to allow collisions between the ships and the player. Rigid bodies were used but gravity was disabled. A simple example of a moon orbiting a planet was also demonstrated.

In the next chapter we will illustrate how to add special effects such as fog, shadows, and particle emitters to a game.

10
Special Effects

Introduction

We have covered several special effects in earlier chapters. In Chapter 6 we demonstrated the use of shadows, and in Chapter 8 we explored the use of water in scenes. In this chapter we will cover a few other special effects including various techniques such as how to create fog, particle emitters, fade in/out, and bloom and glow.

We will start with a discussion of filters and how they are used to achieve special effects. Some of the filters discussed are used to control the depth of field, generate a fog-like appearance, provide cartoon illusions, and generate grayscale scenes.

These are followed by a discussion of particle emitters. These are used to generate effects like smoke, fire, and explosions. Particle emitters are based on a series of images stored in a single file and then displayed in an order to achieve the desired effect.

Fade in and fade out occurs when a scene slowly vanishes into a black background or slowly emerges from a black background. These are demonstrated along with how they can be customized.

Certain objects or parts of a scene can be made to glow. This is referred to as bloom and glow. There are several ways of controlling this effect and how they are applied to different objects. We wrap up the chapter with the application of some of these effects in the Shades of Infinity game.

Understanding Filters

Filters are two dimensional effects that are applied to the rendered scene. Filters take the scene image and apply the filter to the scene in a frame buffer. As you may recall, frame buffers are offscreen GPU renderers. Filters use a shader, or GPU instruction set that assists in rendering, to apply effects to the scene. JME3 filters can be found in the `com.jme3.post` package.

There are several types of filters available. Some of the available filters include: `FilterPostProcessor`, `BloomFilter`, `CartoonEdgeFilter`, `ColorOverlayFilter`, `FadeFilter`, `LightScatteringFilter`, various shadow filters, and the `WaterFilter`. There are many other filters available. You are encouraged to explore the `com.jme3.post` package to see what else is available.

Understanding the `FilterPostProcessor`

The `FilterPostProcessor` is a piece of software that applies one or more filters to alter how a scene is rendered. It manages a list of filters that are applied in the order they were added to the list. Only one `FilterPostProcessor` is needed per application. A filter is added to the `FilterPostProcessor` using the `addFilter` method. The processor is added to the viewport via the `addProcessor` method.

The `FilterPostProcessor` works by adding filters to a scene that has already been rendered. To use the processor, we need to:

1. Instantiate the `FilterPostProcessor` class

2. Add one or more filters to the `FilterPostProcessor` object

3. Add the `FilterPostProcessor` instance to the viewport

As you may recall we used this process in Chapter 6. Next we will take a brief look at some of the popular filters in JME3. To keep things simple, we will reuse the terrain we created in the Creating Code Based Terrain section of Chapter 8. This terrain uses the `Fortress512` heightmap and alpha map.

Understanding Environmental Effects Filters

Environmental filters are used to affect how the environment appears in the game. Some of the effects in this group include fog, blur, and light scattering. In this section we will examine the use of the `DepthOfFieldFilter` and the `FogFilter` classes.

Using the `DepthOfFieldFilter` Class

The `DepthOfFieldFilter` class is commonly used to apply a blur effect to terrain. This type of filter uses specific distances to focus on and then blurs the rest of the landscape. To use this technique, we will need to instantiate the `DepthOfFieldFilter` class and set our desired focus distances using the `setFocusDistance`, `setFocusRange`, and `setBlurScale` methods.

To use the `DepthOfFieldFilter` technique:

1. Create a `FilterPostProcessor` instance

2. Create a `DepthOfFieldFilter` instance

3. Set the distance, range and blur

4. Add the filter to the `FilterPostProcessor` instance

5. Add the `FilterPostProcessor` instance to the viewport

For the next example we will create a `FilterPostProcessor` reference variable called `fpp`. Then we will create a `DepthOfFieldFilter` variable called `dof`. The `DepthOfFieldFilter` class' constructor does not require any arguments.

```
FilterPostProcessor fpp =
    new FilterPostProcessor(assetManager);
```

```
DepthOfFieldFilter dofFilter = new DepthOfFieldFilter();
```

The `setFocusDistance` method sets the distance where objects are clearly in focus. We will call the `setFocusDistance` method with a parameter of `0`. As you increase the focus distance, close objects will become more blurry. Follow this with a call using the `setFocusRange` method with a parameter of `50`. The `setFocusRange` method determines the side-to-side range of the focus distance.

```
dofFilter.setFocusDistance(0);
dofFilter.setFocusRange(50);
```

Next, set the blur using the `setBlurScale` method. The `setBlurScale` method determines how blurry the scene will appear. The default value of `1` will provide an evenly distributed blur. Values higher than 1 will increasingly space out the sampling.

```
dofFilter.setBlurScale(1.4f);
fpp.addFilter(dofFilter);
```

We added `dofFilter` to `fpp`. Next, add `fpp` to the `viewport`.

```
viewPort.addProcessor(fpp);
```

Try varying the values for focus distance, focus range, and blur scale. When you run this program the terrain should appear blurry from a distance and sharp up close. You can see an example of this in *Figure 1 – DepthOfFieldFilter Class Example*.

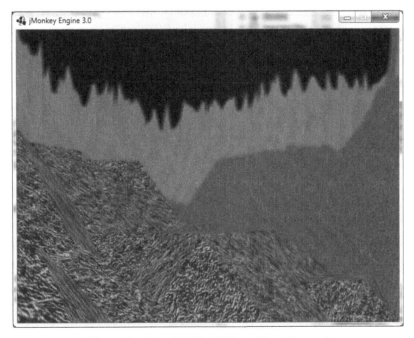

Figure 1 – DepthOfFieldFilter Class Example

Using the `FogFilter` Class

Fog can be a nice effect for making an outdoor scene more realistic. As the name implies, the `FogFilter` class is used to apply a fog effect to the scene. With this type of filter you can set the color, the distance, and the density of the fog using the `setFogColor`, `setFogDistance`, and the `setFogDensity` methods, respectively. To use the `FogFilter` class:

1. Create a `FilterPostProcessor` instance

2. Create a `FogFilter` instance

3. Set the color, distance, and density of the filter

4. Add the filter to the `FilterPostProcessor` instance

5. Add the `FilterPostProcessor` instance to the viewport

To illustrate this approach we will start by creating a `FilterPostProcessor` called `fpp` and a `FogFilter` called `fog` as shown here:

```
FilterPostProcessor fpp =
    new FilterPostProcessor(assetManager);
FogFilter fog = new FogFilter();
```

Next, use the `setFogColor` method to set the color and transparency of the fog. For this example we will use a new `ColorRGBA` with `0.9f` for each of the colors and a transparency of `1`:

```
fog.setFogColor(new ColorRGBA(0.9f, 0.9f, 0.9f, 1.0f));
```

Then, call the `setFogDistance` method with a parameter of `20` as shown next. As the fog distance increases you will be able to see further before the fog blocks out the scene. A low value for fog distance will decrease the distance you can see clearly. Set the fog density to `2` using the `setFogDensity` method. This method controls how thick the fog appears.

```
fog.setFogDistance(20);
fog.setFogDensity(2.0f);
```

As the last step, add `fog` to `fpp`, and `fpp` to the `viewPort`.

```
fpp.addFilter(fog);
viewPort.addProcessor(fpp);
```

When you run the game you will see a fog covering the scene as shown in *Figure 2 – FogFilter Class Example*. To get a better feel for how the appearance of fog can be controlled, experiment with different values for the color, distance, and density of the fog.

Figure 2 – FogFilter Class Example

Understanding Shadow Filters

JME3 has several shadow filters available. You may recall that we examined a few in Chapter 6. Since we already went into some detail about using shadow filters we will only cover one additional filter here, the `SSAOFilter` class.

Using the `SSAOFilter` Class

SSAO stands for Screen Space Ambient Occlusion. Ambient Occlusion refers to the shadows that objects cast on each other while under an ambient light. SSAO approximates the way light radiates in real life. As with previous filters, we need to attach the filter to a `FilterPostProcessor` and add that post processor to the viewport.

Create a simple method called `createBlocks`. This will create a few blocks and add them to the scene as shown here.

```
public void createBlocks(){
    Box box = new Box(1,1,1);
    Material mat = new Material(assetManager,
        "Common/MatDefs/Misc/Unshaded.j3md");
    Geometry geo1 = new Geometry("Box", box);
    geo1.setMaterial(mat);
    geo1.setLocalTranslation(10,3,0);

    Geometry geo2 = new Geometry("Box", box);
    geo2.setMaterial(mat);
```

```
        geo2.setLocalTranslation(5,3,0);

        Geometry geo3 = new Geometry("Box", box);
        geo3.setMaterial(mat);
        geo3.setLocalTranslation(0,3,0);

        rootNode.attachChild(geo1);
        rootNode.attachChild(geo2);
        rootNode.attachChild(geo3);
}
```

The SSAOFilter is created with four float parameters. The first parameter represents the sample radius, or the radius of the area from which samples will be chosen. The default is 5.1f. The second parameter represents the intensity of the created ambient occlusion. The default for the intensity is 1.2f. The third parameter represents the scale, or the distance between occlusion. The default for this is 0.2f. The last parameter is the bias, or the width of the occlusion cone. The default is 0.1f.

The creation of the filter is shown here:

```
        FilterPostProcessor fpp =
            new FilterPostProcessor(assetManager);
        SSAOFilter ssaoFilter = new SSAOFilter(
            12.94f, 43.92f, 0.33f, 0.61f);
        fpp.addFilter(ssaoFilter);
        viewPort.addProcessor(fpp);
```

This filter simulates shadows generated by geometries in the scene. The shadow approximation using this method is fairly crude, but it does the trick. You can see in *Figure 3 – SSAOFilter Class Example* that shadows are being generated based on the unshaded box geometries in the scene.

Figure 3 – SSAOFilter Class Example

Adding the ShaderBlow Library

Many of the best special effects filters are JME3 user community contributions. We can access these filters via the ShaderBlow library that can be downloaded directly using JME3. To do this click on Tools > Plugins as shown in *Figure 4 - Adding the ShaderBlower Library*.

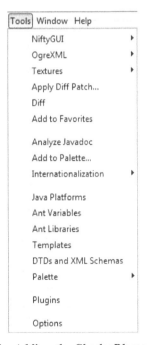

Figure 4 - Adding the ShaderBlower Library

This will bring up the Plugins dialog box as shown in *Figure 5 - Plugins Dialog Box.*

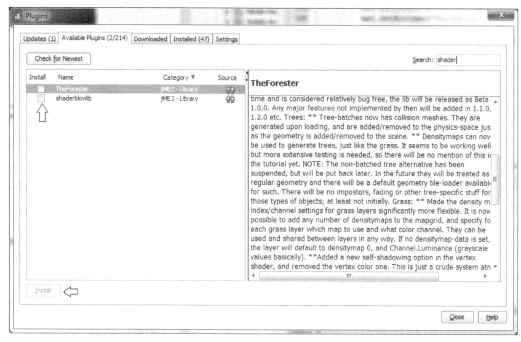

Figure 5 - Plugins Dialog Box

The easiest way to find the library is to click on the search box in the top right of the screen and type *shader*. This will bring up the shaderblowlib on the left side of the screen. Click the checkbox beside the library and select Install.

This will bring up the installation wizard used to install the library. Accept the default values. When completed, you will have access to various special effects filters.

> Remember to add the ShaderBlow library to your project! If you cannot remember how to do this take a look at Adding a Library in Chapter 1.

Understanding Special Effects Filters

Most of the filters we have seen so far are intended to make the scene more realistic. The next set of filters we discuss are intended to do the opposite. They wll reduce the realism of the scene by applying effects such as: a cartoon effect, a grayscale effect, a color scale effect, and an old film effect. These effects are based on the `CartoonEdgeFilter`, `GrayScaleFilter`, `ColorScaleFilter`, and `OldFilmFilter` classes. The

CartoonEdgeFilter is automatically available in JME3. The rest of these filters and many more, are part of the ShaderBlow library that we installed in the previous section.

Using the CartoonEdgeFilter Class

The CartoonEdgeFilter class is used to achieve a cartoon effect in JME3. The cartoon effect is applied to geometries with lighted materials. This particular effect is useful in games which do not aim to be realistic. To use this filter:

1. Create a FilterPostProcessor instance

2. Create a CartoonEdgeFilter instance

3. Apply lighted materials to objects in the scene

4. Add the CartoonEdgeFilter instance to the FilterPostProcessor instance

5. Add the FilterPostProcessor instance to the viewport

To illustrate this technique we will use the Sinbad model. Create the FilterPostProcessor instance as we have in the previous examples, calling it fpp:

```
FilterPostProcessor fpp =
    new FilterPostProcessor(assetManager);
```

Create a CartoonEdgeFilter reference variable called toon. The CartoonEdgeFilter constructor does not require any parameters. We will use the filter's setEdgeColor method to apply an outline color. For this example we will use blue.

```
CartoonEdgeFilter toon=new CartoonEdgeFilter();
toon.setEdgeColor(ColorRGBA.Blue);
```

Since we are using lighted materials we must have a light source attached to the rootNode.

```
DirectionalLight light = new DirectionalLight();
rootNode.addLight(light);
```

For this example create a material called mat. We will use a combination of specular and diffuse maps. We will also set vertex lighting to true as shown next. If you need a refresher on these lighted material components, take a look back to Chapter 5.

```
Material mat = new Material(assetManager,
    "Common/MatDefs/Light/Lighting.j3md");
mat.setBoolean("UseMaterialColors", true);
mat.setColor("Specular", ColorRGBA.Black);
mat.setColor("Diffuse", ColorRGBA.White);
mat.setBoolean("VertexLighting", true);
```

Create a texture, tex, and load toon.png into it. This is a texture JME3 provides for exactly this type of filter. We need to assign tex to mat using the setTexture method.

This method requires a color setting, for this example we will use `ColorRamp`. This color setting allows specular and diffuse values to be mapped together.

```
Texture tex = assetManager.loadTexture(
    "Textures/ColorRamp/toon.png");
mat.setTexture("ColorRamp", tex);
```

Create a basic box to show how a simple object is displayed.

```
Box box = new Box(1,1,1);
Geometry geo1 = new Geometry("Box", box);
geo1.setMaterial(mat);
geo1.setLocalTranslation(10,3,0);
```

Next, load the Sinbad model from the test-data library. We then will apply the material to Sinbad and the box geometry. This will create a cartoon version of Sinbad as well as a cartoon version of the box geometry.

```
Spatial sinbad = assetManager.loadModel(
    "Models/Sinbad/Sinbad.mesh.xml");
sinbad.setMaterial(mat);
```

Attach Sinbad and the box to the scene. Then, add `toonFilter` to `fpp`, and add `fpp` to the `viewPort`.

```
rootNode.attachChild(sinbad);
rootNode.attachChild(geo1);
fpp.addFilter(toon);
viewPort.addProcessor(fpp);
```

When you run this example you should see Sinbad and a box with a blue cartoon effect applied to them as shown in *Figure 6 – CartoonEdgeFilter Class Example.*

Figure 6 – CartoonEdgeFilter Class Example

Using the ColorScaleFilter Class

The ColorScaleFilter class applies a specific color over the entire scene like adjusting the color scale on a television. This type of filter is pretty straightforward. There are probably not many cases when a filter of this type would be particularly useful. However, it is available if you decide you would like to implement this effect in your game.

The ColorScaleFilter class has a setFilterDensity method that is supposed to set the intensity of the color in the scene with a float value between 0 and 1. There is also a setFilterColor method that is intended to change the color of the filter. It is our understanding that the red tint is the only one available at this time. However, we believe these user submitted filters are still being perfected.

```
FilterPostProcessor fpp =
    new FilterPostProcessor(assetManager);
ColorScaleFilter colorScale = new ColorScaleFilter();
colorScale.setFilterColor(ColorRGBA.Yellow);
colorScale.setColorDensity(0.01f);
fpp.addFilter(colorScale);
viewPort.addProcessor(fpp);
```

Using the GrayScaleFilter Class

The GrayScaleFilter class is used to apply a grayscale effect to the scene. There is not much to be said about this filter. This could be a useful feature for many situations (such as in a time-traveling game) where the application of a grayscale could represent a player in the past. Using this filter is pretty simple. All you need to do is create an instance of the GrayScaleFilter class and add it to a FilterPostProcessor. The FilterPostProcessor must also be added to the viewport as with the previous examples.

```
FilterPostProcessor fpp =
    new FilterPostProcessor(assetManager);
GrayScaleFilter grayScale = new GrayScaleFilter();
fpp.addFilter(grayScale);
viewPort.addProcessor(fpp);
```

The result when you apply this filter should be similar to the scene pictured in *Figure 7 – GrayScaleFilter Class Example.*

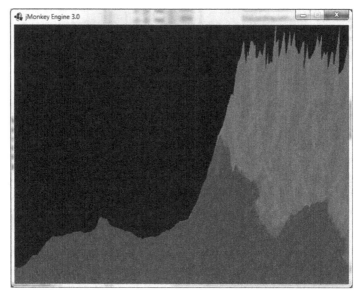

Figure 7 – GrayScaleFilter Class Example

Using the OldFilmEffectFilter Class

The OldFilmFilter class provides an interesting effect that appears similar to an old video camera. This is perhaps one of the most useful filter effects in the ShaderBlow library. Of course the obvious example is a scene where the player is recording on an old camera, or perhaps being watched on an old camera. This would be a particularly useful effect for a horror genre game.

In the following code sequence we will create an instance of the OldFilmFilter called film and add it to a FilterPostProcessor. As we have done in the previous examples we will add the FilterPostProcessor to the viewport.

```
FilterPostProcessor fpp =
    new FilterPostProcessor(assetManager);
OldFilmFilter film = new OldFilmFilter();
film.setFilterColor(ColorRGBA.Blue);
film.setNoiseDensity(1000);
film.setScratchDensity(1000);
film.setVignettingValue(1000);
fpp.addFilter(film);
viewPort.addProcessor(fpp);
```

This filter has a few methods that have not yet been fully implemented, much like the ColorScaleFilter class. These methods include: setFilterColor, setNoiseDensity, setScratchDensity, and setVignettingValue. Currently, calling these methods will have no visible effect on the filter.

Running the previous example will create a scene similar to *Figure 8 – OldFilmFilter Class Example.*

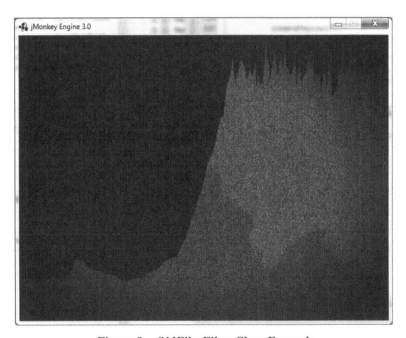

Figure 8 – OldFilmFilter Class Example

Understanding Particle emitters

Particle emitters are used to create special effects such as explosions and smoke. They use a series of small images that are displayed in a particular order to achieve the desired special effect. There are several emitters found in JME3 such as a **spark** and **debris** emitters. A list of these emitters is found in Using a Material with a Particle Emitter.

Particle emitters are based on the `ParticleEmitter` class found in the `com.jme3.effect` package.

The process of creating and using an emitter consists of:

1. Creating a `ParticleEmitter` object
2. Configuring the emitter
3. Attaching it to a scene at a specific location
4. Starting the emitter using the `emitAllParticles` method

To demonstrate the creation and use of a particle emitter, we will create one that produces a flash. The particle emitter uses images that are frequently divided into an even number of rows and columns. Each section contains an image of a slightly different particle. These particles can be debris, streaks, or other partial images. The particle emitter will display these images to create a larger, dynamic sequence of images to achieve the desired effect.

Creating a Particle Emitter

To create an instance of this class, use the three argument constructor whose parameters are listed here:

- Name – A string presenting the name of the emitter
- Type – The type of emitter (`ParticleMesh.Type`)
- Number of particles – The number of particles to create

There are two types available: `ParticleMesh.Type.Point` and `ParticleMesh.Type.Triangle`. These types specify whether the mesh is to be composed on points or triangles respectively. When the triangle type is used, each particle is made up of two triangles creating a quad.

To illustrate the flash emitter, define a `ParticleEmitter` reference variable and a `time` variable as shown next. These need to be declared as instance variables so that we can access them from multiple methods.

```
private ParticleEmitter flash;
private float time = 0;
```

In the `simpleInitApp` method, declare an instance of the `ParticleEmitter` class as shown next. Its constructor takes a name, a type as defined in the `com.jme3.effect.ParticleMesh` package's `Type` enumeration, and an integer specifying the maximum number of particles that can exist at one time.

```
flash = new ParticleEmitter("Flash", Type.Point, 10);
```

Configuring a Particle Emitter

There are numerous methods that are used to effect how a particle stream is emitted. Several of these are listed in *Table 1 - ParticleEmitter Class Methods*. Most of the set methods have corresponding get methods.

Table 1 - ParticleEmitter Class Methods

Method	Effect
emitAllParticles	Starts the emitter
killAllParticles	Stops the emitter
setEnabled	Enables or disables the emitter
isEnabled	Determines if the emitter is enabled or not
setHighLife setLowLife	The low and high life are the boundaries for the duration of the emitter fade.
setStartColor setEndColor	Used to specify the particles' color
setStartSize setEndSize	Specifies the size of the particles. The actual size is chosen randomly.
setGravity	Specifies the direction to use for gravity
setNumParticles	Specifies the maximum number of particles that can exist at one time
setParticlePerSecond	Determines how many particle to create per second
setRandomAngle	Specifies that the particles are to be created at random angles
setSelectRandomImage	Specifies that the images should be selected randomly

The setHighLife and setLowLife methods control how a particle fades. Normally, the minimum value will be less than the maximum value. The duration is randomly selected between these two values. A minimum value less than 1 will result in a more active emitter. A maximum less than 1 will result in short bursts. When the minimum and the maximum values are the same, uneven displays will occur.

> The getInitialVelocity and setVelocityVariation methods are deprecated. Use the ParticleEmitter.getParticleInfluencer class' getInitialVelocity and setVelocityVariation methods instead.

For this example we will use the following code sequence. It uses several of the methods outlined in *Table 1 - ParticleEmitter Class Methods*. The last two methods use a parameter of 2 since this is the number of rows and columns in the image we will use in the next section.

```
flash.setSelectRandomImage(true);
flash.setStartColor(ColorRGBA.White);
flash.setEndColor(ColorRGBA.Red);
flash.setStartSize(.1f);
flash.setEndSize(2.0f);
flash.setLowLife(.2f);
flash.setHighLife(1.0f);
flash.setImagesX(2);
flash.setImagesY(2);
```

Play with these, and other methods, to see how they affect the emitter when this example is fully functional.

Using a Material with a Particle Emitter

A material is needed to support the particle emitter. The material typically used is the Common/MatDefs/Misc/Particle.j3md material definition. However, to be useful, the material needs to be assigned a texture. This texture can be a single image or a sequence of images. Both approaches store the image(s) in a single image file. When multiple images are used, they are arranged in rows and columns.

In the test-data.jar file, there are a number of predefined textures:

- Effects/Explosion/Debris.png
- Effects/Explosion/flame.png
- Effects/Explosion/flash.png
- Effects/Explosion/spark.png

The flash.png image is shown in *Figure 9 - Flash.png*. It consists of 2 rows and 2 columns. When the particle effect is executed, these sub-images are displayed to create the effect of a flash.

Figure 9 - Flash.png

To use a material and texture we need to:

1. Create an instance of `Material` class

2. Assign a texture to it

3. Optionally configure the material

The `Particle.j3md` is used for the material definition and `flash.png` is used for the texture as shown next. The `PointSprite` string and a `true` value are used as arguments to the `Material` class' `setBoolean` method. These are necessary since we are using a point type for the emitter.

```
Material mat = new Material(assetManager,
    "Common/MatDefs/Misc/Particle.j3md");
mat.setTexture("Texture", assetManager.loadTexture(
    "Effects/Explosion/flash.png"));
mat.setBoolean("PointSprite", true);
```

Attaching and Positioning a Particle Emitter

The particle emitter needs to be attached to a scene before it can be used. This is accomplished by:

1. Assign the material to the particle emitter

2. Attach the particle emitter to a node

3. Attach the node to the scene

In addition, to avoid any delay while rendering a scene for the first time, use the com.jme3.renderer package's RenderManager class's preloadScene method. This method takes a spatial that will be preloaded if possible.

```
flash.setMaterial(mat);
Node explosionEffectNode =
    new Node("Explosion Node");
explosionEffectNode.attachChild(flash);
rootNode.attachChild(explosionEffectNode);
renderManager.preloadScene(explosionEffect);
```

Controlling the Lifecycle of a Particle Emitter

Some special effects may last only a few seconds while others may be longer lasting. An explosion typically has a short life but in the case of a volcano exploding, it may consist of a long lasting series of explosions. A flame may burn on and on into the night.

A particle emitter is started using the emitAllParticles method. To stop a particle emitter the killAllParticles method can be used.

To illustrate the use of these methods and to show how to control the duration of the flash, we use the simpleUpdate method as shown next. The time variable keeps track of the elapsed time. When the first second is reached the emitAllParticles method executes starting the particle emitter. After one second has elapsed the killAllParticles method is called to terminate the emitter.

```
public void simpleUpdate(float tpf) {
    time += tpf;
    if (time > 1 && time < 2) {
        flash.emitAllParticles();
    } else if (time > 2) {
        flash.killAllParticles ();
    }
}
```

The emitter is ready to be used. When executed, you will see an effect similar to that shown in *Figure 10 - Flash Example*.

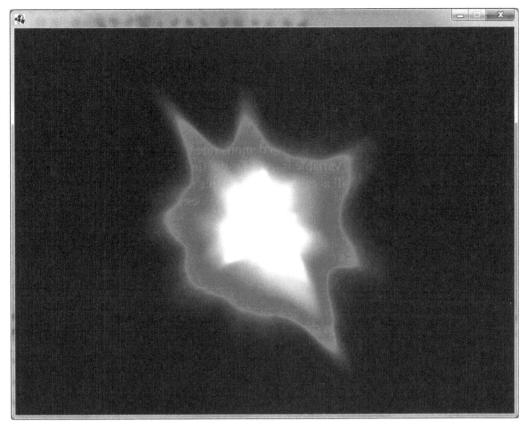

Figure 10 - Flash Example

Using Fade In and Fade Out

One interesting effect is to have a scene slowly fade away to a black screen (and possibly be replaced by another scene that slowly emerges from black). These effects are referred to as **fade in** and **fade out**. JME3 supports this effect for a scene.

The `FadeFilter` class found in the `com.jme3.post.filters` package supports this effect. Its constructor specifies the length of the effect. There is also a value associated with the `FadeFilter` that represents the degree of completion of the fading effect. It is a float value that ranges from 0.0 to 1.0. When the process is complete, the value is set to 1.0. The `getValue` and `setValue` methods will return and set these values respectively.

To create a fade in or fade out effect:

1. Create an instance of the `FilterPostProcessor` class
2. Create an instance of the `FadeFilter` class
3. Configure the `FadeFilter` Instance
4. Invoke the `fadeIn` or `fadeout` methods

To demonstrate the fading effect we will use a scene that consists of a simple cube. A more complicated scene could be used but by keeping it simple, we can focus on the code needed to use the effect. A blue cube will be shown and then it will fade out over a period of 3 seconds. After 4 seconds has elapsed, a red cube will fade in over a period of 3 seconds.

Setting Up the Fade Variables

First, declare the following variables used to demonstrate the fade in and fade out technique. The `simpleBoxGeom` variable is used for the first scene and needs to be an instance variable because we will access it from multiple methods. The `fade` variable represents the `FadeFilter`. The `fadeIn` and `time` variables are used to control when the fade in effect occurs.

```
private Geometry simpleBoxGeom;
private FadeFilter fade;
private boolean fadeIn = false;
private float time = 0;
```

The `createCube` helper method, as shown next, is used to create a cube. We will create 2 cubes, a blue one for the fade out and a red one for the fade in.

```
private Geometry createCube(ColorRGBA color) {
    Box cube = new Box(1, 1, 1);
    Geometry simpleBoxGeom = new Geometry("Cube", cube);
    Material mat = new Material(assetManager,
        "Common/MatDefs/Misc/Unshaded.j3md");
    mat.setColor("Color", color);
    simpleBoxGeom.setMaterial(mat);
    return simpleBoxGeom;
}
```

In the `simpleInit` method use the following code to create a blue cube and add it to the scene:

```
simpleBoxGeom = createCube(ColorRGBA.Blue);
rootNode.attachChild(simpleBoxGeom);
```

Setting Up the `FilterPostProcessor` and `FadeFilter` Instances

Next, we create the `FilterPostProcessor` object and a `FadeFilter` instance as shown next. The fade filter is added to the processor and the processor is added to the viewport.

```
FilterPostProcessor fpp =
    new FilterPostProcessor(assetManager);
fade = new FadeFilter();
fpp.addFilter(fade);
viewPort.addProcessor(fpp);
```

Configuring the Fade Duration

The fade out duration can be set using the `FadeFilter` class' constructor or the `setDuration` method. In this example, set the fade duration to 3 seconds using the `setDuration` method.

```
fade.setDuration(3);
```

Executing Fade Out

The fade out is started using the `fadeOut` method.

```
fade.fadeOut();
```

The blue cube will fade away during the 3 second duration.

Executing Fade In

To demonstrate the fade in process, we will create a new scene consisting of a red cube. The fade in process will start 4 seconds after the application starts.

The `simpleUpdate` method, shown in the following sequence, is used to time these operations. The `time` variable keeps track of their elapsed time. When the time reaches 4 seconds, the `then` clause of the if-statement executes since `fadeIn` was initialized to `false`. The old scene is detached from the root node and a new red cube is created and attached. This allows us to transition between different scenes. The `FadeFilter` class' `setValue` method is called with a value of `0` to make sure the fader is ready to go. The `fadeIn` method is then called and the `fadeIn` variable is set to `true`. Setting the variable to true ensures that the `fadeIn` method is not called again. If it was called, then the fade in process would be continuously restarted.

```
public void simpleUpdate(float tpf) {
    time += tpf;
    if (time > 4 && !fadeIn) {
        rootNode.detachChild(simpleBoxGeom);
        Geometry redBoxGeom = createCube(ColorRGBA.Red);
        rootNode.attachChild(redBoxGeom);
        fade.setValue(0);
        fade.fadeIn();
        fadeIn = true;
    }
}
```

When the application is executed, the blue cube will fade away and the red cube will fade in.

Understanding Bloom and Glow

Bloom is a shader effect that produces a glow around bright areas of a scene, typically light sources. Various effects can be applied to the bloom including blurring. In general, the application of bloom results in part of a scene being brighter and glowing.

We can either select individual objects to glow or have the bright areas of the scene glow. The latter approach uses a **Glow Map** that defines those areas of an image that should glow.

To create a bloom, a `FilterPostProcessor` class is created and used with an instance of a `BloomFilter`. It is found in the `com.jme3.post` package. We will use the `BloomFilter` in conjunction with the `FilterPostProcessor`. The `FilterPostProcessor` is then added to the viewport. This process is summarized here:

1. Create an instance of the `FilterPostProcessor` class

2. Create an instance of the `BloomFilter` class

3. Add the `BloomFilter` to the `FilterPostProcessor` instance

4. Add the `FilterPostProcessor` instance to the viewport

This is demonstrated here:

```
FilterPostProcessor fpp =
    new FilterPostProcessor(assetManager);
BloomFilter bloom =
    new BloomFilter(BloomFilter.GlowMode.Objects);
fpp.addFilter(bloom);
viewPort.addProcessor(fpp);
```

The type of glow is determined by the `BloomFilter.GlowMode` class. It has three enumeration constants:

* `Objects` - The bloom is only applied to objects possessing a *GlowColor* property

* `Scene` - The bloom is only applied to the bright areas of the scene that have a glow map

* `SecneAndObjects` - The bloom is only applied to the bright areas of the scene and objects

Once the processor has been setup, materials that take advantage of a bloom color or glow map will use the processor to display the bloom effect. There are several methods used to configure the glow as listed in *Table 2 - BloomFilter Methods*.

Table 2 - `BloomFilter` Methods

Method	Description
setBlurScale	Specifies the scale of the blur effect
setExposurePower	Affects the roughness of the bloom edges
setBloomIntensity	Sets the intensity of the bloom

To demonstrate the use of a glow, we will create a simple scene consisting of two spheres. One sphere will glow while the other will not. By keeping the example simple, we can focus on the elements that affect glow and allow the glow to be experimented with to better determine how the glow can be controlled.

Using a Glow Color

The steps used are as follows:

1. Setup the `FilterPostProcessor` and `BloomFilter` objects using a `GlowMode` of `GlowMode.Objects`

2. Create an object to use with the `BloomFilter` instance

3. Configure the `BloomFilter` object

The `FilterPostProcessor` and `BloomFilter` objects are created as follows. The `BloomFilter` object is modified using the `setDownSamplingFactor` method. The method's argument is divided into the size of the texture and affects the degree of blur for the glow.

```
fpp = new FilterPostProcessor(assetManager);
bloom = new BloomFilter(BloomFilter.GlowMode.Objects);
bloom.setDownSamplingFactor(3.0f);

fpp.addFilter(bloom);
viewPort.addProcessor(fpp);
```

We will use two helper methods to illustrate the glow effect. The first one, `createSphere`, creates a simple sphere and uses techniques illustrated in previous chapters:

```
private Geometry createSphere() {
    Material commonMaterial =
        new Material(getAssetManager(),
            "Common/MatDefs/Misc/Unshaded.j3md");
    commonMaterial.setColor("Color", ColorRGBA.Green);

    Sphere globe = new Sphere(32, 32, 0.1f);
    Geometry globeGeom =
        new Geometry("Sphere", globe);
    globeGeom.setMaterial(commonMaterial);
```

```
            return globeGeom;
    }
```

The second method, `createGlowingSphere`, differs from the first method in that the `setColor` method is used a second time with a parameter of `GlowColor` and the color `green`. This sets the glow color.

```
    private Geometry createGlowingSphere() {
        Material glowMaterial =
            new Material(getAssetManager(),
                "Common/MatDefs/Misc/Unshaded.j3md");
        glowMaterial.setColor("Color", ColorRGBA.Green);
        glowMaterial.setColor("GlowColor", ColorRGBA.Green);

        Sphere globe = new Sphere(32, 32, 0.1f);
        Geometry globeGeom =
            new Geometry("Glowing Sphere", globe);
        globeGeom.setMaterial(glowMaterial);
        return globeGeom;
    }
```

In the `simpleInitApp` method the two spheres are created and added to the scene. Axes are drawn using the Axes class developed in Chapter 1 to help see where the spheres are located as shown here:

```
        Geometry glowingSphere = createGlowingSphere();
        glowingSphere.setLocalTranslation(1, 0, 0);
        rootNode.attachChild(glowingSphere);

        Geometry sphere = createSphere();
        sphere.setLocalTranslation(-1, 0, 0);
        rootNode.attachChild(sphere);

        drawAxes();
```

When executed, the spheres should appear as shown in *Figure 11 - Glowing Sphere*.

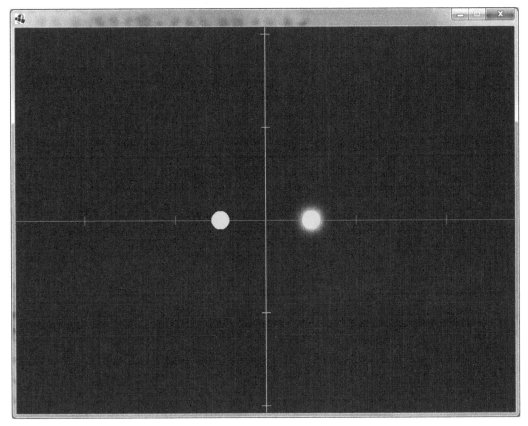

Figure 11 - Glowing Sphere

Using a Glow Map

Using a texture that contains a glow map is easy to do. The `BloomFilter` is setup and modified as before. In this example we will use the `FullskiesBlueClear03.dds` file as shown here:

```
Spatial sky = SkyFactory.createSky(assetManager,
    "Textures/Sky/Bright/FullskiesBlueClear03.dds",
    false);
sky.setCullHint(Spatial.CullHint.Never);
rootNode.attachChild(sky);
```

When added to the glowing sphere example your scene should appear as shown in *Figure 12 - Glowing Sky Example*.

Figure 12 - Glowing Sky Example

Stopping a Glow

To stop the glow, use the `clearTextureParam` method against the glow material as shown here:

```
glowMaterial.clearTextureParam("GlowMap");
```

If a glow color is used, use the `setColor` method instead:

```
glowMaterial.setColor("GlowColor",ColorRGBA.Black);
```

Shades of Infinity Enhancements

While there are several enhancements we can make to the game, due to space limitations (no pun intended), we will simply add the flash effect developed in Understanding Particle emitters to the game when an AI Ship is hit. In addition, we will change the material to `Textures/damagedMetal.jpg` to show the damage.

We will start by adding a few instance variables as shown next. The `timer` and `time` variable will restrict the length of the flash. The `flash` variable represents the particle emitter and the `target` variable is used to update the material hit to a damaged image.

```
private boolean timer = false;
private float time = 0;
private ParticleEmitter flash;
private Geometry target;
```

Next, add a `createFlash` method that returns the flash node as shown next. We do this to make it easy to add the flash effect to the same location as the "boom". The `timer` boolean variable is set to `true` to activate the particle emitter.

```
private Node createFlash() {
    flash = new ParticleEmitter("Flash", Type.Point, 10);
    flash.setSelectRandomImage(true);
    flash.setStartColor(ColorRGBA.White);
    flash.setEndColor(ColorRGBA.Red);
    flash.setStartSize(.1f);
    flash.setEndSize(2.0f);
    flash.setLowLife(.2f);
    flash.setHighLife(1.0f);
    flash.setImagesX(2);
    flash.setImagesY(2);

    Material mat = new Material(assetManager,
            "Common/MatDefs/Misc/Particle.j3md");
    mat.setTexture("Texture", assetManager.loadTexture(
            "Effects/Explosion/flash.png"));
    mat.setBoolean("PointSprite", true);

    flash.setMaterial(mat);
    flash.setEnabled(false);
    Node explosionEffectNode = new Node("Explosion Node");
    explosionEffectNode.attachChild(flash);
    rootNode.attachChild(explosionEffectNode);

    explosionEffectNode.setLocalScale(0.5f);
    renderManager.preloadScene(explosionEffectNode);
    timer = true;
    return explosionEffectNode;
}
```

The `TraverseGraph` class' `visit` method needs to be updated to call the `createFlash` method, return the flash node, and then attach it to the element hit. We also removed the code that was used to attach the boom to the part of the ship that was hit. The `target` variable is assigned the geometry that was hit and will be used in the `controlUpdate` method.

```
public void visit(Spatial spatial) {
    if (closest.getGeometry().getName().equals(
            spatial.getName())) {
        control.decrementHealth(1);
        Vector3f contactPoint = new Vector3f();
        closest.getGeometry().getParent().worldToLocal(
            closest.getContactPoint(), contactPoint);
        target = closest.getGeometry();
        Node node = createFlash();
        closest.getGeometry().getParent().attachChild(
            node);
    }
}
```

The last step is to update the `controlUpdate` method as shown next. The last `if` statement is used to control the behavior of a hit. The `setEnable` method is used to control the life of the flash as an alternative approach to the `emitAllParticles` method. The `setTexture` method is used to change the image of the affected part of the ship.

```
protected void controlUpdate(float tpf) {
    if (spatial != null) {
        if (health <= 0) {
            spatial.getParent().detachChild(spatial);
        }
    } else {
            // Spatial was null
    }

    // Control hit behavior
    if (timer) {
        if (time == 0) {
            flash.setEnabled(true);
        }
        time += tpf;
        if (time > 1) {
            flash.setEnabled(false);
            target.getMaterial().setTexture(
                "DiffuseMap",
                assetManager.loadTexture(
                "Textures/damagedMetal.jpg"));
            timer = false;
            time = 0;
        }
    }
}
```

When executed, a flash and damage will occur similar to that shown in *Figure 13 - Shades of Infinity Damage Example.*

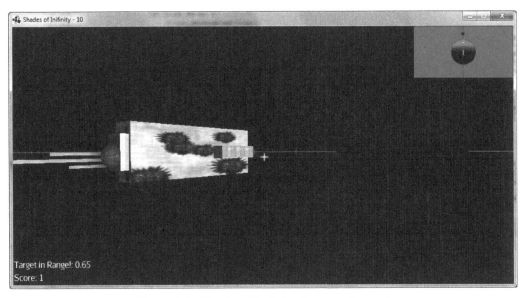

Figure 13 - Shades of Infinity Damage Example

Conclusion

In this chapter, we learned how to apply filters to achieve special effects such as fog, control the depth of field, and add grayscale to mention a few. Filters are used by the `FilterPostProcessor` class to control many of these effects. Only a single instance of the `FilterPostProcessor` class is needed for an application.

The use of particle emitters, fade in/out, and blooms was demonstrated. These can all be customized with some experimentation and achieve desired effects. The particle emitter was also incorporated into the Shades of Infinity Game.

The next chapter will cover concepts related to multi-player gaming and networking.

11

Multiple Players and Networking

Introduction

Games are often more interesting when multiple players participate. They can introduce variety and a level of complexity which can be difficult to achieve in code. Since each player is normally on different machines, it is necessary for players and machines to communicate over a network that interconnects them. JME3 provides support for this communication.

Multiplayer games are built by connecting one or more clients to a single server. The server can maintain and coordinate the game in the background. Each player runs a game client that connects to the central server.

Every client keeps the server up-to-date with its player's actions and movements. Each player's client displays the game state to its player from that player's perspective. The server maintains the game state and relays the current game information to each connected client. This type of network synchronization allows all of the players to exist in the same game state, each with their own perspective.

This server/client relationship is depicted in *Figure 1 - Server Client Network*.

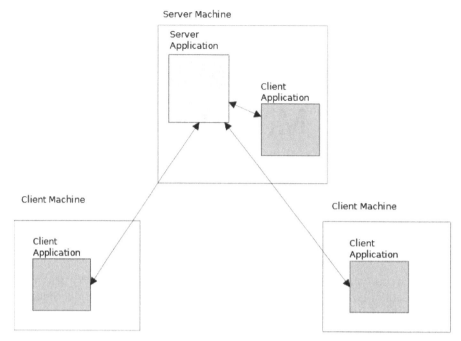

Figure 1 - Server Client Network

There may be more than one server on a given machine. When this happens, we need some way of identifying which server handles which requests. The operating system handles this detail but it needs each server to listen to a different port. A **Port** is a logical construct that identifies a server. A server is associated with a port number. Messages sent to a server are tagged with a port number. This allows the operating system to send the message to the correct server.

In this chapter we will be using port 7000. This selection is somewhat arbitrary. When a port is chosen, care should be taken so that it does not conflict with other ports in use on that server.

SpiderMonkey is the JME3 networking API and supports the server/client paradigm. This API allows us to develop games where several players can interact in real time. The SpiderMonkey API is a collection of interfaces and helper classes found in the `com.jme3.network` package.

There are several approaches to building server/client applications. In this chapter we will demonstrate how a server can maintain the state of a game and calculate the physics interaction between elements of the game. The client renders these elements based on location and transform messages sent from the server.

Understanding the Basics of the SpiderMonkey API

The SpiderMonkey API assists in creating a Server, Clients, and Messages. A message is an object that passes information between the server and its clients. To create and use a client server application:

- Create a server

- Create one or more clients

- Pass information between the clients and server using messages

First we will demonstrate how to create a server. The server will accept remote connections from clients and eventually send and receive messages to and from a client. The client *application* represents the player in the client/server relationship. From the server's perspective, clients are referred to as HostedConnections. The HostedConnection instance maintains client attributes that the server uses to interact with the client and to pass messages.

The SpiderMonkey API possesses several useful tools for tracking changes such as the interfaces MessageListener, ClientStateListener, ConnectionListener, and ErrorListener. You can see the primary components of the API outlined in *Table 1 - SpiderMonkey API*.

Table 1 - SpiderMonkey API

Class/Interface	Usage
Server	Represents a host server
Client	Represents a client
Message	Interface implemented by all network messages
HostedConnection	A connection between the client and server
MessageListener	Use to notify both the client or server when new messages arrive
ClientStateListener	Used to inform the client of changes in the connection
ConnectionListener	Used to inform the server about clients joining or leaving the server
ErrorListener	Used to inform the client about network problems

Creating a Server

A server is created as a headless SimpleApplication. A **Headless Server** is a server that does not use a window nor does it listen to user input. This means that the application will execute simpleInitApp and simpleUpdate normally, but it will not handle user input or use a GUI window. This is the ideal behaviour for a server.

To create a server, create a new application called `ServerApp` as shown next. Inside the `main` method, create an instance of the application as we have done before. When we start the application we make the server headless by providing a `JmeContext.Type.Headless` parameter to `app.start`.

```
public class ServerApp extends SimpleApplication {

    public static void main(String[] args) {
        ServerApp app = new ServerApp();
        app.start(JmeContext.Type.Headless);
    }
}
```

In the `simpleInitApp` method, we need to create an instance of the `Server` class that will provide us access to the network. Create a `Server` class reference variable called `primaryServer` using the `Network` class's static `createServer` method as shown next. The method throws an `IOException` that is handled in a try-catch block. This method takes a port as the parameter. For this example we will use port `7000`. Next, invoke the `primaryServer`'s `start` method.

```
public void simpleInitApp() {
    try {
        Server primaryServer = Network.createServer(7000);
        primaryServer.start();
    } catch (IOException ex) {
        //Handle exception
    }
}
```

The server is now ready to accept clients. The server refers to clients as `HostedConnection` objects. There are few ways we can gain information about clients. These are outlined in *Table 2 - Server Connections*. We do this through the `getConnections` method, called against `primaryServer`.

Table 2 - Server Connections

`getConnections`	Returns a collection of all connected `HostedConnection` objects
`getConnections().size`	Returns the number of all connected `HostedConnection` objects
`getConnection`	Returns a connected `HostedConnection` object based on the order it was added, starting with 0.

To execute the server from the jMonkeyEngine, start the server by right-clicking in the `ServerApp.java` file and selecting Run File. When this server is executed the console window will look similar to that found in *Figure 2 - ServerApp Console Window*. Since this server has little functionality there is little reflected in the window. Use the Stop button to terminate the server.

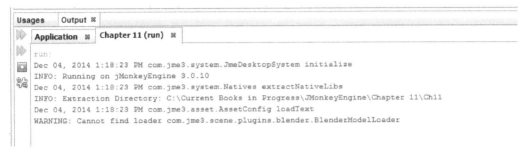

Figure 2 - ServerApp Console Window

Creating a Client

Much like a server, a game client is created by extending SimpleApplication. It uses the Display context type when it is started. This means the simpleInitApp and simpleUpdate methods will be executed, a window will be opened, and user input will be accepted. This is pretty much the same as what we see normally.

To build a client, create a new application called ClientApp that extends SimpleApplication. Set the context type to JmeContext.Type.Display as shown here.

```
public class ClientApp extends SimpleApplication {
    public static void main(String[] args) {
        ClientApp app = new ClientApp();
        app.start(JmeContext.Type.Display);
    }
}
```

The simpleInitApp method must be overridden. Its implementation consists of:

1. Creating a Client instance

2. Starting the Client using the start method

Create an instance of the Client class using the Network class' static connectToServer method as shown next. The parameters for this method are the IP address we are using and the communication port. The client is started using the start method against client1.

```
    public void simpleInitApp() {
        try {
            Client client1 =
```

```
                    Network.connectToServer("localhost", 7000);
                client1.start();
            } catch (IOException ex) {
                // Handle exception
            }
        }
```

For this example, we will use `localhost` for our IP address since the server and the client will be on the same machine. This commonly used network concept refers to the current machine. Instead of using `localhost`, we could have used `127.0.0.1`. Alternately, we would use the actual server's IP address. The port number needs to be the same port as the server: 7000

When the client application is executed it will connect to the server and display a window as shown in *Figure 3 - Simple Client*.

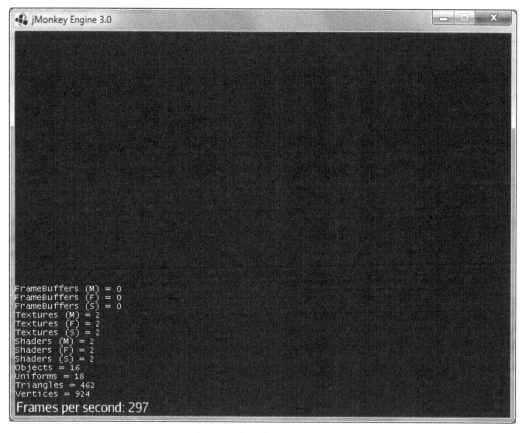

Figure 3 - Simple Client

Before the client and server can communicate, we need to discuss how messages work in JME3.

Creating a New Message Type

Messages are used to transfer data between the server and the client. Messages are often used to interchange information about transformations and game updates. For every type of message we want, we will need to create a message class that extends the `AbstractMessage` class, which is found in the `com.jme3.network` package.

When we create a message type we will need to use the `@Serializable` annotation found in the `com.jme3.network.serializing` package. This marks the class as one that can be saved and restored when transmitting across a network.

In the following code sequence, we define a class called `SimpleMessage` whose purpose is to hold a simple string object. The default constructor is required. Add this class to both the server and the client projects.

```
@Serializable
public class SimpleMessage extends AbstractMessage {
    private String message;

    public SimpleMessage() {
        this.message = "Default";
    }

    public SimpleMessage(String string) {
        this.message = string;
    }
}
```

In order to use a message type in an application, we will have to register each message by calling the `Serializer.registerClass` method with the message class name as the parameter. For the initialization to work properly, we need to use a static initialization block in both the client and the server as shown next. Using a static initialization block guarantees that the class will be registered as the class loads. This way it will be ready when it is needed.

```
static {
    Serializer.registerClass(SimpleMessage.class);
}
```

Using Messages

In order for a message to be properly received, we will need a special type of listener called a `MessageListener`. This listener will listen for incoming messages and is able to access the various parts of a message when it arrives. When a message arrives, its `messageReceived` method is called where it is processed.

In order to communicate, the client and the server will each require their own listener. Each of these classes will either support an instance of the `MessageListener` interface or implement the interface.

Creating a Client Listener

Create a new class called `ClientListener` as shown next. It implements the `MessageListener` interface, which requires us to implement the `messageReceived` method to respond to messages. The `messageReceived` method determines what happens when the client receives a message from the server. In this example, we determine if the message received is a `SimpleMessage`instance. If it is, we will cast and assign the message to the `SimpleMessage` instance variable.

```
public class ClientListener
        implements MessageListener<Client> {
    public void messageReceived(Client source,
            Message message) {
        if (message instanceof SimpleMessage) {
            SimpleMessage simpleMessage =
                (SimpleMessage) message;
            System.out.println(simpleMessage);
        }
    }
}
```

To be able to receive messages, we will need to register the listener to the client. Do this by calling the `addMessageListener` against a client in the `simpleInitApp` method of the client application as shown next. The parameters are the listener and the class of the message type class.

```
        client1.addMessageListener(new ClientListener(),
            SimpleMessage.class);
```

Implementing the `MessageListener` Interface

Create a new class called `ServerListener` that implements the `MessageListener` interface as shown next. Override the `messageReceived` method and determine if the message is of type `SimpleMessage` as we did with the client version of the listener. Notice that instead of a `Client` source, a `HostedConnection` source is used as a parameter type of the `messageReceived` method.

```
public class ServerListener implements
        MessageListener<HostedConnection> {

    public void messageReceived(HostedConnection source,
            Message message) {
        if (message instanceof SimpleMessage) {
            SimpleMessage simpleMessage =
                (SimpleMessage) message;
            System.out.println(simpleMessage);
        }
    }
}
```

Call the `addMessageListener` method against our server in the server's `simpleInitApp` method as shown here:

```
primaryServer.addMessageListener(new ServerListener(),
    SimpleMessage.class);
```

We are now ready to send and receive messages.

Sending Messages

Sending a message is a straightforward task. It involves:

- Creating an instance of the message class

- Calling the `Client` class' `send` method or the `Server` class' `broadcast` method

In the following example, a new instance of the `SimpleMessage` is created. The `client`'s `send` method is then used.

```
Message message = new SimpleMessage("Client Message");
client.send(message);
```

The message is sent from the client to the server where the server's `MessageListener` implementation's `messageReceived` method will be called.

The server uses a broadcast method to send messages to all connected clients. It also accepts a message instance as shown here:

```
Message message = new SimpleMessage("Server Message");
server.brodcast(message);
```

The client application is now ready to be executed. If both the server and the client have been created in the same project, then the server needs to be executed first and then the client. Right-click and select the Run File menu to execute the client as we did for the server.

> When exceptions occur during server and client testing, the port in use may not be properly reset in the testing environment. You may receive a binding or unbinding type of message. When this occurs, make sure that the previous instance of the application has terminated.

Creating a Simple Client/Server Application

To demonstrate the techniques used so far we will create a simple game where a server maintains the state of the game and one or more clients can play. The game starts with a simple block on a playing field. The player will shoot projectiles at the block moving it around. A screenshot of the application is shown in *Figure 4 - Client/Server*.

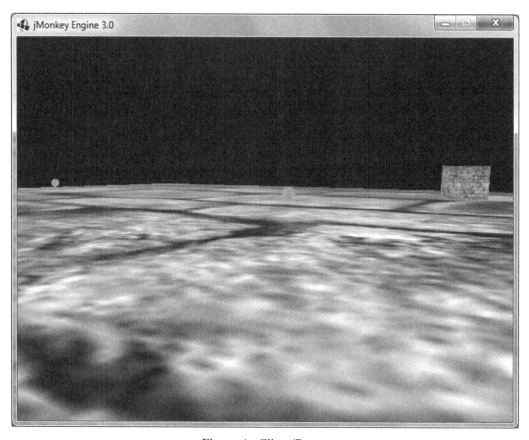

Figure 4 - Client/Server

Creating the `ProjectileMessage` Class

The `ProjectileMessage` class will be used to transfer information between the client and the server. Specifically, the location of the block and the projectiles and any transform information that needs to be passed. We will use this class to send new projectile information to the server and to send block and projectile position information to the client.

The class uses the `Serializable` annotation and extends the `AbstractMessage` class as shown next. The annotation is needed to mark the class as one that can be saved and restored when transmitting across a network. The first two instance variables are used to inform the server of the position and direction a projectile is shot. They are populated by a client and sent to the server for processing. The server will calculate the new position and send it back to the client using the `blockTransform` variable. The `projectiles` variable contains a list of the projectile's positions that have been fired.

```
@Serializable
public class ProjectileMessage extends AbstractMessage {
    private Vector3f projectileLocation;
    private Vector3f cameraDirection;
    private Transform blockTransform;
    private ArrayList<Vector3f> projectiles =
        new ArrayList<Vector3f>();
    ...
}
```

When a message is sent from the client to the server, the `projectileLocation` and `cameraDirection` fields are used by the server to generate a new projectile. When a message is sent from the server to the client, the `blockTransform` and `projectiles` fields are used by the client to update its scene.

Two constructors are used. The default constructor is required for a serialized class. The three argument constructor initialized all but the transforms used by the block. It could have been added as a parameter but is added using a method instead.

```
public ProjectileMessage() {
}

public ProjectileMessage(ArrayList<Vector3f> projectiles,
        Vector3f projectileLocation,
        Vector3f cameraDirection) {
    this.projectileLocation = projectileLocation;
    this.cameraDirection = cameraDirection;
    this.projectiles = projectiles;
}
```

The remaining methods are not shown here but are getter and setter methods. The complete source code for this class can be downloaded from p8tech.com

Building the Server

The server will maintain the state of the game. Clients will send the location and direction of the projectile (when fired) to the server. The server will use this information to generate a projectile and determine how it interacts with the block. The projectile and block transform information is then sent to all active clients.

The declaration of the server follows and is derived from `SimpleApplication`:

```
public class GameServer extends SimpleApplication {
```

The server will need several instance variables and the static initializer as shown next. The instance variables are summarized in *Table 3 - Server Instance Variables*.

```
Server primaryServer;
CharacterControl player;
BulletAppState bulletAppState;
```

```
        Vector3f cameraDirection;
        Vector3f projectileLocation;
        Geometry block;
        private ArrayList<Vector3f> projectiles =
            new ArrayList<Vector3f>();

        static {
            Serializer.registerClass(ProjectileMessage.class);
        }
```

Table 3 - Server Instance Variables

Instance Variable	Usage
primaryServer	Represents the game server
player	Represents the player
bulletAppState	Used for physics
cameraDirection	The direction the camera is pointing. This is passed from the client to the server so the server can correctly control the projectile's trajectory
projectileLocation	The location of the projectile. Also passed to the server along with cameraDirection
block	The block to shoot at
projectiles	A list of the active projectile locations to be sent from the server to the client

The server's `main` method follows:

```
        public static void main(String[] args) {
            GameServer app = new GameServer();
            app.start(JmeContext.Type.Headless);
        }
```

In the `simpleInitApp` method we create an instance of the `Server` class and add an instance of the `ServerListener` class to the server. The `createServer` method can throw an `IOException` so we handle it with a try-catch block. Port number `7000` is chosen as the communication port. An instance of the `ServerListener` is created to listen to messages arriving from clients. This class is detailed in Listening for Messages. The `createScene` method adds elements used to simulate the physics on the server. The server is then started.

```
        public void simpleInitApp() {
            try {
                primaryServer = Network.createServer(7000);
                primaryServer.addMessageListener(
                    new ServerListener(this),
```

```
                    ProjectileMessage.class);
            primaryServer.start();
            createScene();
        } catch (IOException ex) {
            System.out.println("Failure to create server");
        }
    }
```

The `createScene` method will add the floor and block to the scene. While this is a headless server, we want the server to keep track of the position of the block and projectiles. This means we need to create these elements along with the physics used during their interaction.

In the following implementation, physics is added to the application and then the terrain and block are loaded.

```
    private void createScene() {
        //Apply a physicss
        bulletAppState = new BulletAppState();
        stateManager.attach(bulletAppState);

        //Load the terrain and block
        loadTerrain();
        loadBlock();
    }
```

The `loadTerrain` method follows. The details of these methods should look familiar.

```
    public void loadTerrain() {
        Material mat = new Material(assetManager,
                "Common/MatDefs/Misc/Unshaded.j3md");
        Texture brickTex = assetManager.loadTexture(
                "Textures/Terrain/BrickWall/BrickWall.jpg");
        mat.setTexture("ColorMap", brickTex);
        Box box = new Box(100,0.1f,100);
        Geometry terrain = new Geometry("Box", box);
        terrain.setMaterial(mat);
        rootNode.attachChild(terrain);

        RigidBodyControl brickPhysics =
            new RigidBodyControl(0);
        terrain.addControl(brickPhysics);
        bulletAppState.getPhysicsSpace().add(brickPhysics);

        DirectionalLight light = new DirectionalLight();
        rootNode.addLight(light);
    }

    public void loadBlock() {
        Material mat = new Material(assetManager,
                "Common/MatDefs/Misc/Unshaded.j3md");
```

```
        Texture brickTex = assetManager.loadTexture(
                "Textures/Terrain/BrickWall/BrickWall.jpg");
        mat.setTexture("ColorMap", brickTex);
        Box box = new Box(3, 3, 3);
        block = new Geometry("Box", box);
        block.setMaterial(mat);
        block.setLocalTranslation(5, 8, 5);

        RigidBodyControl brickPhysics =
            new RigidBodyControl(5);
        block.addControl(brickPhysics);
        bulletAppState.getPhysicsSpace().add(brickPhysics);

        rootNode.attachChild(block);
    }
```

When a message from a client is received, the `createProjectile` method is called from the `ServerListener` class' `messageReceived` method and will be discussed in the next section, Listening for Messages. In the `createProjectile` method, a sphere is created and attached to the `rootNode` as shown next. The `setLocalTranslation` method uses the `projectileLocation` variable. Physics is added to the projectile and the `setLinearVelocity` method uses the `cameraDirection` variable to sets its initial direction and speed. Since multiple projectiles may be shot, the server needs to keep track of these projectiles and calculate their positions. When a projectile is created, it is added to the `projectiles` list.

```
    public void createProjectile() {
        Sphere sphere = new Sphere(32, 32, 1);
        Geometry projectile = new Geometry(
            "cannon projectile", sphere);
        Material projectileMat = new Material(assetManager,
                "Common/MatDefs/Misc/Unshaded.j3md");
        projectile.setMaterial(projectileMat);
        Texture projectileTex = assetManager.loadTexture(
                "Textures/Terrain/Rock/Rock.PNG");
        projectileMat.setTexture("ColorMap", projectileTex);
        rootNode.attachChild(projectile);

        projectile.setLocalTranslation(projectileLocation);

        RigidBodyControl projectilePhysics =
            new RigidBodyControl(25);
        projectile.addControl(projectilePhysics);
        bulletAppState.getPhysicsSpace().add(
            projectilePhysics);
        projectilePhysics.setLinearVelocity(
            cameraDirection*0.1f);

        projectiles.add(projectile.getLocalTranslation());
    }
```

The following code creates a `ProjectileMessage` instance containing the positions of the block and projectiles. The message is then broadcast to the clients connected to the server. This code can be placed in either the `simpleUpdate` or the `simpleRender` methods.

```
if (!projectiles.isEmpty()) {
    ProjectileMessage message = new ProjectileMessage(
        projectiles, projectileLocation,
        cameraDirection);
    message.setTransform(block.getLocalTransform());
    primaryServer.broadcast(message);
} else {
    // Unknown message
}
```

Listening for Messages

The `ServerListener` implementation is shown next. Its constructor is passed a reference to the server. This is needed so that the listener can modify the server's instance variables. Specifically, when a `ProjectileMessage` is received it sets the server's `projectileLocation` and `cameraDirection` variables. These are set in the `messageReceived` method and will be used by the server to create a new projectile starting at this location and direction. The server's `createProjectile` method is then called to create the projectile.

```
public class ServerListener implements
        MessageListener<HostedConnection> {
    private GameServer server;

    public ServerListener(GameServer server) {
        this.server = server;
    }

    public void messageReceived(HostedConnection source,
            Message msg) {
        if(msg instanceof ProjectileMessage){
            ProjectileMessage message =
                (ProjectileMessage)msg;
            server.projectileLocation = message.getLocation();
            server.cameraDirection =
                message.getCameraDirection();
            server.createProjectile();
        } else {
            //  Unknown message
        }
    }
}
```

When the server is executed, no window appears. It will sit and wait for a client to connect and then process the messages received from one or more clients.

Building the Client

The client is responsible for creating the scene, interacting with the user, and sending a message to the server when it fires a projectile. Periodically, the server will send messages to the client with updated projectile and block positions.

The declaration of the client application, its instance variables, and the static initialization block is shown next. The use of the instance variables are explained in *Table 4 - Client Instance Variables*.

```
public class GameClient
        extends SimpleApplication implements ActionListener {

    private Client client;
    private CharacterControl player;
    private BulletAppState bulletAppState;
    private boolean left = false, right = false,
        up = false, down = false;
    Geometry block;
    Vector3f projectilelLocation;
    private Vector3f cameraDirection;
    Transform blockTransform;
    Geometry projectile;
    ArrayList<Vector3f> projectiles =
        new ArrayList<Vector3f>();
    private ArrayList<Geometry> projectileGeometries =
        new ArrayList<Geometry>();


    static {
        Serializer.registerClass(ProjectileMessage.class);
    }
    ...
}
```

Table 4 - Client Instance Variables

Instance Variable	Usage
client	Represents the client
player	Represents the player
bulletAppState	Used for physics
Left, right, up, and down	Used to control the movement of the player

Instance Variable	Usage
block	The block that is shot at
projectilelLocation	The location of the projectile. Also passed to the server along with cameraDirection
cameraDirection	The direction the camera is pointing. This is passed from the client to the server so the server can correctly control the projectile's trajectory
blockTransform	The block's transform
projectiles	A list of the active projectile locations sent from the server to the client
projectileGeometries	A list of the active projectile geometries sent from the server to the client

The application main method follows. The application is started using the Display type.

```
public static void main(String[] args) {
    GameClient app = new GameClient();
    app.start(JmeContext.Type.Display);
}
```

In the simpleInitApp that follows, an instance of the Client class is created using the connectToServer method with the same port number used by the server, 7000. We dealt with the IOException using a catch block. The scene is then created using the createScene method.

```
public void simpleInitApp() {
    try {
        client = Network.connectToServer(
            "localhost", 7000);
        client.start();
        client.addMessageListener(
            new ClientListener(this),
            ProjectileMessage.class);
        createScene();
    } catch (IOException ex) {
        ex.printStackTrace();
    }
}
```

The createScene method, as shown next, is identical to that of the server application except the player needs to be created. The loadTerrain method is identical to the one found in the GameServer class.

```
private void createScene() {
    //Apply a Physics Space
    bulletAppState = new BulletAppState();
```

```
            stateManager.attach(bulletAppState);

            //Create the terrain and block
            loadTerrain();
            loadBlock();

            //Create the Player and controls
            mapKeys();
            initPlayer();
        }
```

The `loadBlock` is similar to that found in the `GameServer` class and is shown next. It differs in that physics are not included and the `blockTransform` variable is maintained here. The physics have been removed because they interfere when the block needs to be repositioned. The `blockTransform` variable sets the initial configuration of the block.

```
        private void loadBlock() {
            Material mat = new Material(assetManager,
                    "Common/MatDefs/Misc/Unshaded.j3md");
            Texture brickTex = assetManager.loadTexture(
                    "Textures/Terrain/BrickWall/BrickWall.jpg");
            mat.setTexture("ColorMap", brickTex);
            Box box = new Box(3, 3, 3);
            block = new Geometry("Box", box);
            block.setMaterial(mat);
            block.setLocalTranslation(5, 8, 5);

            blockTransform = block.getLocalTransform();
            rootNode.attachChild(block);
        }
```

The `mapKeys` and `initPlayer` methods are used to create and control the player. The code is essentially the same as found in Chapter 9.

The `createProjectile` method is shown next. This is similar to the version found in the `GameServer` class except that the physics components have been removed and the projectile created is added to the `projectileGeometries` list. A list of the geometries needs to be maintained so that they can be rendered.

```
        public void createProjectile() {
            Sphere sphere = new Sphere(32, 32, 1);
            Geometry projectile = new Geometry(
                "cannon projectile", sphere);
            Material projectileMat = new Material(assetManager,
                    "Common/MatDefs/Misc/Unshaded.j3md");
            projectile.setMaterial(projectileMat);
            Texture projectileTex = assetManager.loadTexture(
                "Textures/Terrain/Rock/Rock.PNG");
            projectileMat.setTexture("ColorMap", projectileTex);
            rootNode.attachChild(projectile);
```

```
            projectileGeometries.add(projectile);
            cameraDirection = cam.getDirection().mult(75);
            projectilelLocation =
                cam.getDirection().scaleAdd(5, cam.getLocation());
    }
```

In the `simpleRender` method, shown next, the block and projectiles are rendered. The `projectiles` list and the `projectileGeometries` list should be the same size and not empty before the projectile geometries are rendered.

```
    public void simpleRender(RenderManager renderManager) {
        block.setLocalTransform(blockTransform);
        if (projectiles.size() > 0 &&
                projectiles.size() ==
                    projectileGeometries.size()) {
            for(int i=0; i<projectiles.size(); i++) {
                projectileGeometries.get(i).
                    setLocalTranslation(projectiles.get(i));
            }
        }
    }
```

The client application is now ready to be executed. As we mentioned earlier, if both the server and the client have been created in the same project, then the server needs to be executed first and then the client.

When the client starts up, clicking with the left mouse button will cause a projectile to be created. The projectile and block will be rendered, as determined by the server. One possible scene is shown in *Figure 5 - GameClient Scene*.

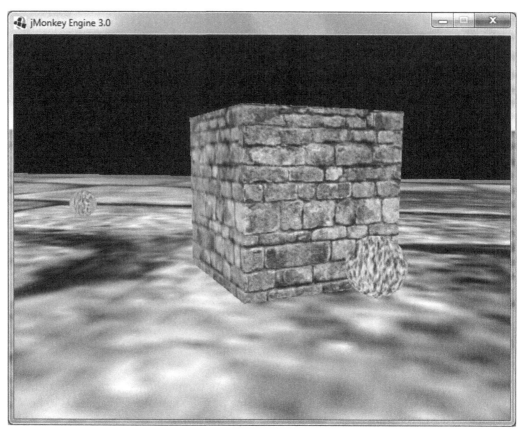

Figure 5 - GameClient Scene

Using the `ConnectionListener` interface

The `ConnectionListener` interface can be used to listen to connection events. This can be useful for debugging an application. In the following implementation, we create a listener for the server where we display message when a connection to the server is added or removed:

```
public class ServerConnectionListener
        implements ConnectionListener {

    public void connectionAdded(Server server,
            HostedConnection conn) {
        System.out.println("Connection made: " + conn);
    }

    public void connectionRemoved(Server server,
            HostedConnection conn) {
        System.out.println("Connection removed: " + conn);
    }

}
```

It is added to the server using code similar to the following:

```
primaryServer = Network.createServer(7000);
...
primaryServer.addConnectionListener(
    new ServerConnectionListener());
```

Using the ErrorListener interface

The ErrorListener interface can be used to listen to error events. This can also be useful when debugging an application. In the following implementation, we create a listener for the client where we display a message when an error occurs. The program stack is also displayed.

```
public class ClientErrorListener implements ErrorListener {

    public void handleError(Object source, Throwable t) {
        System.out.println("Handling error: " + source);
        t.printStackTrace();
    }

}
```

It can be added to the client using code similar to the following:

```
client = Network.connectToServer("localhost", 7000);
...
client.addErrorListener(new ClientErrorListener());
```

Networking with Shades of Infinity

The Shades of Infinity game can be enhanced to support multiple players. However, to incorporate multiple players we have to make a number of changes to the game. This is not unusual as adding some features can significantly impact the design of a game. In this section we will address the more significant changes. The complete version can be found at www.p8tech.com.

We removed some game elements to simplify the game. For example, physics has been removed along with cinematics. These features can be added as necessary.

This version of the game uses a server to:

- Create new ships
- Keep track of which ships have been destroyed

A client will support most of the interaction that exists in the game. It will not create ships except as directed by the server. When a client destroys a ship, it will inform the server which will then broadcast a ship removal message to the other client which will then remove the ship from their list.

New ships are created every three seconds at 'random' locations. Their locations and movement are kept simple for this version of the game. One set of ships is shown in *Figure 6 - Enemy Ships*.

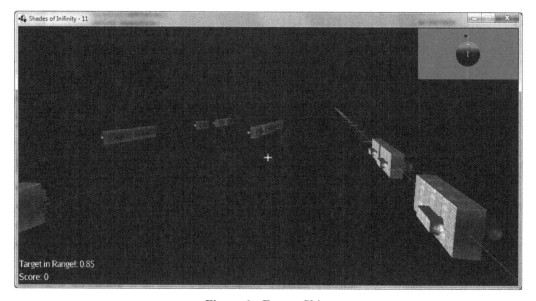

Figure 6 - Enemy Ships

We will divide our discussion into three parts: message, server, and client.

Understanding the SOIMessage Class

The game will use an SOIMessage class for communication. Its intent is to inform clients:

- When new ships need to be created

- To let the server know when a ship has been destroyed

- To inform other clients that a ship needs to be removed

The class is declared as shown next. It follows the general approach as described in Creating a New Message Type. Missing from this sequence are the getter and setter methods for the instance variables.

```
@Serializable
public class SOIMessage extends AbstractMessage {
    private Transform shipTransform;
    private String name;
    private boolean addingShip;
```

```
    public SOIMessage() {
    }

    public SOIMessage(Transform shipTransform,
            String name, boolean addingShip) {
        this.shipTransform = shipTransform;
        this.name = name;
        this.addingShip = addingShip;
    }
...
}
```

Its instance variables include:

- shipTransform – Used to hold the basic transformation information for a new ship

- name – The name of the ship

- addingShip – When true, it means a new ship needs to be created by a client using the previous two fields.

Creating the SOI Server

The server uses several instance variables as shown next. They are used to maintain a list of active ships, determine when to generate a new ship, give the new ship a unique ID, and randomly place it in the scene. The message class is also registered. The static import for the shootables variable is used to make it easy for a client to access it.

```
import static p8tech.Main.shootables;

public class SOIGameServer extends SimpleApplication {

    private Server gameServer;
    private ArrayList<AISpaceShip> shipList = new ArrayList();
    private float tick;
    private int shipID;
    private Random random = new Random();

    static {
        Serializer.registerClass(SOIMessage.class);
    }
    ...
}
```

The main and simpleInitApp methods follow. They create a new server that uses port 7001.

```
    public static void main(String[] args) {
        SOIGameServer app = new SOIGameServer();
```

```
            app.start(JmeContext.Type.Headless);
    }

    @Override
    public void simpleInitApp() {
        try {
            gameServer = Network.createServer(7001);
            gameServer.addMessageListener(
                new ServerListener(this),SOIMessage.class);
            gameServer.addConnectionListener(
                new ServerConnectionListener());
            gameServer.start();
        } catch (IOException ex) {
            // Handle exceptions
        }
    }
```

The `simpleUpdate` method uses the `tick` variable to generate a new ship every three seconds. The `shipID` variable is concatenated with a ship string to create unique names for each ship. A new ship is created, its transform is obtained, and a new `SOIMessage` is broadcast to all of the clients as shown here:

```
    public void simpleUpdate(float tpf) {
        tick += tpf;
        if (tick > 3.0) {
            tick = 0.0f;
            int x = random.nextInt(3);
            String shipName = "Enemy" + shipID++;
            Node node = createShip(shipName, x, 0, 4);
            Transform transform = node.getLocalTransform();

            SOIMessage message =
                new SOIMessage(transform, shipName, true);
            gameServer.broadcast(message);
        }
    }
```

The `createShip` method is very similar to the one used in the previous version of the game. Whilst not shown here, the major difference is that it adds the new ship to the `shipList` list. This list is used instead of individual variables for each ship. This allows us to generate as many ships as we need using a single variable to keep track of all of them.

The other method used by the server is the `destroyShip` method as shown next. It is invoked from the `ServerListener` class. This method will remove a ship from `shipList` when a removal message arrives from a client.

```
    public void destroyShip(String shipName) {
        for (AISpaceShip ship : shipList) {
            if (ship.getName().equals(shipName)) {
```

```
                    shipList.remove(ship);
                    break;
                }
            }
        }
    }
```

The `ServerListener` class follows. It calls the `destroyShip` method when a client removes a ship and then rebroadcasts the message to all of the clients so that they can also remove the ship from their list.

```
public class ServerListener implements
        MessageListener<HostedConnection> {
    private SOIGameServer server;

    public ServerListener(SOIGameServer server) {
        this.server = server;
    }

    public void messageReceived(HostedConnection source,
            Message msg) {
        if(msg instanceof SOIMessage){
            SOIMessage message = (SOIMessage)msg;
            if(!message.isAddingShip()) {
                server.destroyShip(message.getName());
                server.gameServer.broadcast(message);
            }
        } else {
            // Unknown message
        }
    }
}
```

Creating the SOI Client

To create a client we use the `Main` class from the previous version of the game. This class required several minor and significant changes. Here we will only discuss the major changes.

The following instance variables were added to support the client. The `ArrayList` hold a list of the current ships. The `shipToBeDestroyed` string is used to delete ships and the `client` variable represents the `Client` object.

```
    private static ArrayList<AISpaceShip> shipList =
        new ArrayList<AISpaceShip>();
    private static String shipToBeDestroyed;
    private Client client;
```

The `simpleInitApp` has been modified to create a client, add a listener, and to create the scene as shown here:

```
    public void simpleInitApp() {
        try {
            client = Network.connectToServer(
                "localhost", 7001);
             client.addMessageListener(
                new ClientListener(this), SOIMessage.class);
            client.start();
            createScene();
            usePictureInAPicture();
        } catch (IOException ex) {
            ex.printStackTrace();
        }
    }
```

The createShip method is the same one used by the server. The getAIShipByName method has been modified as shown next to accommodate the new ship's name syntax.

```
    public AISpaceShip getAIShipByName(String name) {
        String prefix = name.substring(0, name.indexOf(" "));
        for (AISpaceShip ship : shipList) {
            if (ship.getName().equals(prefix)) {
                return ship;
            }
        }
        return null;
    }
```

Adding New Ships

New ships are only created as directed by the server. To affect this:

- The client will receive a message containing the transform and name of the new ship

- It will call the addNewShip method from the ClientListener class' messageReceived method

- The addNewShip method will then add the ship to the game

The ClientListener class is shown next. It uses a Callable object to invoke the addNewShip method. The client listener executes in a different thread to that of the client. As we will see shortly, the addNewShip method will modify the scene. All scene operations need to be executed from the same thread otherwise an exception will be thrown. To avoid this, the enqueue method will submit the Callable object, containing the call to addNewShip, to the client for execution on the client's thread.

```
public class ClientListener implements
            MessageListener<Client> {
    private Main client;

    public ClientListener(Main client) {
```

```
            this.client = client;
        }

    public void messageReceived(Client source, Message msg) {
        if (msg instanceof SOIMessage) {
            final SOIMessage message = (SOIMessage) msg;
            if (message.isAddingShip()) {
                client.enqueue(new Callable() {
                    public Object call() throws Exception {
                        client.addNewShip(
                            message.getShipTransform(),
                            message.getName());
                        return null;
                    }
                });
            }
        } else {
            // Unknown message
        }
    }
}
```

The `addNewShip` method, shown next, creates a new ship using the transform and the name, adding it to the scene.

```
    public void addNewShip(Transform transform, String name) {
        Node node = createShip(name, 0, 0, 4);
        node.setLocalTransform(transform);
        rootNode.attachChild(node);
    }
```

Destroying Ships

When a ship is destroyed the server needs to be informed. However, this event is determined in the `AISpaceShip` class' `controlUpdate` method. This method will destroy the ship in the current client and then call the `Main` class' `destroyShipByName` method as shown here:

```
    protected void controlUpdate(float tpf) {
        if (spatial !- null) {
            if (health <= 0) {
                spatial.getParent().detachChild(spatial);
                Main.destroyShipByName(spatial.getName());
            }
        } else {
            ...
        }
```

Chapter 11

This `destroyShipByName` method is a static method allowing it to be easily called from the `AISpaceShip` class. This method is shown next. An `Iterator` is used to traverse and remove the ship. The iterator is needed to avoid throwing a `ConcurrentModificationException`. This type of exception can be thrown when a for-each statement is used. The `shipToBeDestroyed` variable is set to the name of the ship so that is can be sent to the server in the `simpleUpdate` method.

```
public static void destroyShipByName(String shipName) {
    Iterator<AISpaceShip> iterator = shipList.iterator();
    while(iterator.hasNext()) {
        AISpaceShip ship = iterator.next();
        if(ship.getName().equals(shipName)) {
            iterator.remove();
            shipToBeDestroyed = shipName;
        }
    }
}
```

The `simpleUpdate` method has been modified to move all of the ships by the same amount as shown next. In addition, if the `shipToBeDestroyed` variable is not `null`, then it sends a message to the server indicating that the ship should be removed.

```
public void simpleUpdate(float tpf) {
    if (shipList != null) {
        for (AISpaceShip ship : shipList) {
            ship.getAIShipNode().move(0, 0, 0.2f * tpf);
        }
    }

    if(shipToBeDestroyed != null) {
        SOIMessage message =
            new SOIMessage(null, shipToBeDestroyed, true);
        client.send(message);
        shipToBeDestroyed = null;
    }
    ...
}
```

To execute the game from the jMonkeyEngine, start the server first by right-clicking in the `SOIGameServer.java` file and selecting Run File. Follow this by doing the same thing to the `Main.java` file to create as many clients as you desire. Another view of the game is shown in *Figure 7 - SOI Planet View*.

336

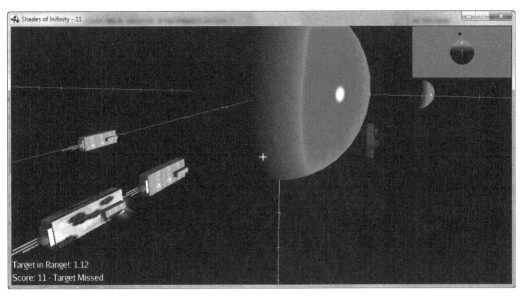

Figure 7 - SOI Planet View

Conclusion

SpiderMonkey supports networked applications using client/server architecture. The server typically maintains the state of the game with one or more client applications connected to the server across a network. Messages are sent between the server and the clients to maintain and synchronize game state information.

We saw how to create a headless server that does not support a GUI interface. The server maintained positional and transform information about the projectiles fired by the clients.

There are several listener interfaces that can be used to listen to connections, messages, and error events. Message listeners play an important part in receiving messages from a server or client.

Message classes must be derived from the `AbstractMessage` class. They must be serializable and implement a default constructor. Before a message class can be used in an application it must be registered using the `registerClass` method. This is best performed in a static initialization block.

Epilogue

Introduction

JME3 provides the necessary tools to build a complete game from start to finish. We have covered the basic building blocks needed to build a compelling game. As you have seen throughout the various topics, JME3 gives you the creative control to mold each game component to fit your needs. Much of JME3's appeal stems from the broad customization and developer control that you have from the beginning.

However, there is much more to JME3 than we were able to discuss. This includes several advanced topics, which we will discuss briefly in the next section. We will also suggest several ways of improving the Shades Of Infinity game and offer a few suggestions with regards to games you may create.

Exploring Other JME3 Topics

There are a number of other topics that can be investigated. These include:

- Enhancing the GUI appearance

- Gaining a better understanding of 3D math

- Managing character movement and animation

- Incorporating multithreading

- Adding Artificial Intelligence

These and other topics introduced here and links to more information is provided.

Enhancing the GUI

As good as graphics can be, there is always room for improvement. One potential improvement is to use Nifty for your HUD. There are a couple of places to start: http://hub.jmonkeyengine.org/wiki/doku.php/jme3:advanced:nifty_gui and http://hub.jmonkeyengine.org/wiki/doku.php/jme3:advanced:nifty_gui_java_interaction.

If you are interested in some of the more detailed aspects of GUI, a discussion of shaders can be found at http://hub.jmonkeyengine.org/wiki/doku.php/jme3:advanced:jme3_shaders. When we created landscapes in Chapter 8 the rendering of the land and its objects can be given further control using different Levels Of Detail (LOD). This topic is addressed at http://hub.jmonkeyengine.org/wiki/doku.php/jme3:advanced:level_of_detail.

Many applications need to support the mobile platform. If you would like to develop an Android based game, then the following link will be a good start: http://hub.jmonkeyengine.org/wiki/doku.php/jme3:android.

Understanding 3D Math

While JME3 hides much of the math used for 3D graphics, it is still useful to understand this math at a lower level. A good introduction to this math can be found at http://hub.jmonkeyengine.org/wiki/doku.php/jme3:math. A slide show specific to JME3 is found at http://hub.jmonkeyengine.org/wiki/doku.php/jme3:math_for_dummies.

Managing Character Movement

Character motion is complex with many different approaches for enhancing character movement. Topics include physical hinges and joints to a character, making characters walk, ragdoll physics to control animation, and the steering of characters around a scene.

- Physical Hinges and Joints - http://hub.jmonkeyengine.org/wiki/doku.php/jme3:advanced:hinges_and_joints

- Walking Character - http://hub.jmonkeyengine.org/wiki/doku.php/jme3:advanced:walking_character

- Ragdoll Physics - http://hub.jmonkeyengine.org/wiki/doku.php/jme3:advanced:ragdoll

- Steer Behaviours - http://hub.jmonkeyengine.org/wiki/doku.php/jme3:advanced:steer_behaviours

Characters are frequently created outside of JME3. There are several tools you can use to create these characters. Blender is one such tool and is discussed at http://hub.jmonkeyengine.org/wiki/doku.php/jme3:external:blender.

Incorporating Multithreading

We used threads in Chapter 11 when we introduced networking. However, there is much more to threading that we were unable to cover. A good starting point is a discussion of the JME3 threading model found at http://hub.jmonkeyengine.org/wiki/doku.php/jme3:advanced:multithreading. When physics is added to a game, performance can sometimes be adversely affected. Threads can help in this situation as discussed here: http://hub.jmonkeyengine.org/wiki/doku.php/jme3:advanced:bullet_multithreading.

Incorporating Artificial Intelligence

To make a game more realistic and enjoyable, the addition of Artificial Intelligence (AI) can be very helpful. The computer's opponent behaviour can be more realistic and challenging. This is a broad topic but a good starting point would be to explore Monkey

Brains (http://hub.jmonkeyengine.org/wiki/doku.php/jme3:advanced:monkey_brains), an AI engine developed for jMonkeyEngine. More specialized topics include Recast Navigation (http://hub.jmonkeyengine.org/wiki/doku.php/jme3:advanced:recast), which deals with path finding.

Other Topics

There are several other topics that are not as easily grouped yet can still be important for most applications. For example, if you desire to make your game playable in different languages and cultures, then understanding how localization is achieved is important. This topic is addressed at http://hub.jmonkeyengine.org/wiki/doku.php/jme3:advanced:localization.

Monitoring and logging an application's behaviour can be useful in the debugging and optimization process. This is covered at http://hub.jmonkeyengine.org/wiki/doku.php/jme3:advanced:logging. Optimization techniques are discussed at http://hub.jmonkeyengine.org/wiki/doku.php/jme3:intermediate:optimization.

There are many additional techniques and resources available online. You can discover many of these techniques through the JMonkey community by visiting the forums available at http://hub.jmonkeyengine.org/forum/. Here you can find discussions of common problems and ask your own questions.

Improving the Shades of Infinity Game

You now have the Shades of Infinity game as a base to build off. This will give you a jumping point to enhance your JME3 skills. This is a good place to practice customization with your own sounds, materials, and objects. Remember, the full code is available for download at p8tech.com

Shades of Infinity can be improved in a number of ways. These include:

- Showing the hits registered on a ship by a different player
- Have the server broadcast a list of all of the ships to allow late-joining clients to see all of the ships
- Adding a more challenging movement to the enemy ships
- Keeping track of players' scores

The reader is encouraged to incorporate these and other enhancements to the game.

Build Your Own Game

Of course building your own game can be fun. It gives you the opportunity to explore a game domain of your interest and to incorporate the features you want. JME3 provides a good framework to use.

As your game grows you may want to consider hosting it on a hub and inviting other developers to contribute. This can be a good learning experience. It allows you to leverage the work of multiple people to develop a game that may not be possible for a single individual to create.

Of course, if you are not quite ready to write your own game you might want to consider participating on other games in development. Regardless, stick with it! Try different approaches and experiment. Ask questions and peruse the JME3 forums. It can be as entertaining and rewarding to develop a game as it is to play one.

> Writing the book has been a fun and enlightening. We hope you enjoyed it and found it to be useful and rewarding. Good luck with your game development efforts!

Index

Index

Index

Index

Java 8
New Features

A Practical Heads-Up Guide

Richard Reese

Java Masterclass

Java Exceptions,
Assertions and Logging

Sam Alapati

Getting Started
with Elastix

A Beginner's Guide

David Duffett

Lightning Source UK Ltd.
Milton Keynes UK
UKOW07f0235260315

248543UK00002B/3/P